# Getting Into
# Medical School

*Other Kaplan Books for Premeds*
MCAT 528
MCAT Complete 7-Book Review
MCAT Flashcards + App

# Getting Into Medical School

## A Strategic Approach

**Selection** • **Admissions** • **Financial**

by **Maria Lofftus, Thomas C. Taylor, and Houman Hemmati**
with a nationwide team
of medical school admissions advisers

**KAPLAN**

PUBLISHING

New York

Published by Kaplan Publishing, a division of Kaplan, Inc.
395 Hudson Street
New York, NY 10014

Printed in the United States of America

10 9 8 7 6 5 4 3 2 1

ISBN: 978-1-61865-895-1

Kaplan Publishing books are available at special quantity discounts to use for sales promotions, employee premiums, or educational purposes. For more information or to purchase books, please call the Simon & Schuster special sales department at 866-506-1949.

# TABLE OF CONTENTS

## Authors

**Jonathan Edwards** is a Kaplan MCAT instructor, content developer and Med School Mentor. During his time at Kaplan, Jonathan has helped hundreds of students prepare for the MCAT and navigate the world of medical school admissions. Jonathan is currently a medical student at the Marshall University Joan C. Edwards School of Medicine. He is a graduate of Princeton University.

**Houman Davd Hemmati, MD, PhD,** completed his MD at the David Geffen School of Medicine at UCLA and his PhD at the California Institute of Technology. He holds a degree in Biological Sciences from Stanford University. Dr. Hemmati is completing his internship in internal medicine at Stanford University and his residency in ophthalmology at the Wilmer Eye Institute of Johns Hopkins Hospital. Dr. Hemmati taught Kaplan's MCAT class for several years and is a former student member of a medical school admissions committee.

**Maria Lofftus, JD,** was recently Kaplan's director of academic services for the health sciences. Prior to that she was assistant dean for admissions at the University of California at San Diego, School of Medicine. During her nineteen years in medical school admissions, Ms. Lofftus held numerous leadership positions within the Association of American Medical Colleges, including serving as a member of the Committee for the Expanded Minority Admissions Exercise, as a trainer-facilitator for the Expanded Minority Admissions Exercise, and as chair of the Committee on Admissions. Currently she is the chief of staff of the Graduate Management School at UCSD.

**Thomas C. Taylor** was recently Kaplan's associate director of academic services for the health sciences. Prior to that he was director of admissions and associate director of student affairs and curriculum at the University of Iowa College of Medicine, and he has also served in admissions and financial aid capacities at the Hahnemann Medical College and the University of Connecticut School of Medicine. A nationally known expert on medical school admissions, Mr. Taylor has held a number of leadership positions in national and regional medical student affairs organizations.

## Contributors

**Michael S. Katz**, financial aid consultant for part six of this book, was recently the university director of student financial aid at the University of Medicine and Dentistry of New Jersey. He has been in the field of financial assistance, primarily in the health professions, for more then 30 years. Mr. Katz has served on numerous state, regional, and national education committees and has given numerous presentations on financing a medical education.

**Cynthia Lewis, PhD**, author of chapters 13 and 15, received her doctorate in zoology from the University of Alberta in 1975, and held postdoctoral fellowships from the National Institute of Dental Research and Scripps Institution of Oceanography before becoming the Preprofessional Health Adviser at San Diego State University (SDSU) for eleven years. She initiated and directed the SDSU Health Careers Opportunity grant for disadvantaged students from 1990–96, and is the founding prehealth adviser for the SDSU Alpha Epsilon Delta chapter and the Collegiate Union for Health Related Education (CUHRE). Currently she is President of Lewis Associates Medical Strategies (www.lewisassoc.com), which provides personal premedical training and coaching to applicants pursuing a career in medicine.

**Allen Maniker, MD**, author of chapter 17, is a board certified neurological surgeon and an associate professor in the Department of Neurosurgery at the New Jersey Medical School in Newark, New Jersey. He received his MD from Wayne State University in 1986. He did an internship and one year of general surgery residency at New York's Beth Israel Medical Center and a residency and chief residency in neurological surgery at the New Jersey Medical School. He was a clinical fellow in neuro trauma at the Medical College of Virginia and a Clinical Fellow in peripheral nerve at the Louisiana State University in New Orleans and the University of Washington in Seattle. Dr. Maniker is director of neurotrauma and head of the New Jersey Peripheral Nerve Center at the New Jersey Medical School. He also holds an undergraduate degree from the Juilliard School in New York.

**Elizabeth "Leah" Parker**, who contributed to chapter 9, was affiliated with the University of California at Irvine College of Medicine from 1980 to 1997, serving as director of admissions for 12 years. During her tenure, she read and critiqued thousands of personal statement essays. Ms. Parker earned a master's degree in public administration from the California State University in Fullerton.

**Chris Rosa**, author of chapter 16, is director of the Office of Services for Students with Disabilities at Queens College, where he coordinates the provision of support services to more than 450 students with disabilities. A member of the Muscular Dystrophy Association's National Task Force on Public Awareness, Mr. Rosa has written several articles published in scholarly journals on the sociology of disability and is a recipient of the Muscular Dystrophy Association's National Personal Achievement Award. He earned a doctorate in sociology at the City University of New York Graduate Center.

**Charles Spooner, Jr., PhD**, contributed to chapter 9. He was involved in every aspect of medical school admissions, from initial recruitment to final selection and admission of students, for 27 years. Dr. Spooner is past national chairman of the Group on Student Affairs of the Association of American Medical Colleges, and has served several times on all the AAMC committees concerning admissions. He is professor emeritus and associate dean emeritus of the University of California at San Diego School of Medicine. He currently lives in rural Oregan, where his community service includes recruiting physicians for under-served areas and specialties, and consulting on local water treatment and management.

# PART ONE

# Is Medical School for You?

# CHAPTER 1

# Making the Decision

The decision to become a doctor can be an intimidating one. As a premed student, you'll be working for at least two years without guarantee of a spot in medical school. It means striving for something that only 45 percent of those applying between 2011 and 2013 got—a position in medical school. After a trying application process, that decision means committing to a labor-intensive course of study, including 4 years of medical school and 3 to 12 years of residency and fellowship.

The large number of applicants per year in relation to the number of open positions makes the admissions process very competitive for applicants. This situation primarily hurts applicants with "borderline" qualifications for admission by decreasing their chances of being offered a secondary application or interview. Between 2002 and 2013, the number of applicants to allopathic medical schools in the United States increased by more than 45 percent, while the number of matriculants increased by only 25 percent. But don't let yourself be fooled by these numbers. The rise in the number of applicants is not large enough to worsen the chances of any one otherwise qualified applicant.

There is no way to predict how the application numbers will change in any given year, let alone how any changes might affect your chances of admission (if at all). The medical school admissions process is not a statistical guessing game, and therefore you should not base your decisions regarding whether and when to apply to medical school on fluctuations in competition.

Getting into medical school will be one of your most difficult challenges in seeking a career in medicine. It is reasonable to assume that many of the applicants who are not admitted each year are good candidates who would make good doctors. Obviously, you will need dedication and careful planning to be successful in this competitive situation.

Two important elements of preparing your application campaign are knowing something about the realities of medicine and understanding why you want to become a doctor; it's likely that you'll be asked to articulate those reasons in your personal statement, as well as in your interview. While some students have a clear vision that they can movingly relate, many students have a more difficult time deciding whether to enter medicine. Some find themselves daydreaming in organic chemistry class, still trying to decide two years into the prerequisites if this is the career for them.

Complicating matters is the fact that many people want to be doctors for complicated, and not purely altruistic, reasons—for example, money, job security, prestige, or parental approval. Are these legitimate reasons to decide to become a doctor? Perhaps. Are these reasons with which an admissions committee will likely be comfortable? Probably not. How then can you figure out what's important to an admissions committee? How can you be honest about goals and aspirations that aren't particularly noble? It's important to address these questions as early as you can in the application process and think through your own personal goals before you apply. If you've never stopped to consider your motivations for pursuing a career in medicine, then these reasons might not be clear to you as an applicant.

---

### Personal Tragedy

"I was 8 years old when my mother died of ovarian cancer. I remember dreaming of being a doctor then, thinking that maybe I could save her. I grew up without her guidance, but losing her sensitized me to the pain of others and played an important part in my decision to become a doctor."

–Univ. of Iowa College of Medicine student; adapted from *Newsweek*/Kaplan's *How to Choose a Career and Graduate School*

---

# WHY GO? GOOD REASONS . . .

There are a number of compelling reasons to become a doctor. Take a moment to consider which of them are motivating you.

## An Intimate Rapport

Being a physician gives you the most privileged listening post a human being can have. A doctor gets to hear the innermost issues of a patient and is privileged to weave those hints and facts into a diagnosis and treatment.

## Unique Responsibility

Doctors are at the top of the "medical food chain." At the hospital level, physicians work on a clinical-care team with nurses, therapists, and technicians. The physician's voice, however, carries the most weight. Physicians are expected to make the tough decisions: to decide when to stop life support, to declare that the slide under the microscope shows cancerous cells, or to carry the weight of the life-or-death consequences that even the most routine decisions—like prescribing a common antibiotic that can sometimes cause lethal reactions—entail. This responsibility can extend outside of the professional realm. If you become a doctor, then on a plane or at a cocktail party, people will come up to you and start telling you things about their skin that no one other than that person should ever know!

## Special Authority

Many people pursue medicine because they want the knowledge of what to do in an emergency and the ability to personally provide care for those in need. Some like the idea of being able to control things that were frightening or nebulous to them as children, while for others, the idea of being in a small town and being the one charged with taking care of the whole town's health is appealing.

## Other Reasons

In a recent poll, physicians reported other elements that lured them into the profession:

- Continuing intellectual challenge
- Intelligent colleagues
- Joy of helping/taking care of people
- Respect of others in community
- Diversity of opportunities
- Enjoyment of working with science or contributing to research
- Job autonomy and security
- Financial reward

As you think about why you are interested in medicine, make sure that you can articulate a goal. While financial reward and job security are indeed important, numerous other careers provide these elements as well. What's important for you personally and as an applicant is that you can explain *why* medicine is your chosen profession.

## REASONS TO RECONSIDER

Many people express interest in becoming a physician well before they are in a position to draw up any conscious list of justifications for their interest. Although it may seem desirable to make a commitment early in life, it's important that you reconsider from an adult perspective decisions you may have made as a child. If you're applying to med school for any of the reasons listed below, critically examine your motivations before you take the plunge.

---

**Gotta Love It**

A college senior we recently spoke to said that he wanted to be a doctor because it was the most difficult thing he could do. He worked hard to ace his MCAT, became volunteer coordinator of his fraternity, and selected his courses on the basis of how they'd look to an admissions committee. Sadly, a real desire to enter the field wasn't there, and admissions committees could tell: He hasn't yet gotten into med school.

---

## Parental Approval

Saying you want to be a doctor, even as a child, pleases many adults. If you're someone who's always wanted to be a doctor, you might be able to remember how your goal was received early in your life. Making your career decision early isn't necessarily bad, as long as you've progressed beyond the approval-seeking stage. Until you've analyzed your commitment with an adult mind, you can't really argue successfully why you believe in it. You need to have a realistic sense of the profession, and of why you want to be a doctor, to convince a committee they should let you in.

## The Longest Path

Another poor reason for pursuing medicine is "the difficulty of the path." It's sometimes the case that high achievers pursue a career in medicine simply because of its competitiveness and arduousness. Although determination and the discipline to accomplish a difficult goal are valuable assets in life and are prized by medical school admissions officers, they alone are not enough. The alchemy of desire and motivation has to precede the chemistry of mixing the right MCAT scores, letters of recommendation, and extracurriculars. Real desire should be there.

## Following in Mom or Dad's Footsteps

Many medical school applicants are children of physicians. Although having a parent who practices medicine may indeed give you a sense of the field, be aware that your folks went to medical school in a different era, and attending med school and starting to practice medicine have changed significantly in recent years. Some med school admissions officers estimate that children of physicians have a higher rate of attrition from medical school than the national average of 1 to 2 percent. It isn't that they can't do the work; it's that they sometimes discover they applied for the wrong reasons.

If you are a child of a physician, give some extra thought to why you want to practice medicine in today's healthcare climate. This climate is characterized by the following:

### Greater Competition

If your mother is in her 40s or 50s, it's likely that she attended medical school around 25–30 years ago. The pool of applicants was much smaller then. The MCAT your parent took was a very different test: It carried far less weight than today's test does, and test takers did not usually prepare for it as carefully. Today, nearly 70 percent of the people who take the MCAT take a test-preparation course. Finally, 25–30 years ago, volunteering in a health-related situation was not on the list of the Association of American Medical College's (AAMC) "Most Important Criteria" for admission. Today, it is one of the big five.

### Changing Medical Climate

Today's medical lingo is peppered with acronyms and phrases—HMO, payor mix, DRGs, prior authorization, PPO, capitation, HIPC—that were not a part of medicine a generation ago. So don't assume that because you grew up with medicine, you know what it's like. Today's private practice work is often signing papers in triplicate—in a public hospital, quadruplicate. Litigation and malpractice worries abound. It is not as easy to make a lot of money in the medical profession as it used to be. Hospital systems and physician practices face enormous financial pressures that are unlikely to ease in the face of an ever-growing need to provide cost-efficient care. Look into these issues so you can go into practice with your eyes wide open.

## THE REALITY OF MED SCHOOL

It's easy to nurture a fantasy of what med school will be like: Within days of your arrival, you'll be caring for patients, following eminent physicians, and—after you're done with a hard but reasonable day's work—leading a social life worthy of an upscale beer commercial.

Not surprisingly, few students report that their experience met their expectations. To many, med school is surprisingly reminiscent of high school—full of anxiety, pressure, and rigid scheduling.

### In a World of HMOs

The spread of managed care is shaking the hierarchy of medical specializations and eroding physicians' incomes. Primary care physicians, who are much in demand by HMOs, are the gainers: Since 1990 their incomes have jumped nearly 30 percent. As a result, more than half of all graduating medical students now enter programs in internal, family, or pediatric medicine.

–Adapted from *Newsweek*/Kaplan's *How to Choose a Career and Graduate School*

## Don't Do It for the Money

"No amount of money is worth this amount of work. Don't get me wrong, there is money to be had, but the money is not worth it as a motivation. The most important advice is to get a life and keep it."

–Medical student, University of California at Davis

## Lingering Worries

After the exhilaration of being accepted and moving to a new place wears off, many students are left with the secret suspicion that everyone else in the orientation room had better scores and grades. The residual fear of "What if I never get accepted?" comes back in the form of "What if they find out I'm a fraud and I'm in that one percent that never graduates?" No matter how often people tell you not to worry, you will. A constant challenge of your medical school experience, particularly during the basic science years, is to push that lingering feeling to the back of your mind.

## Unbending Schedules

As an undergrad, you could choose to skip class or put off reviewing material if you were burnt out. You probably had an hour or two of free time between class blocks. But the medical school format bears a stronger resemblance to high school. In a typical curriculum, all 100-odd of your classmates stay in one room for a 50-minute class. When that class is over, the next professor runs up his PowerPoint presentation, and another 50-minute class on a different subject begins. Afternoon classes may be punctuated by anatomy or histology labs.

## Delayed Gratification

Many students expect to jump right in and start taking care of patients. But the reality is that there's a whole world of knowledge you need before you're really able to care for people's medical needs. After years of dreaming about applying all your schooling, it's difficult to put that off for even longer.

## Stress City

Part of the selection process for med school is designed to find out how you handle stress. For that reason, you may get questions in an interview such as "What's the hardest thing you've ever had to do?" or "How do you handle stress?" Med school is admittedly stressful. The toughest part seems to be the quantity of material to be dealt with. All subjects are important, and there truly is more information than you could possibly learn. Someone else has always learned more than you about something, and—particularly during the first year—there are always acronyms or diseases you've never heard of. Since most medical students are accustomed to being at the top of their class it's hard to get used to being one of the crowd and perhaps no longer at the top.

The students who tend to do best are those who have efficient study habits, don't underestimate the difficulty of the work, have realistic expectations about their ability to retain very significant amounts of material, and make time for regular social events. The ultimate goal is to get through medical school while building the foundation for being a good physician. Perspective on the entire process is critical to your sanity during your four years. Remember, even the person who graduates last in the class is called "doctor."

> ### The Hardest Years
>
> "Before I entered residency, I thought med school was the four hardest years of my life. The amount of information you had to handle was overwhelming at times. Classes were very much like having a nine-to-five job, and then you had to go home and memorize all the information in the evening."
>
> —MD, University of North Carolina, Chapel Hill

## Decent Social Life

For many students, this is a pleasant surprise. Once most people adjust to med school, they find they have about as much social life as they had in college. Of course, this assumes that medical students had a social life during college. For you, it is important to maintain your hobbies and friendships now, so that you can continue to live a balanced and healthy lifestyle during and after medical school. It just has to be more carefully timed. Many mothers and fathers manage to care for their families while doing well in medical school; it's just a matter of prioritizing and scheduling.

> ### As for Residents...
>
> Despite efforts to reform the system, young doctors doing their residencies still work inhumanly long days. "I've operated when I've been up for 24 hours," says Jana Kaplan, who as a third-year ob-gyn resident in Baltimore put in 100-hour weeks even though she was pregnant.
>
> —Adapted from *Newsweek*/Kaplan's *How to Choose a Career and Graduate School*

Life in medical school revolves around the testing schedule. Some schools have all tests on one day three or four times a semester. This means that the weekend after a test day is totally free. Other schools will have tests throughout the year; you'll learn to schedule weekend fun that includes a few hours away from everyone to study for your biochemistry quiz the following Monday.

The changes most medical students notice in their social lives are as follows:

- Having to say no to friends who want to go out
- Losing touch with some peripheral friends
- Becoming aware that their day-to-day vocabulary has become quite different from that of their nonmedical friends
- Giving in to the urge to "talk shop" while socializing, especially when socializing with those with whom you'll spend the most time—other medical students

## Peers and Colleagues

For some people, medical school introduces them to the first social group in which everyone wants to do basically the same things and everyone has had to prepare academically in basically the same way. You'll find you have many things in common with everyone else in your class. There's a flip side, though: While medical schools aim for diversity, your classmates may be a surprisingly homogeneous group. A class consisting of a hundred or so people is usually large enough for you to find a core group you like, but it may make for a less diverse circle of friends than you're used to.

## Married Life

It's no secret that med school can put stress on a relationship. However, plenty of couples happily survive those four years. Most medical schools, especially those affiliated with larger universities, have activities for students' spouses or partners. Married medical students are making up more of each med school class. Since students begin medical school, on the average, at age 24 and graduate at 28, lots of students partner up during their medical school years. Typically, around 9 percent of an entering class will be married. Chances are if you're married or in a committed relationship, you'll be able to find other couples with similar interests from within your own class.

## THE QUALITIES SCHOOLS LOOK FOR

One important consideration in your decision to become a doctor is whether you are well-suited to a medical career. In other words, you have to ask yourself if you will make a good doctor. This can be a difficult question to answer because, for example, a transplant surgeon requires a different set of skills than does a psychiatrist. Each medical school will attempt to enroll a wide variety of students in the belief that this diversity will enrich the experience for all students.

Medical schools do not have a secret formula for the qualities they seek. Rather, they often ask an intuitive question: Would I want this applicant to be my physician someday? Throughout the application process, medical schools will use various parts of your application to evaluate whether or not you possess these qualities. While there is no one model for the ideal medical student and physician, there are a number of qualities that most medical schools find desirable in their applicants. Ask yourself how you rate in each characteristic below.

## Cognitive Ability

Native intelligence is essential. It takes intellectual firepower to understand and retain the body of knowledge required to be a doctor. This is why medical schools place such emphasis on your academic record and MCAT scores.

## Critical Thinking

Knowledge by itself is not enough. Doctors must be able to think critically, to synthesize information, and to solve problems. They must be able to find the answers to puzzles and to tease out a diagnosis from a set of often ambiguous or contradictory facts or symptoms. This intuition—part learned and part innate—separates the good clinician from the great clinician and is part of what has been described as the art of medicine. The format of the MCAT—which challenges test takers with unfamiliar passages and asks questions that require inference, assumption and synthesis of pre-existing knowledge with new information—is an indicator of the value that medical schools place on this quality.

## Curiosity

You need to have a sincere desire to investigate and to learn. Some of what you learn in medical school will be outdated within a few years of your graduation. During your professional career, you'll be asked to continually learn, and—depending upon your practice setting—contribute to new basic science knowledge and the body of clinical best practices and treatments. Do you have a sense of wonder about how the body works? About what causes disease? About how treatments work? Do you follow through to find answers to questions like these?

## Commitment

The rewards of being a doctor are many, but in order to reap those rewards, you must be committed to working harder than most people. The hours are long, and so is the period of training. In fact, as mentioned earlier, your medical education never ends. You must really want to be a doctor and be willing to make the sacrifices needed to become an excellent one. While this may seem obvious, the importance of this statement cannot be overemphasized. The drive should be internal. Your commitment must be a true, personal one, not simply a reflection of your parents' or peers' expectations. You should feel emotionally impelled to be a doctor.

## Compassion

A compassionate person is one who is conscious of others' distress and who has a sincere desire to alleviate that distress. Most people considering careers in medicine say that they want to help people. This is at the heart of medicine. There is no better way to show compassion than by dedicating yourself to helping others regain or maintain their health. Ask yourself what you have done to demonstrate that you are compassionate. Medical schools will want to see some evidence that you possess this quality.

## Communication Skills

A doctor must be able to communicate well. One of the most frequently heard complaints voiced by patients is that their doctors won't listen to them or, conversely, that their doctors won't talk to them. Highly developed communication skills are essential. Communication with patients is important, but effective communication with the medical team is equally important because a majority of medical errors occur as a result of communication failure. Work at developing your communication skills by actively participating in out-of-class activities that allow you to interact with others and require you to be an effective communicator.

## Cooperation

Cooperation means teamwork: Doctors do not work alone. They must be able to work closely and cooperatively with colleagues from many specialties. Healthcare today involves multidisciplinary care teams that include a variety of professionals: attending physicians, fellows, residents, medical students, nurses, therapists, technicians, administrative and support staff, and others. The effective doctor is one who recognizes the contribution each person can make to the care of the patient. Ask yourself how well you work with others. Do you insist on "doing it yourself," or are you willing to involve others?

Check out these cultural awareness and sensitivity resources for physicians and other healthcare providers:

Books
- Galanti, Geri-Ann. *Caring for Patients from Different Cultures*, 4th Edition. Philadelphia: University of Pennsylvania Press, 2008.
- Galanti, Geri-Ann. *Cultural Sensitivity: A Pocket Guide for Health Care Professionals*, 2nd Edition. Oakbrook Terrace, IL: Joint Commission Resources, 2010.
- Spector, Rachel E. *Cultural Diversity in Health and Illness*, 8th Edition. Upper Saddle River, NJ: Prentice Hall, 2012.

Websites
- www.gagalanti.com
- www.hrsa.gov/culturalcompetence

## Cultural Awareness and Sensitivity

As a doctor you will treat patients from many cultures that are vastly different from your own. Their customs, beliefs, social forms, and truths may diverge greatly from the ones you were taught. You will need to be sensitive to those differences in order to effectively help those patients. This goes beyond tolerance of differences; you will need to try to understand those differences.

## Character

Physicians are given a special place in society. Medicine is consistently rated as one of the most highly regarded professions in America. Doctors are granted access to their patients' secrets and are given powers over their patients that few others are privileged to possess. With these privileges comes a high level of responsibility. As a physician, you will be held to an exceptionally high standard of moral excellence and firmness. Your character must be above reproach, your integrity and values unquestioned.

While past failings, including disciplinary actions as a student or a criminal history, won't necessarily preclude an applicant from acceptance into medical school, they do present an extra hurdle that must be overcome. In such situations, the burden falls on the applicant to candidly and fully explain the circumstances of the past transgressions and convince committee members that such experiences aren't negatively reflective of the applicant's potential as a physician.

## Maturity

As a physician, you will have to regularly deal with difficult and challenging issues (as well as people). Death, abortion, euthanasia, and patients unable to pay for medical care are consistent elements of debate surrounding healthcare delivery in the United States. Doctors are counted on by their patients and other members of the medical team to handle these issues professionally and always in the best interests of the patient. Thus, your personal maturity must be exceptionally high.

## YOUR PREMED ADVISER

If you're having doubts about whether med school is for you, or if you're wondering about your chances of getting in, consider talking to your premed adviser. Your premed adviser will have specific data about med school requirements, how students from your school fared in the admissions process, and where students with similar academic backgrounds and MCAT scores were accepted.

### Going It Alone

Naturally, you can apply to medical school without the help of the premed office. But medical schools are usually familiar with the procedures of different undergrad institutions. If they know you had access to a premed office, they will wonder why you chose to bypass it.

At many undergraduate institutions, the premed office handles the letters of recommendation. In some cases, they simply relay the letters to the medical schools. In other cases, the premed adviser or committee writes a letter to the admissions offices on your behalf. This letter can take the form of a "composite letter," which excerpts your recommendations, or it may simply be a cover letter that accompanies the recommendations. Either way, it is imperative that you get to know the people who are going to be writing letters on your behalf. In most such cases, the advisers require a number of meetings with their advisees. Take these meetings very seriously.

Premed advisers are a harried bunch these days. Due to budget cuts resulting from the poor economy, many schools have eliminated or reduced the number of their premed advisers. It's possible that if you're not a particularly strong candidate, you may find your adviser less than enthusiastic about your applying to medical school. She may have legitimate concerns about your competitiveness and may try to dissuade you from applying. Then it's up to you. You may have to go it alone, without the full support of your school's premed office. Be realistic. If everyone agrees your chances are slim, have a backup plan just in case you're not admitted.

If you're a nontraditional student or a transfer who has attended other schools, be aware that you may have access to advisers at your old school. If you do not know if there is an adviser at your school, visit the National Association of Advisors for the Health Professions (NAAHP) at www.naahp.org or email NAAHP.membership@naahp.org.

Be aware that not all premed adviser are created equal. While almost all premed adviser will be well-meaning and most are fantastic resources, some premeds will run across premed adviser who provide incomplete or outdated information. If you find yourself with doubts about the quality of advice you receive, if you have limited access to your adviser, or if you would simply like another opinion or to supplement information you've received from your adviser, take a look at the *Medical School Admission Requirements*, also known as the MSAR—you'll learn more about this valuable resource in chapter 4. Also consider contacting medical school admissions offices directly. Email and telephone contact information for admissions offices can be found readily on most school websites. Admissions offices regularly field calls from potential and current applicants, and most will make every effort to offer specific information about their admissions practices, requirements, and timeline; statistics regarding recently matriculated classes; and, to the extent possible, advice regarding the competitiveness of your application.

# PART TWO

# Planning for Medical School

# CHAPTER 2

# Planning Your Undergraduate Curriculum

Success requires a good plan, plenty of hard work, and a little luck. This is particularly true of the pursuit of a medical career. While there is little we can do about the last two parts of the equation, we can help you develop your plan to apply successfully to medical school.

All plans have a beginning. To be a successful medical school applicant, you need to treat admissions efforts as a strategic campaign. You have to put your best foot forward—first on paper, then in person. The more you understand about the application process, and the more time and care you dedicate to approaching the process (both in research and preparation), the better your chances are of being accepted into a medical school.

## UNDERGRADUATE BASICS

The first step in planning for a medical education is to plan your undergraduate education. Medical schools are looking for well-rounded, broadly educated students. That said, there are still many decisions that you will need to make.

Most medical schools do not require a college degree. Rather, they require that applicants have at least three years (90 hours) of full-time undergraduate work at an accredited college or university. That said, the majority of successful applicants do hold a baccalaureate degree; many hold advanced degrees. Just what degree you are awarded is not important, since there is no distinction made between individual majors or between bachelor of science and bachelor of arts degrees.

## Picking the "Right" Undergraduate College

Premed students and their parents are often concerned with going to the "right" undergraduate school, meaning the undergraduate school that will give the student the greatest chance of getting into medical school. As much as we hate to admit it, there is some validity to this attitude, given that most medical school admissions committees do consider the undergraduate institution attended when reviewing an applicant's academic history. Moreover, opinions on the quality of undergraduate institutions will likely be a more significant contributor to admissions decisions at more selective medical schools.

However, a particular medical school's admissions committee's opinion of an undergraduate institution shouldn't be the litmus test for whether or not you should attend that college. First, it's highly unlikely that a medical school will give you its rankings of undergraduate schools. Second, it would be difficult to get most, much less all, medical schools to agree upon the quality of education at any given undergraduate institution. Third, the four or more years you will spend getting your undergraduate education are more than just a pit stop on your way to medical school. College should be a time of development, a chance to expose yourself to different ways of thinking in a variety of academic disciplines and pursuits. Fourth, as hard as this is to believe, you may ultimately decide you want to do something with your life other than becoming a physician. Finally, and perhaps most importantly, the college one attends is not a limiting factor in the medical school admissions process. Year after year, students are admitted into medical school from nearly every undergraduate institution in the country. The real measure of admissions lies, at its core, with the applicant.

Considering all this, a better way to approach the issue of where to attend undergraduate school is to compile a list of schools you believe will enable you to do your best work. Ask yourself the following questions:

- Do you work better on a quarter system or a semester system? Do you hit the ground running at the introduction to new subject matter but suffer from a short attention span, or do you take a while to warm up to a subject before coming on strong at the end?

- Would you do better with small class sizes (fewer than 100) in which you would be more likely to get individual attention, or do you prefer the stimulation, as well as the anonymity, of a large class size (greater than 250)?

- Would you like to be within driving distance of home, able to enjoy an occasional home-cooked meal and laundry service, or do you need to get as far away as possible from the nest?

## Two-Year versus Four-Year Colleges

Many successful applicants complete part of their undergraduate education at two-year community colleges. The reasons for doing so include an initial inability to gain admission to a four-year institution, financial considerations, course selection and availability, and issues of convenience. While you certainly can take some courses at a two-year school, whenever possible, complete your prerequisite science courses at a four-year institution. Many admissions committees look to your performance in undergraduate science courses as being a good predictor of your potential to negotiate the preclinical medical school curriculum. Therefore, you should strive to perform well in the most academically challenging environment available to you. Typically, although not always, this means completing prerequisite coursework at a four-year school.

An additional thing to consider is that many admissions committees do not consider grades earned from community colleges when evaluating your composite GPA. If you have taken all of your science courses at a community college and you apply to a medical school that does not consider community college grades, you could find yourself without a science GPA for the purposes of that particular medical school.

These are just some of the many issues you might consider when deciding whether a particular school is right for you. Remember, it doesn't do you any good to go to the "right" school if you crash and burn because it wasn't the right school for you.

Once you've made a list of potential schools, you should consider how the institutions rate with medical schools. You can do this by asking the premed office what percentage of premed applicants were accepted over the past five years. Compare that number to the percentage accepted within the state as well as across the country (both of which are available in the MSAR). Ideally, the school you attend should have acceptance rates equal to or higher than both the state and national averages.

## Choosing an Undergraduate Major

As we've already said, admissions committees look for well-rounded, broadly educated applicants. Successful candidates demonstrate a high level of scholastic achievement and intellectual curiosity, as well as an aptitude for the sciences.

---

**Do What You Like**

Don't choose a major because you think it will get you accepted to med school. Choose something you're really interested in studying. You'll probably get better grades if you study what interests you most.

---

As a rule, admissions committees do not take into account an applicant's undergraduate major. Therefore, aside from doing well in the required premedical courses, it is important for you to choose a major of your liking. First of all, your overall academic record will probably be stronger if you take classes you enjoy; and secondly, if you choose not to go to medical school, you will have a major that will help you in gaining employment or in applying to graduate school.

This said, science majors often have a significant academic advantage in medical school over their classmates who did not major in science. The first two years of medical school intensively cover the basics of anatomy, physiology, behavioral science, biochemistry, microbiology, immunology, pathophysiology, and pharmacology. Science majors are far more likely to have studied some of these subjects in detail during their upper-division coursework. Those students often find the first two years of medical school less demanding and occasionally are asked to tutor other medical students in their areas of expertise. To add to the benefits of majoring in science, biology majors at most colleges automatically fulfill much of their premedical coursework requirements simply by completing their major requirements. Still, the only applicants to medical school who *must* major in science are those interested in entering a joint MD/PhD program.

In its listing of information regarding the majors of successful medical school applicants, the MSAR notes that 52.6 percent of successful applicants were life science majors; science majors in general composed more than 75 percent of those accepted to med schools in 2012. This might lead you to believe that medical schools prefer science majors. This isn't the case, however. The proportion of accepted applicants with life science and science majors in general remains roughly in line with their percentage of the total applicant population.

What these statistics indicate is that if you're a non-science major, you're not at a disadvantage. The more important basis for admission to med school is your undergraduate transcript, no matter what your major is. If you're not a science major, your work in both science and non-science courses will be evaluated. However, with fewer courses on which to judge your science ability, your grades in the core science courses will take on greater importance, both qualitatively and to your science GPA.

On the other hand, a science major who has taken the minimum number of non-science courses may in fact be at some disadvantage: Medicine is a people profession, and many admissions committees look for applicants with demonstrated interests in the world around them, which may be illustrated in part by a broad selection of courses.

## BASIC COURSE REQUIREMENTS

The faculty at each medical school is responsible for establishing courses required for admission. In some cases, required courses reflect courses needed for licensure as a physician in the state in which the medical school is located; in other cases, prerequisites reflect institutional requirements.

In general, current requirements include one year of biology, one year of physics, one year of general chemistry, and one year of organic chemistry—as well as each subject's related lab work, with some variation from school to school as to the specific number of hours required to satisfy the lab work requirement. Additionally, many medical schools also require math and English, with specific requirements for each varying. The best sources for specific information on prerequisites are the MSAR and the American Association of Colleges of Osteopathic Medicine's (AACOM) *Osteopathic Medical College Information Book*, which include requirements for all of the programs.

Some schools, especially California schools, prefer Spanish proficiency, although it is usually not a requirement. Because of changes to the MCAT with the introduction of MCAT 2015 in the spring of 2015, many schools are changing their basic course requirements for students entering in 2016 and later. Almost all schools that don't already require entering students to have completed courses in biochemistry, psychology, and sociology will have those requirements for students entering in 2016. Many schools will require a statistics course. The MSAR and AACOM's *College Information Book*, along with individual school websites, remains the best resource to stay abreast of changes to course requirements.

### Prerequisite Courses

When enrolling in your required premed courses, you must almost always choose between two different course sequences: courses for students majoring in that particular discipline, and courses for everyone else. For example, when you register to take the one-year general physics requirement, you will have the option of taking one-year, calculus-based general physics sequences intended for engineering and physical science majors or a one-year, algebra-based general physics sequence intended for other majors and often taken by life science majors. If you happen to be in a major that requires the calculus-based sequence, the decision is easy—you take the sequence designed for your major. But what if you have a choice?

In general, medical school admissions committees state that when two course sequences are available, you should take the more academically challenging of the two. That said, there are still some practical realities of life that you might want to consider. First, be sure that the course you choose to take appropriately covers those topics commonly presented on the MCAT. In the previous example, for instance, many two-semester, calculus-based physics sequences cover only mechanics and electricity and magnetism, while most two-semester, algebra-based college physics sequences also include topics such as thermodynamics, geometric optics, sound, and fluids that are tested in the physical sciences section of the MCAT. Second, the reason many college subjects are divided into two distinct tracks is that the subject matter is difficult. Courses designed for students majoring in that discipline are filled with students who live, eat, and breathe the stuff and are therefore presumably good at it. The competition will be stiff. If you think you can do well, go for it. But if you think you will have to work very hard—too hard—to perform well, it is probably wiser to take the sequence for the nonmajors. But be careful: Some schools offer a "watered-down" course sequence for non-science majors, like "Physics for Poets." These should be avoided at all costs, as they are unlikely to satisfy most medical school course requirements and will ill prepare you for the content tested on the MCAT.

This brings us to another practical reality of life: It is unlikely that the medical school admissions committee reviewing your application will be fully versed in the course sequences offered by your undergraduate institution, or that it will actually reward you for having chosen the harder sequence for each premed requirement. What is more likely to be true is that your application will be considered based upon your academic performance without regard for whether or not you took the more difficult sequence. Of course, it is best to get an A in the more challenging course, but it's better to get an A in an easier course than a C in a more difficult course.

Does that mean you should try to "pad" your GPA by taking the easiest courses available? Of course not. But it does mean you should use your head. Challenge yourself, yes. Push yourself to develop your potential, yes. But don't put yourself in a position where you have no hope of succeeding academically no matter how hard you work.

While your GPA is only a number and not wholly reflective of your academic experience, it remains a vitally important measure in the admissions process.

A related issue concerns choice of instructors. It may be that the same class, taught by different instructors, is offered on different days or at different times. If you have a choice, by all means find out all you can about the instructors and their teaching styles. Read the course evaluations on file with the course department or student services, or talk to upperclassmen or your premed adviser. Then, pick the instructor who is best for you and your learning style.

Unless you are in a structured postbaccalaureate program, you should try to pace the completion of your prerequisite courses over your four undergraduate years, but with an eye toward completion of those courses covering information tested on the MCAT ahead of your planned test date.

Here is a course schedule that would prepare you for taking MCAT 2015 (the new version of the exam, which launches in the spring of 2015) during or after your junior year. It takes into account other courses that are required or recommended by a large number of medical schools (two-semester sequence in writing or English, and mathematics, up to second-semester calculus). Keep in mind that this schedule does not take into account your own school's requirements, Advanced Placement (AP) exam scores besides calculus, or courses required for your major. It also does not take into account extracurricular activities, which may play a significant role in which classes you'll be able to fit in during a given semester.

| YEAR | FALL SEMESTER | SPRING SEMESTER |
|---|---|---|
| *Freshman* | Biology I<br>General Chemistry I<br>Writing/English<br>Calculus I | Biology II<br>General Chemistry II<br>Writing/English<br>Calculus II |
| *Sophomore* | Organic Chemistry I<br>Psychology<br>*2 open courses* | Organic Chemistry II<br>Sociology<br>*2 open courses* |
| *Junior* | Physics I<br>Biochemistry<br>*2 open courses* | Physics III<br>*3 open courses*<br>*Start preparing for the MCAT* |
| *Senior* | *4 open courses*<br>*Apply to medical school!* | *4 open courses*<br>*Apply to medical school!* |

## Biology

Most medical schools require a two-semester sequence in introductory biology as adequate preparation for the MCAT and medical school. These two courses should be scheduled during your freshman year of undergraduate school for a couple reasons. First, if you're not positive that medicine is the right path for you, biology is the science most clearly connected to the content physicians think about every day. Second, premedical students who are science majors (especially biology majors) will often have to take higher-level biology courses as part of their studies. Even if you're a non-science major, consider taking higher-level biology courses during undergrad.

## General Chemistry

Most medical schools require a two-semester sequence in introductory general chemistry as adequate preparation for the MCAT and medical school. It is very important to schedule these two classes during freshman year since they are prerequisites for organic chemistry and biochemistry. While studying general chemistry in undergrad, focus on themes and trends rather than just the math. Not only is this more in line with what the MCAT will test, but it also just makes the material more memorable for midterms and finals, as well as over the long term.

## Organic Chemistry

Most medical schools require a two-semester sequence in organic chemistry as adequate preparation for the MCAT and medical school. Organic chemistry is ideally scheduled during sophomore year, since it is usually a prerequisite for biochemistry courses. Learning organic chemistry is like learning a new language. You'll find the same thing in medical school, too. Additionally, the terminology of organic chemistry is important for the MCAT. It's not common to see questions on the MCAT ask directly for nomenclature, but jargon is used in passages and questions with the assumption that you can understand what's being said. Isomerism, for example, uses terms like *structural/constitutional isomer, stereoisomer, conformational isomer, diastereomer, enantiomer, geometric isomer, epimer* and *anomer.* You need to understand what each of these terms means and be able to use these terms accurately.

## Physics

Most medical schools require a two-semester sequence in introductory physics as adequate preparation for the MCAT and medical school. You can take physics during sophomore year; alternatively, you can push it back to junior year to lighten your course load during the first two years of undergrad. Similar to general chemistry, many undergraduate physics classes are focused heavily on solving problems mathematically. Often they require calculus as well; the MCAT does not expect you to apply calculus at all during the exam. And while it's more common to have plug-and-chug questions in physics than in general chemistry, they're still not the norm.

# PREPARING FOR MCAT 2015: BIOCHEMISTRY, PSYCHOLOGY, AND SOCIOLOGY

The three sciences listed here constitute the material that is being added to the 2015 MCAT. While there are some ways to circumvent taking these courses and study the material on your own, this should not be your primary strategy.

## Biochemistry

Most medical schools do not require biochemistry for entrance to their institution, although many schools do highly recommend such a course. For the MCAT, the AAMC recommends one semester of college-level biochemistry. Since both general chemistry and organic chemistry are usually prerequisites for biochemistry, you will likely have to take this course during the fall semester of your junior year as you prepare to study for the MCAT during spring semester that year.

Many students are nervous about biochemistry because of how intricate and detailed the subject matter is. But this shouldn't be a deterrent to you—the human body is just as complex (indeed, metabolism is essentially just the application of biochemistry to human physiology), and it's this complexity that makes medicine so interesting. This anxiety about biochemistry may flow out of the fact that many undergraduate biochemistry classes focus ostensibly on the memorization of reaction pathways: glucose is converted into glucose-6-phosphate by glucokinase or hexokinase, which is converted into fructose-6-phosphate by phosphoglucose isomerase, and so on. This is one way of considering glycolysis, but it's not the way the 2015 MCAT is likely to test this information.

## Psychology

Most medical schools do not require psychology classes for entrance to their institution. For the MCAT, the AAMC recommends one semester of introductory psychology. Since psychology is not a prerequisite for any of the other premedical courses, you can choose to take it any time before the MCAT. However, we suggest taking psychology sooner as opposed to later in your college career—perhaps during fall semester of sophomore year. You don't want to put off taking psychology because it has connections to critical analysis of research. Psychology has its roots in strong research design, and creating a robust psychological study is actually quite difficult. Controlling for lurking variables, assessing for sampling and generalizability errors, and finding creative ways to present data are some of the major challenges of this line of research and will be major parts of the 2015 MCAT.

An introductory-level course should suffice for the material that you'll be expected to know for the MCAT. The breadth of psychology material that the AAMC is adding for the new 2015 MCAT is vast. It includes everything from cognitive processes (development, attention, language, and perception) to behavioral models (attribution theory, discrimination, nonverbal communication, and attachment) to abnormal psychology (mood disorders, psychosis, and personality disorders). Therefore, it would be optimal to take the broadest introductory-level class, rather than multiple courses covering more narrow topics at a deeper level, such as Abnormal Psychology or Developmental Psychology.

## Sociology

Most medical schools do not require sociology classes for entrance to their institution. For the MCAT, the AAMC recommends one semester of introductory sociology. Since sociology is not a prerequisite for any of the other premedical courses, you can choose to take it any time before the MCAT. However, it may be best to take it as soon as you've completed psychology, during spring semester of sophomore year. By continuing with behavioral sciences in the same year, you can create connections between the material of psychology (studying the mind and behavior at the individual level, and how the individual interacts with society) and the material of sociology (studying the mind and behavior at the societal level, and how society interacts with the individual).

An introductory course in sociology should suffice for the material you'll be expected to know on Test Day. While the sociology material on the MCAT is again quite broad in scope, the depth is not as great as that of other science material included on the 2015 MCAT. Much of sociology may make intuitive sense to you, but it's important to know how to translate that intuition into the terminology the testmakers will use on the MCAT.

# VERBAL REASONING / CRITICAL ANALYSIS AND REASONING SKILLS

Most medical schools require two semesters of writing or English as adequate preparation for medical school. There are no formal recommendations of specific types of writing or English classes as preparation for the MCAT. Further, there is no outside knowledge required for this section; all information necessary to answer the questions is included in the passage.

So how do you prepare for Verbal Reasoning on the current MCAT or Critical Analysis and Reasoning Skills (CARS) on the new MCAT? The answer is simple: Read and think. This direction is intentionally vague, because you want to expose yourself to as much information (especially opinionated, potentially biased information) as possible. Read academic journals both in topics that you enjoy and in topics you sometimes struggle with. Watch the news and critique the arguments of political pundits and the popular media. Question the validity of advertisements. Challenge your professors (tactfully!). By honing your skills in constructing an argument, you can start to *deconstruct* the arguments you'll see on Test Day.

## Waiving Requirements

Many applicants want to know whether requirements can be waived. Requirements cannot be waived if they are licensure requirements. However, institutional requirements may be waived depending on the institutional policy. Your best bet is to complete the prerequisite courses of those medical schools to which you plan to apply. If you are unable to complete a requirement, check with each relevant institution regarding their waiver policy.

## AP Credit

Many applicants receive high school AP credit for lower-division science lecture courses and, in some cases, for laboratory courses. AP credits can often satisfy prerequisite requirements. However, because this is an institutional decision, contact each school you're applying to regarding its policy.

The most commonly acceptable AP credits for medical school purposes are math (calculus and statistics) and physics credits.

## Study Abroad

Many applicants study overseas during their undergraduate careers. If you are lucky enough to do so, congratulations: The chance to live, work, and play in a different culture will be one of the great experiences of your life. Because you will undoubtedly want to travel while you are abroad, it is advisable that you not overload your academic schedule. To this end, you should save any outstanding prerequisite courses until you return to your home undergraduate campus. You may also want to consider taking your courses on a pass-fail basis, particularly if you are studying in a country where the language spoken is not your native tongue.

Another important consideration is that you will most likely be applying to medical schools during your senior year. Since all medical schools require personal interviews, if you are engaged in study abroad during your application year, you may be required to return to the United States for interviews. Make sure that you (and your budget) allow for this possibility.

## POSTBACCALAUREATE PROGRAMS

Postbaccalaureate programs are academic programs specifically designed to help applicants improve their chances of gaining admission to medical school. While there are several types of postbac programs (discussed in chapters 12 and 13), one type is for students who decide to apply to medical school after graduation from college and need to fulfill prerequisite course requirements, or who wish to retake courses to improve their performance.

If you're considering entering a postbaccalaureate program, bear in mind that postbaccalaureate work is automatically averaged in with the undergraduate GPA on the American Medical College Application Service (AMCAS) application. The extent to which the postbac work is ultimately considered depends on the degree to which individual admissions committees consider it relevant to the evaluation process. In order to view a partial list of programs, see the AAMC Student Hub at http://services. aamc.org/postbac.

# CHAPTER 3

# Extracurricular Activities

Medical school admissions committees select applicants who have demonstrated intelligence, maturity, integrity, and a dedication to the ideal of service to society. Of these qualities, your intelligence is the easiest to measure objectively. Assessment of the other three is tricky and subjective. But rest assured, admissions committees *will* make this judgment about you.

One way that admissions committees can assess your nonacademic qualities is by looking at how you have lived your life, as reflected in your medical school application. To this end, many committees review the list of extracurricular activities with which you have been involved. As you participate in these activities, keep in mind that you will have many opportunities to elaborate upon them in varying levels of detail throughout the application process. You will choose some of them to discuss in your personal statement. Others you will describe in short essay responses as part of your secondary applications. For some activities, such as clinical experience and research, you will likely wish to ask for a letter of recommendation from your supervisor or adviser. And in your interview, you will have the chance to have a dialogue about some of these experiences. Most admissions committees consider the nature and depth of the extracurricular activities you have undertaken to offer insight into you and your motivations and to be a significant factor in your admissibility to medical school.

# CLINICAL EXPERIENCE

Of all the activities you could be involved in, the one that is most likely to be considered essential by a medical school admissions committee is clinical experience. Over 90 percent of matriculating students in 2012 volunteered and/or worked in healthcare prior to beginning medical school. As a general trend, clinical experience has become increasingly important for admissions purposes. As recently as ten years ago, interviewers would ask, "Do you have any clinical experience?" Now they say, "Please discuss your clinical experience." After all, you are applying to medical school—not business, law, or graduate school. It is not unreasonable for the committee to want to see some evidence that you know firsthand what you're getting into. The standard answer applicants give when asked why they want a career in medicine is, "I want to help people." While there is nothing wrong with that answer (one sure way to be eliminated from the competition is to say "I don't like helping people"), clearly you can help people and have a lot more fun as a cruise director than as a physician. Sick people don't feel well; they get cranky, and they may forget to say thank you. Admissions committees want proof that you have some sense of a profession.

---

**Try the Hospital**

"I recommend doing hospital volunteer work. It gives you the chance to find out if you like the work environment, being around sick people. And, best of all, it's fun. You'd be surprised how few prospective medical students list volunteer-work experience."

—Soni J. Anderson, University of Alabama School of Medicine, adapted from *Newsweek*/Kaplan's *How to Choose a Career and Graduate School*

---

While medical schools do not "officially" require healthcare experience, applicants are finding it increasingly hard to be admitted without it, or at least without being able to speak cogently about the realities of healthcare. So it pays well to be sure you include this experience in your college, and even high school, years.

## *What's the Best Experience?*

The quintessential clinical experience an applicant can have is to work in an emergency room. Emergency rooms are plentiful, and they're always looking for a few good volunteers. That said, the experience is seldom a good use of your time, even if it does make for a decent story to recount in an interview. The reason for this is that ERs tend to be busy places. You don't know anything about emergency medicine. Therefore, what you'll most likely end up doing is running errands for someone—not the best use of your time, given that the goal is for you to gain insight into the role that a physician plays in the healthcare delivery system.

Your time would be much better spent if you volunteered for a chronic-care activity. By this we mean working with people who have a chronic illness or disability. Because these patients have long-term conditions, volunteers get put to real use as support individuals within the healthcare team. Additionally, you are likely to work with the same patients and their families for weeks, if not months, at a time. This can give you the opportunity to experience healthcare over time from multiple perspectives—that of the patient, his family, the physician, and other members of the healthcare delivery team.

### How to Find It

The best way to find such an experience is to call those organizations in your community that work with the chronically ill or disabled. Such organizations may work with people who have conditions such as multiple sclerosis, cystic fibrosis, mental retardation, and spinal cord injuries, or they may work with battered women and children, drug-addicted babies, AIDS patients, and so on. Pick an organization of interest to you and go for it. Remember that you may be asked to make a commitment of up to one year, but in return, you will be made a real member of the team.

Remember: Clinical experience is very valuable during the application process. Applicants will have a chance to discuss it in the personal statement and during interviews and to receive a letter of recommendation from a clinical supervisor.

One of the most critical aspects of any clinical experience is that you enjoy it. If you don't like chronic care, try working in a small clinic in an underserved area, or find another area of medicine that suits your interests. Not every experience is perfect for everyone.

> **Stand Out**
>
> "Med school is so competitive that you have to find a way to distinguish yourself. I was an English major, had a musical background, and worked as an undergraduate, and I think these things all helped me stand out. Admissions people don't talk about applicants as 'the person with a 4.0 and great MCAT scores.' Virtually every applicant is at the top of his or her class, has great recommendations, and was in an honors society. Admissions people remember the applicant who worked with handicapped children, started a soup kitchen, or had an art exhibit."
>
> —MD, Jefferson Medical College

## RESEARCH EXPERIENCE

In general, the only time research experience is an absolute must is if you are planning to apply to MD/PhD programs or are representing yourself as someone who is interested in an academic or research career.

But that doesn't mean you wouldn't benefit from a research background if you're planning a purely clinical career. In fact, almost 60 percent of matriculating students in 2013 served in a laboratory research apprenticeship. As a future physician, your job will involve research, either as you seek to determine your patients' medical conditions or through the process of continuing education, in which you study other individuals' research efforts. Research experience demonstrates to medical schools that your thirst for scientific knowledge does not end in the classroom. Curiosity and a sense of lifelong learning are essential qualities of a good medical student and physician.

Most applicants obtain their research experience during their undergraduate years. There are three paths that can be taken. The first involves taking a class for academic credit that is designed to allow the student to work one-on-one with a faculty member on an independent research project. The second path involves applying and being accepted to participate in a sponsored summer research program. The final path entails volunteering in a laboratory and working your way up to a position of greater responsibility. This final path is the one most often taken by students with no prior lab experience.

## TEACHING EXPERIENCE

A third category of extracurricular activity common to many successful applicants is teaching. One of the most important roles that a physician plays is that of a teacher, as she communicates medical information and frames complex medical decisions for patients; teaching patients enables them to play a more active role in their own healthcare, a proven factor in healthcare outcomes.

The diversity of teaching experiences of medical school applicants during their undergraduate years is very broad. Such experience might include teaching Bible study in your place of worship, leading swimming or musical instrument lessons for children, or becoming a teaching assistant in a lower-division class in which you did exceptionally well. Teaching can become part of almost anything that you enjoy doing. All you need to do is share it with others in a structured, organized manner.

# EMPLOYMENT

Many undergraduate students need to work throughout their college years in order to stay in school. Many admissions committees recognize that the time you work reduces the time you have for your studies and other forms of extracurricular activities. These committees understand that maintaining academic performance while holding down a job is hard work. If an applicant has been able to do both well, it is an indication that he will be able to handle the academic workload faced by medical students, when work demands are significantly decreased or eliminated but academic pressures increase.

# OTHER ACTIVITIES

Other activities that may be considered noteworthy by admissions committees include participation in campus or community governance, membership on a varsity or intramural sports team, excellence in the arts, or commitment to a socially meaningful activity such as medical mission trips or participating in the Peace Corps or AmeriCorps. In whatever you choose to do, however, you should emphasize quality over quantity. Leadership positions are especially valuable, but even more importantly, be able and prepared to communicate the personal significance of your activities in writing on primary and secondary applications and in an interview setting.

Again, while not all admissions committees consider extracurricular activities a part of the evaluation process, many do. One warning, though: No amount of participation in extracurricular activities will forgive a poor academic record. Your first priority must be to demonstrate academic excellence. Don't expect great understanding from committee members if your grades suffer as a result of participation in non-academic activities. The committee's reaction is likely to be that you showed poor judgment in setting your priorities.

# PART THREE

# Selecting a Program

# CHAPTER 4

# Your Basic Choices

Choosing the medical schools to which you will apply is perhaps the single most important decision of the admissions process. It's important that you take the time to faithfully research medical schools in which you're interested, so you'll be able to determine how good a fit each is for you. After reviewing this chapter, you'll be prepared to start drafting your list of schools.

## THE BASICS

Unfortunately, many applicants know very little, if anything, about the medical schools to which they apply. They enter the application process blindly and base their decisions on "common knowledge" or "school reputation." This is a naive way of planning a future. Before plunging into the actual logistics of the application process, you need to review some of the main criteria for selecting schools.

### MSAR: Your Premed Bible

There are currently 141 accredited medical schools in the United States—including 4 in Puerto Rico—and 17 medical schools in Canada. *Medical School Admission Requirements,* often referred to as the "MSAR," provides comprehensive information on all of these schools. The information published in this online database

**Straight from the Source**

For a complete listing of accredited schools, get access to the MSAR directory:

Association of American Medical Colleges

Website: www.aamc.org

Cost $25.00

comes from the horses' mouths—the schools themselves. It isn't filled with second-hand accounts or student opinions. It's the official stuff.

The MSAR provides profiles of all the Liaison Committee on Medical Education (LCME)–accredited schools in the United States and Canada. It's worth the $25 you'll need to purchase access to the searchable database for one year. Each school profile in the MSAR provides information on all of the following:

- Enrollment and class data
- Selection factors
- Application procedures and deadlines
- Curricular information
- Basic course requirements
- Applicant volunteer and research experience
- MCAT & GPA data
- Costs of attendance and financial aid information
- Data on applicant volunteer and research experiences
- Research opportunities
- Information on combined degree programs
- Graduates' specialty choices

In chapter 5, we'll tell you how to make the most of this excellent resource.

## NARROWING DOWN YOUR LIST

At some point, you're going to have to pare down your list of schools. While there is no magic number of schools to apply to, the average in 2013 was 14 schools. Naturally, if you're going to apply to lots of very competitive schools, you may need to construct a more extensive list. Work with your premed adviser and browse MSAR to select schools that make sense for you. Check to see where students from your college with your GPA and MCAT scores have been accepted. Also check what the median and 10th–90th percentile ranges for MCAT scores, GPAs, and science GPAs are at the schools to which you're considering applying. Also, inquire whether your school has had a feeder relationship with a particular medical school.

While you're agonizing over which schools to keep on your list, consider the following issues:

- Competitiveness
- Cost
- Accreditation
- Curriculum
- Teaching hospitals
- Location
- Affiliation with undergraduate institutions
- Student body
- Public versus private schools

## Competitiveness

As we mentioned in the introduction to this section, competition to get into medical school is very intense. You need to be realistic about your admission chances. There are many qualified applicants who won't be accepted. Don't take anything for granted; apply to schools of varying degrees of competitiveness.

The entire notion of ranking schools is, of course, a highly subjective and controversial exercise. However, rankings can provide an idea of how competitive it is to gain admission into a school. For instance, so-called Top Ten medical schools (e.g., UCSF, Hopkins, Harvard, Stanford) are very competitive. For a somewhat more objective method of evaluating a particular school's competitiveness, check the MSAR.

> ### Humane Medical Philosophy
>
> In osteopathic school, you get the same training as an MD does, as well as additional training in muscular and skeletal manipulation, and alternative forms of treatment. DO's can go into DO residencies in all medical specialties, as well as many MD residencies. They can also prescribe drugs and perform surgery. Some also say osteopathy is a more humane medical philosophy, treating a patient as a patient, not as a disease.

It's helpful to view schools in categories: highly competitive schools, middle-tiered schools, and the backup, or "safety," school. (Remember, however, when it comes to med school, there really is no such thing as a safety school.) You should not take the risk of applying only to the most competitive schools—the outcome may be rejection from all of them.

By the way, don't get too hung up on a school's reputation. All LCME-accredited schools provide a solid medical education and, no matter where you go, you get the magical MD after your name. And, while residency-program directors certainly have their individual opinions about the quality of medical schools, most will agree that United States Medical Licensing Exams Step 1 and Step 2 scores—the "board" exams that you will take in medical school as part of the requirements for eventual medical licensure—are among the most important factors in their decisions regarding how to rank applicants to their residency programs. The availability of such an objective measure of your mastery of the basic medical science and clinical knowledge necessary for success as a resident in many ways levels the playing field for applicants from less competitive medical schools when applying for residency spots in competitive specialties and programs.

---

### Pros and Cons of the Military Option

"I applied for the Health Professions Scholarship Program with the Army. They pick up just about every cost that you can imagine and give you a living stipend. In return, I had to go through officer basic training and rotations with the Army. The military is interested in keeping you happy, and you get to choose what sort of rotations you do. I have no regrets about following this path. If it wasn't for the financial support of the military, I'd probably be changing tires somewhere."

—MD, Jefferson Medical College

"One problem with the military route is that we had very little real-world exposure. In the military, you tell someone to take medicine—it's an order. People are more likely to follow rules. It's different in the civilian world. We were taught how to deal with war, famine, and exodus. It's intimidating that at some point I will have to deal with the HMO world."

—MD, Uniformed Services University of Health Sciences

## Cost

You may have already taken out loans to pay your undergraduate education, or you may have mortgages or high rents to pay. Tuition to medical school will only add to your financial burden. Of the 141 LCME-accredited medical schools in the United States, the majority are state sponsored. The difference in cost between attending a state and a private medical school can be striking. For example, consider the tuition at a state institution such as the University of Texas Southwestern. In 2013–2014, tuition for a resident was $17,843. Compare this to a private institution such as Georgetown Medical School. The tuition at Georgetown ran $53,102 for 2013–2014. If you were a resident of Texas, the difference in tuition costs of about $35,000 would translate into an additional $140,000 over four years.

Remember, we're comparing only tuition. This doesn't figure in fees or the cost-of-living (room, board, entertainment, etc.). As an example from the case above, according to one cost of living calculator, living in Washington, D.C., costs approximately 50 percent more than living in Dallas, Texas.

The solution seems all too obvious, right? Everyone should attend state schools! The problem: limited slots and strict residency requirements. State schools often strongly favor those applicants who are state residents (i.e., those who are already paying taxes to support the existence of the school). Unfortunately, residency requirements differ from state to state, so there is no one set way of establishing residency and, in many cases, those procedures that are in place make establishing residency difficult. The reported tuition price of medical schools might not provide a complete picture of the costs of attending particular school. The amount of merit and need-based aid will vary from medical school to medical school, as will the demographic and statistical profile of students receiving such aid. One rough way to estimate the real cost difference between attending various medical schools is to compare the average debt load of graduates as reported in MSAR and in other AAMC publications. Nonetheless, when considering the economics of going to medical school, state residency will more than likely be a significant consideration. It is important that you decide which state schools are feasible for you and that you clear up any misconceptions concerning residency requirements well before you apply.

## Accreditation

It is essential that the medical school you attend meets the standards established by the Liaison Committee on Medical Education (LCME), the body that is responsible for accrediting MD-granting programs in the United States. The LCME is made up of representatives appointed by the AAMC, the Council on Medical Education of the American Medical Association, the Committee on Accreditation of Canadian Medical Schools, and representatives of the general public.

LCME standards state that a medical school's curriculum must be designed to provide a general professional education, while recognizing that this alone is insufficient to prepare a graduate for independent, unsupervised medical practice. The LCME requires schools to have a program that provides a minimum of 130 weeks of instruction, usually over at least four years, and that allows students to do the following:

- Learn the fundamental principles of medicine
- Acquire the skills of clinical judgment based on evidence and experience
- Develop an ability to use principles and skills wisely in solving problems of health and disease
- Acquire an understanding of the scientific concepts underlying medicine
- Be introduced to current advances in the basic sciences, including therapy and technology, changes in the understanding of disease, and the effect of social needs and demands on medical care

The LCME goes on to specify a number of basic science and clinical areas that each medical school's curriculum must cover, but it does not specify exactly how that curriculum must be organized. As a result, medical schools differ widely on how they present their educational programs.

## Curriculum

Medical school alone will not prepare you to practice as a physician. What it will do is give you the basic training that you need to continue into residency training (graduate medical education) in the specialty that best suits your talents and interests. Only after you have completed residency training and have met other licensure requirements will you be ready to enter medical practice on your own.

Because medical school lays the foundation for the rest of your medical career, the curriculum of the medical school you attend is one of the most important criteria in selecting schools to which you will apply.

For most of the twentieth century, medical school was divided into two phases: preclinical (basic sciences) and clinical. Until recently, students were exposed to a two-year intensive dose of the basic sciences before having any meaningful patient contact. The preclinical (also called basic science) years were followed by two years of patient contact composed of clerkships and electives. The distinction between preclinical and clinical years has blurred somewhat in recent years, as medical schools introduce students to patient and simulated-patient contact earlier, often at the beginning of the first year of medical school in the form of clinical-skills classes and time spent in the hospital in various capacities.

Here are some of the ways in which the medical school curricula of today differ from those of years past:

- Length
- Organization of the preclinical years
- Use of problem-based learning
- Organization of the clinical years
- Earliest patient contact
- Primary care focus
- Innovative educational methods and new technologies
- Student evaluation

- United States Medical Licensing Examination (USMLE) policies
- Special programs and opportunities
- Emphasis on research

## Length

The LCME requirement that schools offer a curriculum of at least 130 weeks of instruction has resulted in a standard four-year program at nearly all medical schools. A few schools offer the opportunity for at least some students to take additional time (usually five years) to complete the program, usually incorporating dedicated research time. Programs of fewer than four years are relatively rare, but a few three-year programs do now exist, with several other schools considering implementing such programs.

## Organization of the Preclinical Years

Until relatively recently, the preclinical years of the medical curriculum were referred to as the basic science years. Students took traditional courses in disciplines such as anatomy, biochemistry, physiology, microbiology and immunology, pathology, pharmacology and therapeutics, and preventive medicine. Instruction consisted of long hours of lecture and laboratory work, and possibly some small-group discussions.

A newer approach employed by some schools replaces the discipline-based curriculum with one organized on an interdisciplinary, organ-system basis. In this type of curriculum, students study all aspects of each organ system before moving on to the next. Instruction is interdisciplinary, with faculty members from many departments forming teaching teams. Proponents of this approach believe that the organ-system model provides better integration of the material to be learned.

Some schools use a hybrid of the two curricular models. For example, the first year may be organized with traditional, discipline-based courses, while the second employs the interdisciplinary organ-system approach. Alternatively, elements of both may be mixed during parts of the curriculum.

## Problem-Based Learning

A relatively new arrival on the medical education scene is Problem-Based Learning (PBL) or, as it's sometimes called, case-based learning. In PBL, case-oriented problems are reviewed by small groups of medical students working together as a team under the direction of a faculty member. The PBL teams review the case material presented, identify learning issues, and assign those issues to group members. Each group member researches the issue assigned and reports back to the group at a subsequent meeting. As the cases unravel, the students not only begin to learn the basics of clinical medicine (the vocabulary, normal lab values, etc.), but they're challenged to understand the basic physiology, pathology, and pharmacology of the disease as well.

Some medical schools employ PBL almost exclusively. Others use PBL in conjunction with more traditional approaches, selecting the best approach for the material to be covered. The latter schools endeavor to coordinate the PBL cases with material covered in the traditional courses.

### Organization of the Clinical Years

The second year (in a handful of schools with a one-year basic science curriculum) and, more typically, the third and fourth years of medical school are designed to equip you with the knowledge, skills, attitudes, and behaviors necessary for further training in medicine. This is done by providing you with clinical experiences in a variety of clinical settings. You can expect some exposure to emergency medicine, family medicine, internal medicine, obstetrics and gynecology, pediatrics, neurology, psychiatry, and surgery. Some schools will require you to complete these core experiences, called clerkships, before moving on to other areas of medicine. Other schools will provide more flexibility in scheduling and may permit some electives or selectives during the third and, more typically, the fourth year. Schools will also differ in the extent to which they will permit off-campus, and even international, electives during the clinical years.

### Earliest Patient Contact

There is a trend toward providing patient contact early in the curriculum, often as early as the first few weeks of the first year. Proponents of this approach argue that medical students will find their studies more meaningful if they are combined with the chance to work with patients right from the start of medical school. Those who advocate delaying such contact point out that students can do little but observe until they have obtained enough training to be of real help to their patients. Medical schools differ as to when and how they provide this contact.

## Primary Care Focus

Some medical schools clearly state that their mission is to increase the number of primary care (family practice, general internal medicine, general pediatrics, and possibly obstetrics and gynecology) physicians in practice. These schools structure their curricula to emphasize opportunities in primary care and may attempt to select applicants who show a higher likelihood of entering primary care specialties.

## Innovative Educational Approaches

Medical education is evolving rapidly, and new approaches are being tried at many schools. Simulated patients are used by many schools to help students learn to conduct patient interviews, examine patients, and simulate various normal and pathological physical findings. Self-instruction, also referred to as self-directed learning, is emphasized in many schools. New methodologies are being developed regularly.

Computer-assisted and online instruction is widely utilized at medical schools. As the adoption of electronic medical records systems and medical information databases increases, many medical schools have decided to require medical students to own their own computing devices for accessing these resources. The requirements vary from one medical school to another and can include a laptop computer or a table. As with the rest of the population, the use of smartphones by medical students, residents, and attending physicians has risen dramatically over the last few years. Electronic resources such as Epocrates and popular books like *Harrison's Principles of Internal Medicine* have become available for smartphones and tablets. In many cases, medical schools will either provide such technology or consider the costs of required technology purchases and licenses in their financial aid calculations.

## Student Evaluation and Grading

An essential component of the curriculum is the method by which you will be evaluated. One way in which medical schools differ is in the grading systems they employ. Grading systems can vary from a simple pass-fail system to a five-step system, such as A-B-C-D-F. Others use a numerical system. A three-point system of honors-pass-fail is common; some have a more elaborate pass-fail-honors system with high pass (A), pass (B), marginal pass (C), low pass (D) and fail (F). Some schools use different systems for different parts of the curriculum, such as honors-pass-fail for required courses and pass-fail for electives. Some schools will employ Objective Structured Clinical Examinations (OSCE) during the clinical years, a practical exam of a mock patient, while others will emphasize standardized written "shelf" exams. The pass-fail system tends to be the least competitive, but the traditional letter-grade system encourages students to learn as much as possible.

### United States Medical Licensing Examination Policies

As mentioned earlier, the USMLE is the series of examinations required of all applicants for a medical license in any state in the United States. The USMLE is actually made up of three steps. Step 1 is usually taken at the end of the second year of medical school; Step 2—composed of two components, a Clinical Knowledge (CK) exam and a Clinical Skills (CS) exam—during the fourth year; and Step 3 at the end of the first year of residency. The majority of medical schools require their students to pass Step 1 to be promoted to the third year or to graduate. Many schools also require Step 2 passage for graduation. Most residency programs consider your scores on Step 1, and sometimes also Step 2 CK, closely when you apply for residency.

### Special Programs and Opportunities

One of the ways in which medical schools differentiate themselves is with the special programs they offer. These may be in the form of research opportunities, opportunities for community involvement, international educational experiences, or in other ways too numerous to mention. Joint-degree programs have been gaining popularity over the last decade. Traditionally, the most popular of these programs has been the MD/PhD program, designed for students who intend to pursue careers in academic medical research. However, during recent years, other programs such as MD/MBA (75 programs), MD/JD (26 programs), and MD/MPH (98 programs) have become attractive options for medical students who seek mastery of business, law, or public health in addition to their medical studies. In deciding to apply to any of these programs, it is important to be willing to devote, in many cases, the extra years (and extra money) to complete a joint-degree program and research requirements of specific programs.

### Emphasis on Research

As advances in science contribute increasingly to patient care and our understanding of disease, some medical schools are responding by making participation in research an integral component of their curricula by, among other things, building in dedicated research time. Some other medical schools encourage research involvement without making it a requirement. The substance and degree of research experience for medical students varies from one medical school to another. While 9 medical schools require participation in a long-term research project and presentation of a thesis at the end of the project, 103 schools encourage medical students to participate in clinical or basic science research during the summer and present a brief report of their research findings. Medical schools affiliated with large urban medical centers are more likely to place an emphasis on research than are smaller or more rurally based medical schools.

These are all important issues for you to consider. Be sure to consult school web pages, call admissions offices to request catalogs, review the MSAR, and even ask questions at the interview stage to find out what approach is used at the schools you're interested in. You should know how the schools you're interested in differ in each of the ways discussed. Weigh the pros and cons of each factor and decide which is most appropriate for your learning style. Remember, each medical school will ask you to articulate why you have chosen it.

## Teaching Hospitals

Just as important as the basic science curriculum that a medical school offers are its affiliated teaching hospitals. You'll be doing your clinical rotations predominantly in those hospitals and clinics that are designated as teaching hospitals of that school. Your first clinical experiences will be shaped, in large part, by the types of hospitals to which you are exposed. For example, if a medical school is primarily associated with city hospitals, you'll probably be exposed to a disproportionate amount of trauma and emergency medicine. Likewise, if Veterans Affairs hospitals predominate, you may encounter many cases of emphysema, heart disease, and post-traumatic stress disorder. What you experience during your clinical rotations may greatly influence your choice of specialty.

> **Unique Considerations**
>
> "I was interested in studying epidemiology within the confines of a structured MD/PhD program. I didn't want to be the odd one out in some other program, without the support you get from having others around you who are doing the same sort of thing. There were only four or five schools in the country that met these requirements."
>
> —Medical student, University of Washington

## Location

Location is another important consideration in deciding where to apply to medical school. Most premedical students, however, are so concerned about whether or not they'll be accepted by any school that they fail to consider if they'll be happy spending four years wherever that school is located. Applicants tend to understandably evaluate the medical schools lists based on reputation, prestige, cost, and the statistical profiles of accepted applicants, rather than location and lifestyle. Don't make the mistake of completely ignoring these factors. The bottom line is that medical school is hard and often isn't very much fun, so, in addition to the costs of your education and the reputation of the degree which you'll earn, you should consider where you'll be happy and comfortable for four years. Take the following location-related factors into account when making your choice.

### Safety

Many medical centers are located in inner cities with high rates of crime. It's obviously an added stress to be in an area in which you feel unsafe. Some medical centers will provide escorts and other security services. Keep this in mind when you're visiting schools and inquire about safety issues.

### Housing

Remember that in addition to tuition, you'll have to pay for housing, food, and transportation. Unfortunately, due to the location of some schools, nearby housing is either unsafe or unaffordable. In some inner-city schools, the majority of the student body resides in dormitories. These dorms are often expensive and have inadequate kitchen facilities. Nonetheless, they may be the best alternatives given the medical school's location.

In contrast, students who decide to attend equally good programs that are based in small towns may be pleasantly surprised to find inexpensive housing near the school. Crime will not be as big a problem in these areas.

### Transportation

This is obviously important as it pertains to housing and community shops. If there isn't housing near the medical center or its affiliated

---

**Read All about It**

If you're considering a particular locale, get your hands on its newspaper or visit the newspaper's website. Also try visiting a cost-of-living calculator website. This will give you a better handle on the cost of living, available transportation, and local issues.

---

hospitals, then you'll need to have a car. If you don't, it is important that there be adequate public transportation.

### Proximity to Family and Friends

If there are special people in your life with whom you enjoy spending time, it may be important for you to live near them. Medical school doesn't afford you much free time, and the time it takes to travel can easily make frequent or lengthy visits difficult if not impossible.

## Affiliation with an Undergraduate Institution

It's of great benefit to you if your medical school is part of a larger institution. Typically, the undergraduate institution allows the graduate students to enjoy the same privileges as the undergrads. This will include gym facilities, movies, and libraries.

## Student Body

Some schools are known for having a competitive atmosphere, in which students feel little camaraderie with one another. At other schools, a sense of "We're all in it together" prevails. Think about how much the attitude of other students matters to you. You can probably get a sense of a school's "flavor" by visiting schools and speaking to current students.

You may also want to find out about the schools' gender and ethnic balances. While most schools strive to create a diverse student body, the diversity of student bodies varies. The MSAR is a good reference point for determining class demographic data.

## Public versus Private Schools

For most students, with the exception of MD/PhD candidates, discussed at the end of chapter 6, the best chance for admission is to a public medical school located in their home state, where they're likely to receive preference in the admissions process because of their residency status. Medical schools have different methods for determining residency status for admissions purposes, and those methods may differ from the way in which schools determine residency for tuition purposes. For this reason, you should

> ### "Med-Student Friendly"
>
> "When I visited medical schools, one thing I felt while interacting with students was an overshadowing sense of pressure. I think you are often expected to be a med student first and a person second. In contrast, UNC drew me in because it was such a supportive environment very accommodating to human needs and thus an atmosphere that seemed to be very conducive to learning."
>
> —MD, University of North Carolina, Chapel Hill

take a close look at schools located in your home state as you consider schools to which you will apply.

While a few private schools give some preference to in-state applicants, most do not. Since the majority of applicants apply to at least some private schools, most private schools receive large numbers of applications, sometimes over 10,000, for an entering class of fewer than 200 seats.

Unless you are an exceptionally strong candidate, your chances of gaining admission to a public school located outside your home state are relatively small, quite probably worse than your odds of admission to most private institutions. Since most public schools give preference to in-state applicants (some are prohibited from admitting nonresidents), the competition for admission to these schools as a nonresident is very keen. On the other hand, a few public schools will admit a reasonable number of nonresidents, and, for residents of states with especially competitive public schools, applying to out-of-state public schools along with private schools should bear at least some consideration in your application strategy. If you are a relatively strong applicant and have an interest in a particular public school, you should consult that school's admissions office for advice about your application's competiveness.

---

**Go State!**

Attending a state school may seem like the answer, but make sure you meet the school's residency requirements. If in doubt, consulting the admissions offices at your schools of interest is a good idea.

---

The individual school entries in the MSAR describe schools' residency preferences and list the number of applicants and matriculants by residency status. This is an excellent place to start looking for schools that might consider you if you're application search extends to out-of-state public schools.

## Personal-Academic Life Balance

One important issue that applicants to medical school frequently overlook is the ability to balance personal life with academic life. This factor is especially critical to students with children, spouses, or other individuals to whom they are responsible. You should research each medical school to learn what special accommodations, if any, are available to fit your needs. For example, some medical schools offer flexible exam or class schedules, viewing of recording class sessions in lieu of optional lecture attendance, and brief absences for family reasons. Some others have a five-year graduation timeline available to students who have other demands during medical school.

The balance between personal and academic life does not only apply to students with families. Much as some undergraduate colleges have "hard-core" reputations, while others have reputations as being "laid-back" or "party schools," medical schools vary widely in terms of the amount of time they'll ask you to spend in class, their curricula outside the classroom, and the social culture of the school and student body. If you prefer to study independently, a school that allows you flexibility to study from home rather than mandating lecture attendance might better fit your learning style. Additionally, there are medical schools that actively encourage fun and relaxation by ending classes early on Fridays, regularly sponsoring parties or weekend trips, or funding medical student–led cultural or social interest groups. By talking to current and former medical students and reading websites like www.studentdoctor.net, you can learn crucial details that will affect your life, not just your academic career.

## EARLY DECISION PROGRAM (EDP)

A little more than half of the medical schools in the United States offer early decision programs. For an EDP, you apply to only one medical school—the one you wish to attend—through AMCAS. Such programs have an August 1 deadline for applications, and many schools have specific GPA and MCAT requirements for EDP applicants. You are prohibited from applying to any other schools until the school has rendered a decision on your EDP application or until, upon your request, the school releases you from your early decision agreement. If you're accepted, then you must attend. Under the terms of the agreement, schools notify EDP candidates of their acceptance, rejection, or (more commonly than rejection) deferral to the general application pool by October 1. Upon notification or after the October 1 deadline passes, EDP applicants are free to reenter the general application pool and designate additional medical schools to receive their AMCAS application.

Early decision programs are appropriate only for very competitive applicants who have a strong preference for one particular school. These applicants benefit in that they save considerable money on applications, interviews, and travel. In addition, they know where they're going to med school by October.

### First Choice, Only Choice

Apply early decision only if you feel strongly about your first choice and only if you're certain that if you're accepted, you'll attend. If you apply early decision but don't get in, you'll be playing application catch-up.

If you apply early decision but are not accepted, you'll be behind your peers in the application process. It's not a decision—or a possible consequence—to be taken lightly. You should definitely sit down with your premed adviser and decide if this option is appropriate for you.

## FOREIGN MEDICAL SCHOOLS

An important distinction must be made between the 158 American and Canadian allopathic medical schools accredited by the Liaison Committee on Medical Education (LCME) and the remaining medical schools around the globe (foreign medical schools).

In general, you should consider applying to domestic medical schools first and applying to foreign medical schools only if you were not accepted to a domestic medical school during your first or second attempt. Aside from the likelihood that barriers such as language and culture will impede your education at foreign medical schools, there is a possibility that the educational experience at foreign schools will not match up to that of domestic schools. These schools can vary widely in quality since they do not need to adhere to the strict accreditation standards of domestic medical schools. Moreover, graduates of foreign medical schools traditionally have a lower medical licensing exam pass rate and are given less favorable consideration by domestic residency programs (which are under pressure to give priority to graduates of medical schools at home). That said, there are several medical schools located abroad that have strong reputations and a lengthy track record of high licensing-exam pass rates and placement of graduates at American residencies. Some of these medical schools have classes that are taught entirely in English, have mostly American students, and enable medical students to complete many of their fourth-year clinical electives at American hospitals. On the other hand, some foreign medical schools are simply for-profit organizations whose graduates often fail to earn American medical licenses and residencies.

In researching foreign medical schools, you should insist on receiving information about graduation and USMLE pass rates as well as the percentage of students who match into American residencies. Ideally, obtain a list of residency programs into which graduates have matched over the last several years. Be aware of tuition, travel, and living costs and inquire about specifics regarding the availability of financial aid programs. In addition, you should read about these schools on www.studentdoctor.net

and attempt to contact current or former students at those schools. Your premedical adviser will often know a good deal about which foreign medical schools to consider and which ones to avoid. Attending a foreign medical school could be a viable option for you, especially if you haven't succeeded in being admitted to a medical school at home.

## OSTEOPATHIC MEDICAL SCHOOLS

Doctor of Osteopathy degrees are virtually indistinguishable in practice from medical doctor degrees. DOs work alongside MDs or in their own practices. Like allopathic medical school, the osteopathic course of study spans four years: two years of basic education and two years of clinical rotations. After they obtain their degrees, DOs also complete residency. Osteopathic medicine more typically focuses on the whole person, leading DOs to practice more often in primary care fields, such as internal medicine, family practice, and pediatrics. They are licensed to prescribe medicine, and they can admit patients to hospitals in the same fashion as do their MD colleagues.

The difference between allopathic and osteopathic practice lies in focus and reputation. Osteopaths believe that a problem in one body part will cause distress in another. In addition, according to osteopathic medicine—which subscribes to a "whole person" philosophy—the body can regulate and heal itself if conditions allow for it to do so. The biggest obstacle to this healing process is physical or emotional stress. To osteopaths, musculoskeletal health is key to preventing and overcoming illness and disease. By treating the musculoskeletal system, the disease cycle can be interrupted. Osteopathic medicine focuses on relaxation of muscles, tendons, and connective tissue.

Although osteopaths are highly regarded, especially as the United States focuses on primary healthcare needs, a DO degree may make it slightly more difficult to get a highly competitive residency because historically, only a few DO-only residency programs accredited by the AOA existed, offering relatively fewer seats per capita in competitive specialties than were available for allopathic medical students. However, beginning in 2015, AOA and the American Council on Graduate Medical Education (ACGME)—the accrediting body for MD residency programs—will initiate a single, unified accreditation system for all residency programs. Following integration of the two accrediting processes, expected to be completed in 2020, all medical school graduates, MD and DO, will be able to apply to any residency program.

In general, the median MCAT scores of entering classes to allopathic medical schools are higher than those of osteopathic entering classes. Average GPAs for the two types of schools are usually closer.

On a percentage basis, it is somewhat more competitive to get into osteopathic schools: Less than one in five applicants is accepted. This is in part reflective of the number of osteopathic medical school seats versus the number of allopathic medical school seats available for applicants. As of 2013, there were nearly five times as many students enrolled in allopathic medical schools in the United States than students enrolled in osteopathic schools. However, from 2000 to 2015, the growth in the number of osteopathic medical students will have outpaced the growth in the number of allopathic medical students. The *Osteopathic Medical College Information Book* gives a brief description of each of the 30 osteopathic medical colleges, including admissions criteria, minimum entrance requirements, supplementary application materials required, class size or enrollment, application deadlines, and tuition.

You can download the book for free or purchase a printed copy for $15.00 plus the cost of shipping by contacting AACOM:

American Association of Colleges of Osteopathic Medicine–AACOM
5550 Friendship Boulevard, Suite 310
Chevy Chase, MD 20815-7231
Phone: (301) 968-4100
Fax: (301) 968-4101
Website: www.aacom.org/resources/bookstore/cib/Pages/default.aspx

# CHAPTER 5

# Researching Medical Schools

Although it may be tempting to apply to schools without having researched them, succumbing to this temptation may get you into trouble later in the process. Medical school admissions committees are most interested in an applicant whose decision to apply to their school is an informed one. You should demonstrate enough specific interest and knowledge in the school that the committee believes you would accept its offer over one from another school.

The goal of your information gathering is not just to formulate a list of medical schools for the general AMCAS application, but to be able to take each medical school on your list and cite several specific reasons you have decided to apply there (and not just "Well, it's in the top twenty" or "I think I can get in"). This approach will serve you well at two important points in the application process: secondary applications and interviews.

Variations on the question "Why have you decided to apply here?" appear in many of the secondary applications that you'll receive from schools. This is the admissions committee's first attempt to plumb the depths of your motivation to not only go to medical school but go to *its* medical school. A strong, enthusiastic, specific statement of the reasons you're excited about their school will immediately place your application in a more favorable light. If you're informed, you can write at length about what specifically attracts you to the school: its innovative curriculum, the emphasis on problem-based learning, its great location, your ties to the community, the opportunities to spend time doing research with famous professors X and Y, the chance to spend an elective studying abroad in India, etc.

Researching a particular medical school and being able to make a persuasive case for why you and the school are a good match can help you with that school's secondary application. If you apply to a large number of medical schools, you're likely to be completing an equally large number of secondary applications. Avoid the temptation to cut and paste generic responses to each. Know something about the schools to which you're applying and be sure that your secondary applications reflect this. Knowing and saying something about the school to which you're applying is likely to be even more important during your interview. There are a multitude of ways to find out everything you want to know about medical schools. They range from official AAMC-produced publications, to commercial and online sources, to word of mouth and student forums.

## MILK THE MSAR

As we said in chapter 4, it's worth your while to pay for access to the MSAR from the AAMC as soon as you get a chance. The MSAR is as close as you can get to a premed bible, especially considering the fact that the information it contains on all of the medical schools comes directly from the schools themselves.

The MSAR contains information about the admissions process and financing your education, statistics about applicants and acceptees, and profiles of all the accredited schools in the United States and Canada.

### Curricula/Programs

The curricula of many medical schools have undergone or are undergoing major change; the trend is toward some degree of incorporation of problem-based learning and organization around organ–system–based approaches. Each medical school typically outlines the different components of its curriculum, including the progression of courses over the first two years, the exposure to clinical medicine, and electives. The school may offer more than one curriculum, and often the school's MD/PhD option is mentioned here.

### Requirements for Entrance

With changes regarding prerequisite course work requirements, this information has become more important than it once was. For example, many schools have a one-year English requirement, and a few require a year of humanities. Others will vary in terms of the amount of organic chemistry they require. Other schools have responded to MCAT 2015 by eliminating strictly defined basic course requirements, allowing applicants to choose from a "menu" of courses to satisfy their matriculation requirements. Skip this section at your own risk; you might not have fulfilled all of the requirements for your dream school.

Sometimes an admissions committee will go out of its way to assert that it will consider applicants who have majored in any field, as long as the work done in that major was exemplary. Some schools even state that they do not give any preference to those who majored in the sciences. Good news, if you're an English or history major.

### Selection Factors

Look here for important data such as the mean GPA and MCAT scores for the most recent entering class, the distribution of applicants or entrants by undergraduate major or school, the mean age of students, and the percentage of women and minorities in the entering class. Many schools will not disclose their numerical criteria for selection, since they make an effort to judge students as individuals, not as numbers.

Your GPA and MCAT scores are by no means the only factors that go into an admissions committee's decision, and most schools take the opportunity here to sketch out the qualities they like to see in an applicant. However, the numbers they publish for GPA and MCAT can be used as a crude but powerful indicator of how competitive a school is to get into. A school whose students have a mean GPA of 3.9 and a mean MCAT score of 36 is probably more competitive than a school whose students have a mean GPA of 3.6 and a mean MCAT score of 30. Also, notice the 10th–90th percentile ranges for GPA, Science GPA, and MCAT score provided. This gives an indicator beyond the median numbers of the range of applicants that were admitted in the previous class.

If a school systematically gives preference based on geography, whether it be to in-state applicants only or to applicants from nearby states as well (as is the case with the University of Washington at Seattle), you should find a statement to that effect in the "Selection Factors" section.

### Expenses and Financial Aid

Information is provided regarding expenses and school resources in terms of scholarships and loans available to medical students. Often a school will also indicate the percentage of the student body that receives financial aid. (Note: When you decide which medical school to attend, you should work closely with that school's financial aid office. You'd be surprised at the number of loans, grants, scholarships, and fellowships—both institutional and external—that are available.)

Several points come up often in the "Financial Aid" section of the school profiles:

- Some schools state a preference that their students not be otherwise employed while in school.
- Non-US citizens without permanent-resident or visa status are not eligible to receive financial aid and often must be able to prove their ability to pay.
- Many assert that financial need has no bearing on whether an applicant will be accepted.

### Information about Diversity Programs

Most schools are deeply committed to the active recruitment of underrepresented minority and socioeconomically or educationally disadvantaged applicants. In fact, this demonstrated commitment to programs that contribute to the diversity of medical school student bodies is part of LCME's accreditation and maintenance-of-accreditation process. Schools offer specific programs and incentives (which might include reimbursement for interview travel expenses) that are designed to support and encourage such applicants.

Admissions committees typically have significant minority representation and, as such, have personnel such as minority student advisers. Some medical schools have dedicated admissions committees that review only the applications from minority and/or disadvantaged applicants.

### Application Processes and Requirements

This section of the school profile provides you with some key pieces of information:

**AMCAS Deadline.** Traditionally, AMCAS schools want you to file during a period starting June 1 and ending sometime in October or November.

**School Application Fee.** This is the fee you will have to pay in addition to the AMCAS fee. Most schools require you to pay this when you submit their secondary applications. Pay attention to the way the school application fee is listed. You can infer from information here whether a school reviews your application before it sends you a secondary application. Some schools have an "application fee to all applicants"; other schools, including the University of California programs, say that they charge an application fee after "screening." Those in the latter category will be doing an initial review of your application before they send you a secondary application and request the application fee. If you apply and receive a secondary application from such a school, you can give yourself a pat on the back for making the first cut.

**Oldest Acceptable MCAT Scores.** Schools vary widely in their willingness to accept old scores, so if you took the MCAT a couple of years ago but have held off on applying, you should look at this closely—you may have to retake the MCAT to get into the school of your choice. Most schools will take scores that are two or three years old, but a few will accept only scores received in the four administrations immediately preceding entry into schools. With the new format of the MCAT exam, this is an especially important consideration for applicants who took the exam in pre-Spring 2015 format.

**Early Decision Program Deadlines.** As we described in the last chapter, slightly more than half of the medical schools in the United States offer early decision programs. With early decision, your primary application is transmitted to the one medical school you wish to attend, with a deadline of August 1. You can't apply to any other school until the EDP school has rendered a decision on your application or released you from your EDP commitment. If you're accepted, you must attend. Most schools notify the candidates of their decision by October 1.

**The MSAR also contains information on the following:**
- Earliest dates for acceptance notices
- Availability of option to defer
- Amount of deposit to hold place in class
- Estimated number of new entrants
- Starting date of classes
- Interview format
- Combined-degree programs
- Financial information

### Information on Previous Year's Classes

Here is yet another opportunity to figure out how partial a school is to in-state residents, since two sets of numbers (in-state and out-of-state) are given for the categories of "number of applicants," "number of applicants interviewed," and "new entrants."

This section also serves as a very general barometer of how difficult it is for an applicant to obtain admission to the school, since you can use the numbers to calculate the percentage of applicants who are granted interviews and the percentage of those granted interviews who are actually admitted. One caveat, however: You have to take into account the fact that one school's applicant pool may well be stronger than another's if you are trying to compare them. If Harvard and Podunk U. Med both take five percent of their applicants, this clearly does not mean that they are equally competitive.

## READ THE RANKINGS

You've probably heard about the rankings of medical schools in *U.S. News & World Report*. These rankings do indeed contain some valuable information, such as the following:

- Amount of NIH-funded research for each school
- Faculty-to-student ratio
- Out-of-state tuition
- Percentage of graduates who have gone into primary care fields

From the rankings, you can also get a pretty good sense of how prestigious schools are as well as how difficult they are to get into. This information can be useful when you are formulating your overall application strategy and trying to determine your particular "dream" and "safety" schools.

Take rankings with a grain of salt, however, because they are pretty subjective. Make sure you read the explanations of the methodology employed in putting each ranking together so that you understand exactly what you are getting. You should also review rankings from previous years in order to see how they and their underlying methodologies have recently changed.

Of course, rankings leave out a lot of important information. They tell you nothing about how well a particular school treats its students as a whole (this does vary from school to school), what the professors and the students are like, what special offerings the school's curriculum might have, or what the social life and housing arrangements are like. You shouldn't assume that a school's high ranking automatically means it would be a good choice for you.

## Hospital Rankings

In addition to its yearly rankings of medical schools, *U.S. News & World Report* also publishes rankings of hospitals affiliated with medical schools (you can find these in a separate issue entitled *America's Best Hospitals*). The rankings go specialty by specialty, so you'll find them particularly useful if you already have an interest in a specific branch of medicine. The teaching hospitals are, after all, where you will be receiving your clinical training during your clerkships (the third and fourth years at almost every medical school).

The rankings include information on the following:

- Hospital reputation
- Mortality rate (for specialties for which this is applicable)
- Ratio of residents, doctors, nurses, and inpatient operations to beds
- Number of high-tech services available

# ASK ON-CAMPUS SOURCES

Visiting a med school you're considering attending or asking around the university you currently attend can give you great insight into a school's particular flavor, including the kind of student who's been accepted into the med school.

### *Med Students*

If you attend a university that has a medical school, you're in luck; you can't help but get an idea of what the medical program is like, and you may well have some contact with the med students, even if only in the cafeteria. Ask them how they got accepted to medical school, what they did as an undergraduate, and where else they applied (and were accepted or rejected).

> **Inside Scoop**
>
> Ask current med students about the schools they attend and how they got in. Not only will you get info on what worked for them in the application process, but you'll also get a sense of whether a particular school is right for you.

They've been through the process; no doubt they're proud of being accepted to med school, and you know how willing people are to discuss their achievements. You'll learn things about medical schools that you could never pick up from a book.

### PhD Students

In addition, universities with medical schools typically have affiliated programs that grant PhDs in the biomedical sciences. PhD students often will not hesitate to comment on their own program (you may be interested in doing an MD/PhD), their professors (who may also be on the medical school faculty), the research at the university, and the medical students.

### Premed Seniors

If you are not so fortunate as to have a medical school nearby (and even if you are), be sure to seek advice from the premed seniors at your college before they graduate. They have gone through the process of applying and are interviewing and making their decisions as the school year progresses. They will be an extremely good source of up-to-date information about medical schools; after all, the admissions process has taken up a considerable amount of their time and mental energy in the past year.

### Your Premed Adviser

As mentioned earlier, don't forget about premed advisers as a source of information about medical schools. Advisers who have held their positions for a substantial amount of time have built up links and personal contacts with admissions officers at different medical schools—which means they have gotten feedback from them in one form or another about applicants they sent to them in the past. They know which schools may overlook a disastrous freshman year if they see a trend of improvement; which schools will accept large numbers of nontraditional students (that is, older students changing careers); which schools are known to give sons and daughters of alumni and faculty preferential treatment; and, most important, which medical schools like to accept students from your college or university.

Premed advisers are also the individuals best suited to give you the information you may want—more than anything else—about a particular school: your chances of getting in. They can roughly judge how competitive you will be as an applicant because they have already advised students with your approximate profile (GPA, MCATs, extracurriculars) and they know how these previous applicants have fared. They may even have compiled statistics on those who have gone before you in order to help make such evaluations. Of course, bear in mind that you are a unique candidate and your premed adviser is not the one making the admissions decisions.

The typical premed advisory office also has a wealth of information in the form of catalogs, brochures, and announcements. They may also have videos on the AAMC and on some of the medical schools.

## AMSA

An excellent organizational resource, AMSA (American Medical Student Association) has many premed chapters as well as a huge annual national convention that attracts hundreds of med students and premeds from every school. Visit www.amsa.org for events and information.

## WEBSITES

Reading med school websites can give you great insight into the specifics of a school. You should carefully read the information on the website of each school to which you're applying. The admissions committee will expect you to have read and familiarized yourself with the school's website before you complete the secondary application—certainly before you show up for the interview. Many med school websites have added personalized features that allow you to track the status of your application online.

### Reading the Website

Keep in mind that the medical school website is a marketing tool as well as a repository of information. Schools are interested in attracting the best students they can, so they put their best foot forward. (Undergraduate schools do the same thing, of course; take a look at the current brochure your undergraduate institution puts out and compare it with your personal experience.) Take the photos with a grain of salt: Although they can provide some valuable information, a good photographer can make a medical center situated in the middle of an urban war zone look like a country club.

Many websites also profile some of the school's students. While the students profiled may be outstanding in some way or another, they are not necessarily representative of the average student at the school. So don't assume that you won't be a competitive applicant just because you didn't spend two years deep in the heart of Brazil learning about the medicinal properties of rare plants, as the student profiled on the website did.

In addition to the admissions-related sections on the websites, you should look around on pages designed for current medical students. On those pages, you will receive more inside information regarding the curriculum, the organization of the school, faculty and administrators, residency match results, social activities, and other issues or opportunities that the admissions office chose not to discuss on the admissions office website.

Glossy photos and student profiles notwithstanding, the website does contain a lot of information that is not only necessary to know for interviews but will also help you compare that school to others you are interested in. Here are some things to look for.

---

**Research versus Service**

Even schools that are heavily into research value a diverse student body, so don't hesitate to express a commitment to public service to a school known for its excellence in research.

---

### Educational Priorities

Schools differ in their emphasis on primary care versus research/specialization. The current trend is to encourage greater numbers of graduates to go into primary care, since there is a recognized shortage of primary care in this country. However, some schools with a long tradition of producing leaders in research and academic medicine continue to recognize their responsibility for training the next generation of biomedical scientists.

Once you have read and compared a few websites, you will be able to discern each website's underlying message concerning the school's educational priorities. One website will devote a single paragraph to "Research Opportunities" but boast right in the introduction that over 45 percent of the graduates do their residencies in primary care. Another will devote pages and pages to the "Special Study and Research Experiences" available and go on at great length about the amount of NIH funding the Nobel laureates on the faculty receive yearly. Considering this, it's not hard to tell where each school stands. Websites will be especially useful in determining the general educational orientation of the many schools that do not appear in rankings or on commercial lists.

### Application Requirements

The section on requirements offers another chance for you to make sure that you've taken all of the courses required by a school and that your application contains all the necessary components. Read any information concerning letters of recommendation very carefully. You're usually safe with admissions committees if you are submitting a packet of letters or a composite letter from your undergraduate school's preprofessional committee. If you're not, though, each medical school has specific requirements about the number and distribution (in terms of academic departments, professors who have taught you in class, research advisers and principal investigators in the laboratories in which you've worked, physicians and supervisors in clinical or work settings, etc.) of recommendations they want you to send them, and these requirements do vary from school to school. Be aware that many osteopathic medical schools require a letter of recommendation from an osteopathic physician. Also, if you have been away from your undergraduate school for some time, you may be expected to submit recommendations from employers or graduate school professors. If you have any questions about recommendation letters, ask your premedical adviser, who will have handled this issue with many previous students.

### *Where Students Come from, Where They're Going*

Many medical schools list their recent graduates and where those graduates are doing their residencies; some also give statistics on where their first-year students went to college. The list of residencies gives you a general indication of the reputation of the medical school among residency directors, and you can compare the relative success of students from different schools. You will probably want to ask a medical student or doctor whom you know or consult *U.S. News'* "Best Hospitals" issue to determine the reputation of the teaching hospitals where the graduates are doing their residencies and the relative competiveness of obtaining residency spots in various specialties. Information about the first-year students' undergraduate school of origin may be important, since a medical school's admissions committee may well have had favorable results from accepting students from your college in the past and may therefore, be that much more willing to consider your application.

### Matchmaker, Matchmaker

A statistic many schools cite is the percentage of students who match at one of their top-three residency choices. The "match" is a process by which senior med students and residency programs rank each other via, most commonly, the National Resident Matching Program (NRMP). A computer algorithm matches a student with a residency program based on the rank lists submited by both programs and applicants. The results of the match are announced annually on Match Day in March. It's prestigious for a school to have a high percentage (> 85 percent) of their students match at their first choice of residencies. You can read more about the match at the NRMP website, www.nrmp.org.

### Curriculum

Every medical school website contains a detailed description of the curriculum. Some have graphs that lay the whole four years out for you very nicely. Take note of any changes that have been made in the past few years, such as reorganization of how material is presented into an organ-system format, earlier exposure to patients, and the institution of problem-based learning. You will also find information about combined-degree programs, electives you can take abroad, research tracks, and other special opportunities.

No doubt you'll be interested in how students are evaluated in their coursework and whether or not you'll be ranked numerically within your class; this will be in the school's catalog, along with a host of other school policies.

### Faculty and Research

Not all schools list their faculty on the website, but most do, and if they do, you can look up the names of both basic science and clinical faculty members in the field or department in which you are interested. Many school websites will include biographical entries that detail faculty research interests. You can also do an online search of *MEDLINE*, the medical journal database, to read about the research they have published recently. This is particularly important to do if you are applying to combined-degree programs or if you plan to apply to a competitive specialty. In such cases, applicants are often advised to incorporate research as part of your medical education.

### Student Resources and Services

How are the school's libraries and computer resources, recreation facilities, and student health service? Can you find decent, affordable housing in the area? What help will the school give you in your housing search? If the school is located in a dangerous part of town, is there a student shuttle to take you where need and want to go? What about guidance on course selection and career planning? The school catalog can provide at least partial answers to these and other practical questions. You may have to wait until you visit the campus for the interview to get the whole picture, but catalogs often provide the addresses and telephone numbers of the school housing office, the libraries, and other resources that will help get you started.

### *Student Organizations*

Medical schools like to accept individuals who have been involved in extracurricular, community, and volunteer activities, so it's no surprise that they typically offer a wide range of student organizations and activities. If the catalog describes an organization or activity that appeals to you, tell the admissions committee about your interest, especially if you have something in your background to suggest that you would truly be committed to it. If you were deeply involved in student government in college, for example, and would want to continue by serving in medical student government, let them know.

## THE INTERNET

In addition to medical schools' own websites, you can use the Internet to learn more about the professors in your research field at each school, to read the insights and advice of medical students who have made it through the process, and to prepare for interviews by perusing the comments of former interviewees at different schools.

Some excellent resources can be found at the following websites:

- www.studentdoctor.net: An online message board where premeds, medical students, residents, and doctors exchange and share information regarding interview experiences and applications, as well as giving inside pointers on applying to specific schools. Use caution when reading this site, since information is unofficial and can be inaccurate. Verify information with an official source whenever possible.
- www.kaptest.com: A centralized resource for medical school application and MCAT preparation information, with links to admissions consulting services that will guide you from planning your application to writing your personal statement and excelling at your interviews.
- www.aamc.org: The official website of the Association of American Medical Colleges. This website is filled with updated information regarding changes to the MCAT as well as admissions statistics, and it also contains a searchable database of programs at all US allopathic medical schools.
- www.usnews.com: The magazine's popular website contains an annual ranking of medical schools and hospitals, plus information on application deadlines, fees, acceptance rates, average MCAT scores, and tuition.

Use your Web browser to search for sites by using "medical school" or the name of the school you want to learn more about as the search terms, and you'll be off and running.

A word of caution: While the information you get from the Web can be extremely helpful, some of it may be incomplete or inaccurate. For example, admissions advice from a medical student reflects only that student's personal experience and may not accurately reflect how the admissions process works at all medical schools.

## MAKING YOUR LIST AND CHECKING IT TWICE . . .

Now comes the fun part: making your list. As you begin selecting the schools you will be applying to, keep in mind everything you learned poring over medical school catalogs, learning the MSAR by heart, studying this chapter, and listening to the sage advice of your premed adviser. While everyone should have a few schools that constitute a "wish list" (Hey, it could happen!), you basically have to remember to use your head when you select schools to apply to. Remember that more is not necessarily better, but it is more expensive.

**PART FOUR**

# Getting In

# CHAPTER 6

# Meeting
# Admissions Requirements

Though you started the college application process in the fall or, in some cases, in the early winter of your senior year of high school, the medical school application process starts considerably earlier than your senior year of college. The decision to apply to medical school is not one to be made lightly. Med schools have a whole set of prerequisites for admission that you may not yet have taken as an undergraduate.

Researching med schools early in the process means knowing exactly what courses you need to take before you apply. You'll also learn what courses you can take during the 18-month application period, as well as what courses you should have completed before you take the MCAT. Since some courses are both grueling and key to getting accepted, you should plan your schedule accordingly to avoid overloading yourself.

## COURSE REQUIREMENTS

Nearly all schools require work in the biological sciences, chemistry (two years, including general and one or two semesters of organic), biochemistry, and physics with laboratory. Sixty percent of schools require English, 10 percent require social sciences, and 9 percent require calculus. A small number of schools have no specific course requirements. For more information on course requirements and prerequisites, see Chapter 2: Planning Your Undergraduate Curriculum. Bear in mind that since the MCAT covers material from the commonly required courses, you will need to take courses whether they are required by medical schools or not; otherwise, you will need to plan to learn this material independently in preparation for taking the MCAT. Nevertheless, many students are surprised to learn that the list of courses required by medical schools is so small.

The best sources for specific information on prerequisites are the MSAR, which includes requirements for all accredited allopathic medical schools, and the *Osteopathic Medical College Information Book,* which contains similar information on all of the country's osteopathic medical schools. These publications will also tell you of each school's other admission requirements, such as minimum semester hours required and whether a bachelor's degree is mandatory for matriculation.

Since the list of courses required by medical schools is short and somewhat varied, you will need to decide what else to take. Many of your decisions will be governed by the requirements of the major and degree you are seeking. Even so, you will probably be faced with at least some choices every semester or quarter. You will need to choose specific courses within your major, and you will have to select various electives. In the interest of preparation for the medical school basic science course that you will take, consider enrolling in upper-division biology courses, such as human anatomy, physiology, biochemistry, immunology, and histology and pathology.

How should you choose which specific electives to take? One approach is to broaden your education by considering at least some humanities electives if you are a science major. Conversely, if you are a non-science major, consider taking at least some additional science courses. Think about subjects that parallel the content that you'll see in medical school. And to the extent possible, take courses that interest you.

## THE MCAT

For nearly all schools, the MCAT carries significant weight in the admissions process. Administered by the Association of American Medical Colleges, the MCAT is a relatively objective way to compare you with other applicants. Medical schools use MCAT scores to assess whether you have the foundation upon which to build a successful medical career. Although it's hard to believe that a single test could indicate how good a doctor you'll be, the evidence seems to indicate that the MCAT (especially taken in context with your undergraduate GPA) does predict how good a medical student you'll be, at least in the sense that your MCAT performance strongly correlates to your likelihood of passing the USMLE Step 1 on your first attempt. Although that's not the final word on your future medical competency, it does give medical admissions committees a way to approximate your potential in the medical arena. It also gives these admissions committees a level of comfort that if they offer you admission to their schools, you'll be capable of handling the academic demands that will be required.

The MCAT is not a straightforward science test; it's a test of critical thinking and analysis in the context of physical, biological, and social science and verbal reasoning passages. This means that the test is designed to let you demonstrate not only your breadth of knowledge but your thought processes as well.

## MCAT 2015

The AAMC decided to change the MCAT for all administrations into a computer-based exam beginning in 2007. The MCAT remains an exclusively computer-based test (CBT). The exam is offered at small, climate-controlled testing sites worldwide. Test takers must bring one government-issued ID that includes a photo and signature and has an expiration date. (Valid examples include a driver's license, military ID, or passport.) In addition, the test center will take an electronic photo of the test taker, as well as fingerprints. The computer-based MCAT is typically administered on several dates in January, March, April, May, June, July, August, and September. For the latest information on test dates and a current list of testing sites, visit www.aamc.org.

The MCAT is not a computer-adaptive test (CAT), in which the computer chooses a harder question to follow a correctly answered question and an easier question to follow an incorrectly answered question. Unlike on a CAT, on the MCAT, you can return to questions in the same section and change your answers. You have the ability to strike out answer choices and highlight text selections on the computer screen during the test. Beginning in spring 2015, the MCAT will undergo its biggest revision in 20 years. The test will be longer and contain new content like biochemistry, psychology, and sociology. For more information about the MCAT 2015 exam, visit www.aamc.org.

### What's on the Test

Beginning in Spring 2015, the MCAT will consist of four sections: Biological and Biochemical Foundations of Living Systems; Chemical and Physical Foundations of Biological Systems; Psychological, Social and Biological Foundations of Behavior; and Critical Analysis and Reasoning Skills. Test Day will last approximately seven hours, with all questions being multiple-choice. The scores for each of the four sections will sum to the total score. Total scores will range from 472 to 528, with 500 being the mean score. Individual section scores will range from 118 to 132, with a mean score of 125.

**(optional 10-minute break)**

| Chemical and Physical Foundations of Biological Systems | |
| --- | --- |
| Time: | 95 minutes |
| # of Questions | 59 questions Score between 118 and 132 |
| What it tests: | 25% Biochemistry, 5% Biology, 30% General Chemistry, 15% Organic Chemistry, 25% Physics |

| Critical Analysis and Reasoning Skills | |
| --- | --- |
| Time: | 90 minutes |
| # of Questions: | 53 questions Score between 118 and 132 |
| What it tests: | 50% humanities passages, 50% social sciences passages |

| Biological and Biochemical Foundations of Living Systems | |
| --- | --- |
| Time: | 95 minutes |
| # of Questions: | 59 questions Score between 118 and 132 |
| What it tests: | 25% Biochemistry, 65% Biology, 5% General Chemistry, 5% Organic Chemistry |

**(optional 10-minute break)**

| Psychological, Social, and Biological Foundations of Behavior | |
| --- | --- |
| Time: | 95 minutes |
| # of Questions: | 59 questions Score between 118 and 132 |
| What it tests: | 60% introductory psychology, 30% introductory sociology, 10% introductory biology |

## How It's Scored

As with the previous, pre-2015 MCAT, each of the multiple-choice questions is expected to have the same value, and the number of your correct answers is converted into a "scaled" score and a percentile (how you did relative to everyone else who took the exam).

The average scaled score for each test on the pre-2015 MCAT is between 8 and 9. In 2013, the mean MCAT score for all administrations was 25.3, with a standard deviation of 6.5. What's a good score? In 2013, the mean MCAT score of allopathic medical school applicants was 28.4, while the mean MCAT score of accepted applicants was 31.3. Given these averages, you should aim to be above the mean score in each section and even higher above the mean for top-tier schools. The 2015 MCAT will have each section scored in the range of 118–132, with 125 being the mean score. This means that on the MCAT administered in 2015, you'll want to aim for a score above 125 on each section, and a score above 500 overall. (The highest score one can achieve on the 2015 MCAT is 528).

Receiving a lower MCAT score in a section isn't necessarily an application killer, but it can be a significant obstacle to acceptance. Bear in mind that schools report the average MCAT score of their students. So if a school reports an average of 125 per section, this clearly means that plenty of its students scored 125 or lower. However, the range of MCAT scores for applicants accepted to a given school is typically rather narrow. In other words, if a med school's average accepted MCAT score is 500, you're not going to see many accepted students with scores in the 470s and 480s. Take a look at median section score and the 10th–90th percentile total score ranges for accepted applicants reported in the MSAR. This data should give you a better feel for the score floor for total MCAT scores and an indication of the likelihood of acceptance with low individual or composite scores.

You'll be receiving four different scores for the four sections. If you aced one or two sections but fell a bit in one or two others, your total score will still look pretty good. Even students who receive perfect scaled scores usually get a handful of questions wrong.

It's important to maximize your performance on every question. Just a few more correct or incorrect questions can make a big difference in your scaled score.

## Prepping for the MCAT

You wouldn't run a marathon without training for it; similarly, you don't want to go into the MCAT without having thoroughly prepared. You can prep in a variety of ways—through live courses, software, or books. Nearly 65 percent of matriculating students in 2011 took an MCAT prep course. Prepping for the test will help you accomplish four things:

- Learn or review the content on the test
- Learn how to apply the content to specific question types
- Build endurance needed to face over seven hours of testing
- Gain confidence in your ability to manage the material, the computer interface, and the stress of test day

The MCAT tests your basic knowledge of physics, general chemistry, biology, organic chemistry, biochemistry, psychology, and sociology. So make sure you take one year or semester of each before taking the MCAT.

## Test Information and Registration

For information, contact the AAMC (email is preferred):

**Association of American Medical Colleges**
Medical College Admission Test
2450 N Street, NW
Washington, DC 20037
Phone: (202) 828-0690
Email: mcat@aamc.org (Do not send attachments.)

For registration information, visit
www.aamc.org/students/applying/mcat/reserving/

# When to Take the MCAT

The MCAT is currently offered approximately 26 times a year (note that the number of test administrations is likely to change with the new exam in 2015). Test dates fall in January, March, April, May, June, July, August, and September. See www.aamc.org for the most current test dates. When deciding when to schedule your exam, be sure to leave yourself lots of lead time so you can prepare thoroughly.

There is no easy answer to the question of when to take the MCAT. There are advantages and disadvantages to each administration.

### January, March, April, May, June, or July Advantages

- The timing is right. Many applicants take the MCAT near the end of their junior year of college. This is when all of the common prerequisite courses have been completed, and these students feel better prepared to take the test.
- You'll get it out of the way so you can concentrate on preparing your AMCAS application.
- You will receive your scores earlier, and this may help you to decide on how many, and which, schools to apply to.
- If your scores are below your expectations, you can repeat the test in late summer or early fall. Remember, schools will see both scores.
- You must take the MCAT by spring of your junior year if you wish to apply to your first-choice school under the Early Decision Plan.
- Medical schools receive your scores along with your AMCAS application instead of having to wait until September or November to receive late summer or early fall scores.

### January, March, April, May, June, or July Disadvantages

- You may not be ready because you have not completed all of the prerequisite courses.
- You may feel MCAT preparation will take time from your studies and adversely affect your grades.
- Your work schedule may not permit adequate preparation time.

### *August or September Advantages*

- You may not have completed all of the prerequisite courses until then.
- You may have the entire summer to prepare for the test with fewer distractions.
- It may fit into your personal schedule better.
- One of the best options is to take the MCAT during the late summer or early fall after sophomore year, assuming that you have almost completed physics; you'll have the benefits of a late summer or early fall test date and the opportunity to take the test again if needed.

### *August or September Disadvantages*

- Your scores will reach medical schools later in the application season. Verified applications will begin to be delivered to allopathic and osteopathic medical schools via their respective application services (AMCAS and AACOMAS) shortly after July 1. Schools vary in terms of when they begin to send out secondary applications to applicants from whom they receive verified applications, but many will do so shortly after receipt of the primary application. While submission of applications and verification of submitted applications can occur without having scores, schools will be unable to act on an application without a score. Remember also that it will take 30–35 days from Test Day before your scores are available for release and able to be made available to schools. Your application file may become complete later in the application year, thus delaying a decision to send supplemental materials to your or to invite you for an interview.
- You will not have the chance to repeat the MCAT during the current application year.
- Preparation may limit your other summer options.
- You will not be able to take advantage of the Early Decision Plan.

## Score Reporting

The MCAT has a policy of "Full Disclosure," in which an examinee's full testing history is reported. All MCAT scores are automatically released to AMCAS and included in the MCAT Testing History Reports (THx Reports, formerly known as Additional Score

Reports) that are sent to other medical and professional schools at the examinee's request.

THx Reports are free. Also, the THx system shows scores, not just test dates. That way, students can find out their scores as soon as the information is available to the AAMC. In order to report MCAT scores to postbaccalaureate programs, foreign medical schools, non–AMCAS participating medical schools, and osteopathic schools, you will need to manually release your scores to those services through the MCAT THx site.

## How Long Are MCAT Scores Valid?

Most medical schools accept scores no more than two or three years old, though this can vary slightly. Consult the individual school entries in the MSAR to determine the oldest MCAT scores they will accept. With the transition to MCAT 2015, this is an especially important consideration for applicants with scores from the older version of the test.

## Tips for MCAT Success

Here are some tried-and-true strategies for doing your best on the exam.

- Learn the test components inside and out.
- Consider enrolling in an MCAT prep course.
- Review the content outlined in the MCAT student manual.
- Build up your test-taking stamina. This is approximately a seven-hour test with additional time devoted to administrative details and breaks. It's not a good idea to think you can just waltz in and keep alert for what can easily be an eight-hour Test Day!
- Take all the MCAT practice tests you can. Practice with shorter, focused tests first to increase your accuracy; then tackle longer ones.
- Focus on taking computer-based practice tests that simulate the interface of the real MCAT. You should learn how to highlight, strike out, and skip around between questions using a computer prior to test day.

- Do not focus study time on learning or memorizing content. Rather, focus on applying the content to practice exam questions/passages. Content mastery is necessary, but not sufficient to perform well on the MCAT. You must become comfortable with answering the information and drawing upon the skills tested by the MCAT in the manner in which it's actually tested on the exam.

- Figure out in practice how much time you can spend on each question in each section. Practice moving more quickly so if you fall behind on the test, you've practiced catching up, too.

- Keep building up your confidence in your test-taking ability. Confidence feeds on itself and results in higher scores. If you've reached your target score on the exam many times on practice tests, you'll be better able to manage the stress of Test Day.

## HEALTHCARE EXPERIENCE

According to a recent survey of medical schools, knowledge of healthcare issues and commitment to healthcare were among the top five variables considered very important to student selection. (The other four were medical school interview ratings, GPA, MCAT scores, and letters of recommendation.) While having experience in healthcare—most likely some type of volunteer experience—is not exactly a requirement, you should be as active in healthcare activities as possible as a premed student. For many schools, such experience is an unstated requirement. If nothing else, healthcare experience will help you articulate in your personal statements and interviews why you want to pursue a career in medicine.

## JOINT DEGREE PROGRAMS

Many medical schools offer joint degree programs, the most common one being the joint MD/PhD in an area relating to medicine. Approximately eight out of nine schools allow students to pursue the MD and PhD in an area pertinent to medicine, such as biochemistry, biomedical engineering, immunology, molecular biology, neurosciences, and pharmacology. MD/PhD programs are long—at least six years, usually seven years, and sometimes longer—and require a high level of commitment.

Some MD/PhD candidates see the joint degree as a way of achieving balance between clinical medicine and scientific research. Your chance of admission into a joint degree program is based in part on your commitment to both clinical work and research/teaching. If you're considering applying to a joint degree program, make sure you can articulate the reasons why you want to pursue both degrees.

As an applicant to MD/PhD programs, you must demonstrate your research commitment in several ways. You must have had at least one lengthy and significant research experience in which you showed substantial intellectual as well as technical involvement. MD/PhD admissions committees value coauthorships on papers or abstracts very highly. They will ask you to write an additional personal statement, in which you will describe your research experience and how earning two degrees fulfills your career goals. Moreover, you will need to submit a detailed letter of recommendation from each of your research advisers outlining your involvement in research projects and your capacity to conduct independent research in the future. Finally, most MD/PhD programs will put you through numerous interviews (as many as ten) in up to two separate rounds of interviews. On the bright side, some MD/PhD programs pay for or subsidize travel expenses to attend interviews, and many waive the in-state residency preferences of their medical schools.

Also popular today, as doctors become more business savvy, are MD/MBA programs. Some doctors, particularly those entering public service or epidemiology, pursue a master's degree in public health along with their MD.

# CHAPTER 7

# Letters of Recommendation

Letters of recommendation are typically submitted with the secondary applications, in the latter part of the application process. However, it's important that you start to think about potential letter writers and approach them sooner, rather than later, in the process.

Admissions committees are generally very specific about whom they want to submit letters on your behalf. Many committees require letters from either a premed committee or from science professors who have taught you in a class. Don't take these requirements lightly. You should do everything you can to give the medical schools exactly the kind of letters they have requested; after all, there is a reason they ask for certain recommenders. So the questions are these: How do you know what kind of letters you will be asked to submit, and how do you go about soliciting these letters?

To learn the types of letters you are likely to be required to send to a particular medical school, consult the MSAR, visit individual school admissions websites—most schools' websites detail the kinds of letters they require—or visit your premed office. The advantage of the last approach is that you can get a jump on establishing relationships with the people best suited to write your recommendation letters, especially if your school writes premedical committee letters.

## PREMEDICAL COMMITTEE LETTERS

It is fairly typical for a medical school to ask you for a "premed committee letter." If your undergraduate school has a premedical committee, most medical schools will prefer to receive it over individual letters. These letters are typically of two types: either an original letter written by your undergraduate premedical committee on your behalf or a summary of excerpts of comments made by individuals who have submitted letters (at your request) on your behalf. The premed committee letter used to be a standard component of any applicant's application. In recent years, many schools have eliminated the premed committee. If your school has done that, med schools will accept individual letters in lieu of a committee letter.

## INDIVIDUAL LETTERS

An applicant who is not submitting a premed committee letter will typically be asked to submit three individual letters of recommendation. Generally some, if not all, of these letters must come from science faculty members who have taught you in a class. A letter written by a teaching assistant carries far less weight than does a letter from a senior faculty member, and you should probably not ask a TA to write you a letter of recommendation if a letter from a writer with more professional gravitas is available. However, letters cosigned by both the teaching assistant and the professor are generally acceptable.

In addition to recommendations from science faculty, some medical schools request that non-science majors submit letters from a professor in their major. They may also give you an option of submitting an additional letter or letters from professors outside of science or outside your major. Additionally, many medical schools permit letters from research advisers and from physicians or other individuals whom you've shadowed or worked with in a clinical setting. Typically, applicants to MD/PhD programs are required to submit letters from research advisers or principal investigators in the labs in which they have been meaningfully involved. Most osteopathic medical schools require a letter of recommendation from an osteopathic physician.

You'll be able to submit as many letters of recommendation as you like to AMCAS and electronically designate the schools to which you would like individual letters to be delivered. For applicants interested in submitting more than the required number of letters of recommendation, remember that letter quality is better than quantity. A greater number of lesser-quality letters is probably less effective than the required number of well-written, detailed letters from recommenders who know you well.

# HOW TO SOLICIT LETTERS

Having to approach a professor to ask for a letter of recommendation can be daunting. This is particularly true if you are planning to approach a professor whose class you attended years ago or who taught a class in which you were only one of 300 students. The concern, and it is a very real concern, is that letters solicited under these circumstances will be no more than glorified form letters and will be written with very little insight.

Your job, therefore, is to put yourself in a position in which the letter writer can get to know you. Notice that we didn't say "put yourself in a position in which you can get to know your letter writer." While polite, that misses the point. You're not writing your professor a letter of recommendation; she's writing one for you. So how do you help your professor get to know you? Step one: Start early.

> ### I Like What's-His-Name
>
> Beware the impersonal recommendation. Be sure to ask potential recommenders if they can write a strong letter. If not, move on.

While you're completing your premed requirements, visit your professor during office hours if you have any questions regarding course material. Students will often seek out their TAs for assistance, but they seldom seek out their professors. Chances are that if you go to see your professor during office hours, you will be one of only a handful of students present. Consider getting a cup of coffee with your professors. Many undergraduate institutions sponsor something called "Take Your Professor to Lunch" to encourage faculty and students to intermingle. What a deal: Not only do you get a free lunch, but you also get to know your professors outside of the classroom. And if you do well in a particular class or have an especially positive experience, apply to become a teaching assistant the following year or volunteer to work in that professor's lab. The possibilities are limitless; you just need to put forth a little effort to get the relationship started.

When you approach someone to write a letter of recommendation, don't hesitate to ask whether he can write you a strong letter of support. If the person hesitates in any way ("I'm going to be out of town"; "I'm really very busy now"), look elsewhere. While this may be the truth, this may also be a way to tell you that he can't, or won't, write a letter on your behalf. Although this may be embarrassing, it will hurt you a lot more in the long run to have someone's late recommendation force you to withdraw your application, or worse yet, to have a lukewarm letter of recommendation submitted.

Assuming the individuals you ask express pleasure and honor at being requested to write a letter on your behalf, be prepared to give them a copy of your résumé or an outline of your personal, professional, and academic background and accomplishments to provide a complete picture of you and your interests. If you have a strong academic record, you may want to include a copy of your transcript or at least a summary of courses taken and grades received. Any articles or papers that you think may be helpful should also be offered. Be specific in the information you provide. This is usually the raw material from which recommenders will construct their letters. The material that you provide letter writers often closely matches the final letters that they compose. Finally, always provide recommenders with addressed and stamped envelopes to either your premed adviser/committee or the school in question and transcript request forms along with your AMCAS and AACOMAS ID numbers (as appropriate). Individual school secondary applications and the primary medical school application services provide additional specifics.

## NONTRADITIONAL APPLICANTS

Applicants who have been out of undergraduate school for several years face special issues when it comes to obtaining letters of recommendation. Generally speaking, medical schools will still request that you submit letters from undergraduate science professors from whom you took a course. However, it might also make sense for nontraditional applicants to submit letters from employers. Whether you're still in college or long graduated, do everything in your power to provide medical schools with whatever letters they request. When given flexibility in the decision regarding letter writers, think deeply about who will best be able to write a letter painting you in the light in which you wish admissions committees to see you.

As a nontraditional applicant, you have two options as to how to go about obtaining letters from professors: You can go back to your undergraduate professors, or you can take additional postbaccalaureate science classes at a four-year institution and ask your professors there to write recommendations.

The latter may be the best option for two reasons. First, you may have unfinished premedical course requirements that you'll be required to finish. Second, some medical schools require that prerequisites be done within a certain time frame; these facts alone may mean that you'll need to go back to school to take additional courses. Additionally, depending on the length of time since you last saw your professors, it's possible they're not going to remember you, no matter how sterling your personality.

Letters are usually sent directly, either via mail or electronically to AMCAS, to individual schools, or to a third-party document management service such as Interfolio.

## CONFIDENTIAL OR NONCONFIDENTIAL LETTERS?

When you initially open a file with your premed office, you will be asked to decide whether you want an "open" or "closed" file. Individual medical schools may ask you this question again on their secondary applications. If you choose to have an open file, you will have access to your letters of recommendation. If you do, admissions committees may question whether or not you've "censored" your letters by including in your packet only those that paint a very positive picture of you. Admissions committees want to have assurance that they are receiving a complete, unedited picture of you from those who wrote your letters of evaluation. From the medical schools' perspective, therefore, it is preferable that you have a closed file and that your letters be confidential. Some schools will require this.

## WHAT MAKES A GREAT RECOMMENDATION?

Keep in mind the purpose of recommendation letters: They serve as outside endorsements of your medical school candidacy. The more personal the letter, the better off you are.

Schools fully expect these letters to be glowing endorsements. Anything less may be a concern. Admissions committees are looking for applicants who have demonstrated intelligence, maturity, integrity, and a dedication to the ideal of service to society—all the things that you'd look for in a physician. To this end, a glowing letter of recommendation generally begins by detailing the circumstances under which the letter writer has come to know the applicant. This includes the length of time and the nature of the association. It then evaluates the candidate on the nature and depth of scholarly and/or extracurricular activities undertaken, the candidate's academic record and performance on MCATs, and the personal and emotional characteristics of the candidate. The letter ends with the letter writer's overall assessment of the candidate's suitability for the medical profession.

> **Do the Waive**
>
> Conventional wisdom dictates that you should waive your option to review your recommendations. Med schools prefer that you not have any hand in what is written about you in these letters.

The admissions committee may react negatively to a letter of recommendation that focuses solely on the academic qualifications of the applicant and gives little or no attention to the candidate's nonacademic strengths and characteristics, as this may imply a lack of familiarity with the candidate.

## TIMING IT ALL

Don't wait until the fall to ask for letters of recommendation. You don't want to be crushed in the fall rush, when zillions of premeds are scrambling and science professors are overwhelmed. Waiting until the last minute means that it's likely that the quality of the letters will suffer.

Keep track of the status of your letters. It will be easy to monitor electronically when they've been received by application services or Interfolio. Additionally, most schools that allow letters of recommendation to be delivered to them directly have some sort of web portal through which you can view the receipt status of application-supporting documents. If they're late, politely call or email and check on the writer's progress. But don't harass your recommenders; if you make a pest of yourself, it could negatively impact what they will end up writing about you. Once you've confirmed that your letters have been sent, it's nice to send thank-you notes (or at least a thank-you email) to the writers. Personal visits are in order after you've been accepted.

# CHAPTER 8

# Completing Your Application

The medical school application is your single best opportunity to convince a group of strangers that you would be an asset both to the school and to the medical profession. It's your opportunity to show yourself as something more than grades and scores. Granted, every person who applies will have strengths and weaknesses. But it's how you present your strengths and weaknesses that counts.

So what's the best way to present yourself on the application? We all know that some people are natural-born salespeople in person, but the med school admissions process is written, not spoken. The key here is not natural talent but rather organization—carefully planning a coherent presentation from beginning to end and paying attention to every detail in between.

## AMCAS SCHOOLS

The AMCAS (the American Medical College Application Service) is a centralized application processing service that was developed to simplify and standardize the process of applying to allopathic medical schools. All but a handful of US med schools currently participate in this service.

What this means is that you submit just one application to AMCAS no matter how many schools you apply to. AMCAS then assembles your application file, verifies it and forwards it to your designated medical schools. Instead of having to complete individual applications for every school, you complete just one AMCAS application.

The AMCAS uses an entirely Web-based application, and students are required to submit their applications electronically via the Internet. Students are given accounts on the AMCAS servers at the time they register for the MCAT, and their applications are saved on those computers until they have been completed. After payment and receipt of your primary application along with supporting transcripts, applications enter the verification process. After verification, students notify AMCAS that their applications are verified and ready for submission to their designated medical schools.

## The AMCAS Application

The AMCAS application is available via the AAMC website at www.aamc.org/students/applying/amcas. The application can be accessed 24 hours a day, beginning around May 1. For the Early Decision Program for all schools, the deadline is August 1. The sooner you open an application file on the AMCAS server, the sooner you can complete it; the sooner you can send it in, the better off you'll be. It's advisable to make sure all transcripts are received prior to June 1 and that the application is complete and submitted as close to June 1 as possible. Historically, verification wait times have hovered between four and six weeks, with wait times being much shorter in June and considerably longer during peak application time in late summer. Remember, applications can't be considered by your designated medical schools until your AMCAS application has been verified.

---

### Important AMCAS Application Tips

1. Unless you are applying for a combined MD/PhD, there is only one essay on the application, the Personal Statement. See chapter 9 for a full discussion of the personal statement.
2. Applicants who consider themselves "disadvantaged" are also asked, "Briefly describe any social or educational challenges that you believe have affected your educational pursuits." This response must be no longer than one-quarter of a page.
3. Fees for the 2014 entering class in AMCAS are $160 for one application and $36 for each application thereafter. On average, students apply to 14 medical schools.
4. Email will be your primary mode of communication with AMCAS, so make sure to keep your email address up-to-date at all times. You can change it as often as necessary on your Web application.
5. To access the AMCAS application, go to www.aamc.org/students/applying/amcas/. Start by downloading the Application Worksheet file, which is an outline of the questions for which you'll have to prepare.

---

The application contains six main sections: biographical information, postsecondary experiences, essay, schools attended, transcript requests, and coursework.

### Biographical Information

The information requested is what you would find on any kind of application. Avoid the "throw everything in and the kitchen sink" mentality. Spotlight those activities and honors that are most important to you and that you hope will distinguish your application.

### Postsecondary Experiences

This section is where you'll list your work and extracurricular experiences, honors, or publications that you want to highlight. Experiences should be listed either chronologically or by experience type. Make sure to list only significant and relevant items.

> **Follow Directions**
>
> Admissions officers are amazed at how many applicants simply refuse to follow directions. Don't think that you're an exception to any rule. If the application asks for X, give them X, not Y.

### Essay

The personal statement has significant weight with many admissions committees. It should be approximately one full page. AMCAS provides a specific maximum word count. See chapter 9 for more details about this essay.

### Schools Attended

The information required in this section is basic factual information about the institutions you have attended.

### Transcript Requests

To complete your AMCAS application, you must arrange to have official transcripts sent to AMCAS from all the college-credit granting institutions which you've attended. Generally, colleges charge a fee for this service. You will be able to print out an AMCAS Transcript Request Form to send to the registrar's offices at your prior schools. You are strongly advised to use this form when requesting your official transcripts, as it contains your AAMC ID and will increase the speed with which received transcripts can be registered to your application. Make sure to inform the registrar's office to attach this form to the transcripts when they are mailed back to AMCAS. If you're no longer physically located near the school from which transcripts are being sent, it may be necessary for you to fax the form to the appropriate number, and then follow up with an explanatory phone call to the office responsible for sending transcripts at that institution.

---

**Apply Early**

It really does pay to go to the trouble to apply early, particularly in this era of rolling admissions. If you delay and submit your applications late in the season, schools may have fewer, if any, openings left.

---

It is also strongly advisable to request unofficial school transcripts for your personal use if this information isn't available to you through a school website, as you'll need dates of attendance, credit hours, and specific information regarding your degrees and coursework (see below). You will also want to confirm the accuracy of your transcripts.

### Coursework

In this section, you'll enter details on any postsecondary course you have ever taken, regardless of whether you earned credit. You must enter courses exactly as they appear on the original school transcripts, in addition to the official transcript grade and AMCAS grade for each course. Courses should be entered in chronological order.

---

**Lone Star State Schools**

The state of Texas has its own application form for state schools. To apply to the UT system, contact:

Application Service, Texas Medical and Dental Schools
Phone: (512) 499-4785
Website: www.utsystem.edu/tmdsas

---

# NON-AMCAS SCHOOLS

There are a few schools that do not participate in AMCAS. These schools require that you complete their own individual applications. This must be done for each non-AMCAS school that you apply to, and the applications can differ significantly. Do not send the AMCAS application to a non-AMCAS school.

The following schools must be contacted individually or via other application programs:

- Texas A&M University System Health Science Center College of Medicine
- Texas Tech University Health Science Center School of Medicine
- Texas Tech University Health Sciences Center, El Paso, Paul L. Foster School of Medicine
- University of Texas Southwestern Medical Center at Dallas Southwestern Medical School
- University of Texas Medical School at Galveston
- University of Texas School of Medicine at Houston
- University of Texas School of Medicine at San Antonio
- Canadian schools of medicine (17 schools)

Not surprisingly, the non-AMCAS school applications tend to be similar to the AMCAS application. These applications also contain general information pages, and of course, an essay (one or more). The major difference may be that a non-AMCAS school simply requests a copy of your transcript rather than making you compute yearly and subject GPAs, as is the case with the AMCAS application. Since there is so much overlap, once you have completed the AMCAS application, you shouldn't have much difficulty cranking out the non-AMCAS applications. You probably can take most of your personal statement from the AMCAS application.

## DEADLINES

Many schools have a rolling admissions system, which means that those applicants who are reviewed first will be given the first interviews and subsequently be granted admission before other candidates. If you're using the AMCAS, try your best to get your application in as soon after June 1 as possible. Even if you're taking the August MCAT, try to submit your application early so the verification process can begin. That being said, if you can't submit it in June or early July and you find that working on it really cuts into your MCAT prep time, put it away until after the test. You need to focus on getting the best possible MCAT scores, and it isn't detrimental to get the AMCAS application in later (but no later than September), since schools won't consider it until they have your August MCAT scores anyway.

Although some schools don't employ rolling admissions, they nonetheless begin assessing applications as soon as they are received, and consequently, they will begin to offer interviews to those they feel are qualified candidates. This is a major advantage: If you send your materials in too late, you will be given an interview later in the application season. Some admissions committees will discuss candidates they have discussed at previous meetings. So, if you have interviewed in October, you could be reviewed five times; if you interview in March, you've got one shot. Again, the moral of the story is do not procrastinate.

## APPLICATION DOs AND DON'Ts

1. *Triple-Check Your Application for Spelling Errors.*

   You lose a certain amount of credibility if you write that you were a "Roads Scholar." Ask a family member or friend to read through your application as well.

2. *Check for Accidental Contradictions.*

   Make sure your application doesn't say that you studied abroad for a semester in 2013 when it also says that you shadowed a physician in the United States during the same dates.

3. *Prioritize All Lists.*

   When you're asked to list your honors or awards, don't begin with fraternity social chairman and end with Phi Beta Kappa. Let the admissions committee know that you realize what's important—always list significant scholastic accomplishments first.

4. *Account for All of Your Time.*

   If you have been away from school for longer than a semester, did not enter college directly from high school, have been out of college for some time, or had other breaks in your education, be sure that your application shows what you were doing during that period. Don't leave gaps.

5. *Don't Overdo Listing Extracurricular Activities.*

   Don't list every activity you ever participated in. Select the most significant and, if necessary, explain them. Admissions officers are suspicious of people who list 25 time-consuming extracurriculars and yet still manage to attend college. Ask a close friend to help you select the most significant activities to list and discuss.

6. *Don't Mention High School Activities or Honors.*

Unless there's something very unusual or spectacular about your high school background, don't mention it. Yes, this means not stating that you were senior class president. However, do list health-related work or volunteering.

7. *Clear Up Any Ambiguities.*

On questions concerning employment, for instance, make sure to clarify whether you held a job during the school year or only over the summer. Many applications ask about this, and it may be an important point to the admissions officer.

## SECONDARY APPLICATIONS

So you finally finish your AMCAS and/or non-AMCAS applications. You relax and congratulate yourself on completing all that darned paperwork. You put away the credit card and sit back to await your interview invitations. Well, don't get too comfy, because there's more paperwork on the way!

Nearly all schools will forward a secondary application after they receive your AMCAS or non-AMCAS applications. Some schools will send secondaries to all applicants, while others will screen their candidate pools before sending secondaries. What do the secondaries entail? Well, they can vary from requesting just a bit more biographical data to asking for a full-fledged essay. The one thing they almost uniformly request: more money (surprise, surprise). Most schools require a secondary application fee between $25 and $100. It's usually at the secondary application stage that you'll be asked to forward your letters of recommendation as well. Again, in secondaries you explain your interest in individual schools, so do your research.

## MANAGING YOUR CAMPAIGN

*When* you submit the various components of your application is as important as *what* you submit: If you miss deadlines or omit a piece of necessary information, your stellar GPA and MCAT scores, brilliant personal statement, and glowing recommendations are all for naught. The moral: Keep yourself organized.

## OSTEOPATHIC MEDICAL SCHOOLS

The American Association of Colleges of Osteopathic Medicine provides a centralized application service for all 30 accredited osteopathic medical schools. Through this service (called AACOMAS), you can file one application, one set of official transcripts, and one set of MCAT scores. AACOM then verifies and forwards these to each of your designated schools.

Like admission to allopathic medical schools, admission to an osteopathic medical school is competitive. So, despite the fact that most osteopathic medical schools have later deadlines than do allopathic schools, it's still advisable to apply early. Most schools are on a rolling admission basis, and some offer "early decision" programs. For more information, contact AACOMAS:

American Association of Colleges of Osteopathic Medicine (AACOM)
AACOMAS Application Service
Phone: (301) 968-4190
Website: https://aacomas.aacom.org

# CHAPTER 9

# The Personal Statement

When you submit an AMCAS application, you have the opportunity to "talk" to the admissions committee members via your one-page "personal statement." You may use this space to write about anything you want. Applicants often wonder whether their statement is actually read by the admissions committee. Not only will it be read, but it will be read again and again during the application process.

While your academic history is a reflection of your potential to successfully negotiate the medical school curriculum, your personal statement is the first step in developing a portrait of who you are as a person and whether or not you have the personality traits and characteristics necessary to be a physician.

While it is impossible to know what each medical school is looking for when it reviews your personal statement, your statement is nonetheless the one area into which you can infuse a little bit of personality. Your goal is to make yourself a "real person" to the admissions committee and not just an "academic profile." Using your life story to illustrate the points you are trying to make is an excellent way of doing this.

## WHAT TO WRITE

When many applicants write their personal statements, they try so hard to sound impressive to the admissions committee that their writing style becomes stilted and artificial. These applicants wind up portraying themselves as overstuffed, pompous characters no committee member would want to spend much time with— instead of real people with goals and ideals.

Here are some important points to consider, as well as common pitfalls to avoid when writing your statement.

---

### Weave a Story

Use vignettes and anecdotes to add interest to your essay. Why did you decide to go into medicine? Was it because of an experience you had in school? Have you or family members had an experience with the medical community that left a lasting impression? Be creative.

---

- The personal statement is not the place to recount all your activities and honors in list-like fashion. Avoid writing the rehashed résumé or typical biographical essay ("I was born in a small fishing village . . .").

- Make it personal. This is your opportunity to put a little panache into the application. Show the admissions committee why you decided to go into medicine.

- Be yourself. This is not the time to try on a new persona, nor is it the time to fall back on clichés. Unless you're one of the five people in the world who is naturally funny, it is probably not a good idea to start your personal statement with a joke.

- Don't name-drop; no one will be impressed.

- Don't write in the third person. Normal people do not write about themselves as though they were writing about someone else.

- Don't begin every sentence with the pronoun *I*, since doing so makes you sound egotistical.

- You probably want to avoid delving into any controversial topics, such as abortion or euthanasia. If you do decide to include one, though, definitely avoid being dogmatic or preachy. You don't want to take the risk of alienating a reader who may not share your politics.

- Try not to make apologies for your past. For instance, if you received a C in physics (hey, it could happen), don't feel compelled to justify it somehow. However, there may be events in your past for which you believe the circumstances truly do merit some mention. When this is the case, briefly state the relevant facts, but don't make excuses. What you don't want to do is provide the admissions committee with a road map to your weakness by making the problem bigger than it really is. On the other hand, if there really is a weakness

in your application, avoiding the issue will not prevent the admissions committee from finding it on its own. If you haven't provided a context in which
to view the issue, you may not have an opportunity to do so again. If you feel
further information is needed, talk to the admissions offices at the schools to
which you're applying. They can provide direction as to whether, and what
kind of, additional documentation might be required

- You can't take liberties with margins or fonts with the electronic applications, since margins will be preset and fonts will be standardized. That
  means that you'll have to write a personal statement of the appropriate
  length—no rambling on for pages or trying to turn a paragraph into a page.

## The Five Most Common Mistakes

We asked a medical school admissions officer for the five most common mistakes
students make in writing their personal statements. Here's what she told us:

### Underestimating the Importance of the Essay

It appears to be a common misperception that a stellar academic record will overcome
other deficiencies in a student's application, including a poorly written personal statement. This is often glaringly evident when a student writes a few hastily constructed
paragraphs, leaving most of the allotted page blank. In other less obvious examples,
students simply don't allot enough time to polish the essay.

### Using Excessive Detail–the "Overwhelm and Conquer" Approach

The common misperception that more is better results in an essay that generates
groans from the unfortunate reader on the admissions committee. Unfortunately, it
is such an unpleasant experience for the reader to wade through this essay that the
entire application often goes to the bottom of the pile.

### Failing to Make the Essay Personal

A common mistake is to use the essay to recite a list of activities and accomplishments, without really addressing the question, "Why medicine?" When students fail
to convey what they learned from their experiences, they fail to communicate to an
admissions committee how they see themselves as an asset to the medical profession.

Ask your mother and your best friend to review your personal statement to make sure they can hear your "voice" in it.

### Embellishing the Essay

Students often avoid the personal approach entirely by writing an overly creative or philosophical treatise, hoping to impress the committee with their unique approach. While this approach may make for interesting reading, it does not leave the reader with a compelling reason to recommend the student for an interview. There is a place for creativity in the essay, but overall, the personal statement should not deviate from the standard essay format.

### Failing to Proofread the Essay

Attention to detail often eludes the medical school applicant. The failure to proofread can be a devastating omission, as nothing destroys the credibility of an application faster than misspelled words and faulty grammar. Admissions committees place a high value on strong communication skills—both written and verbal—and expect high-quality writing in the personal statement.

## Writing Drafts

Because the personal statement is such an important part of your application, it shouldn't be done overnight. A strong personal statement may take shape over the course of weeks or months and will require several different drafts. Write a draft and then let it sit for a few weeks. With the Web-based AMCAS application, you can save your draft on the AAMC server and edit it as often as you'd like. Time gives you valuable perspective on something you've written. If you leave it alone for a significant period of time, you may find (to your astonishment) that your first instincts were good ones; on the other hand, you may shudder at how you could ever have considered submitting such a piece of garbage.

Allow at least a month or so to write your statement, and don't be afraid to overhaul it completely if you're not satisfied. Most important, get several different perspectives. Have close friends or relatives read it to see if it really captures what you want to convey, asking them about their initial reactions as well as their feelings after studying it more carefully. Once you've achieved a draft that you feel comfortable with, have it read by a few people who barely know you. Since they haven't heard the story before and don't know the characters, they're often able to tell you when something is missing or confusing.

The bottom line is to let a reasonable number of people read the essay and make suggestions. To avoid being overly influenced by an individual reader, try to read all of the comments at once. If certain criticisms, crop up consistently then they're probably legitimate. But don't be carried away by every suggestion every reader makes. Stick to your basic instincts—after all, this is your personal statement.

> **Proofread!**
>
> Proofreading is of critical importance. Don't be afraid to enlist the aid of others. If possible, let an English teacher review the essay solely for spelling and grammar mistakes. Nothing catches an admissions officer's eye more quickly than a misspelled word.

## The Interview Connection

Interviewers often use your personal statement as fodder for questions. They may focus on a couple of key points mentioned in your essay and use these as springboards for discussion. If you have included experiences and ideas that are dear to you or that you feel strongly about, you will have no problem speaking with passion and confidence. Nothing is more appealing to admissions folks than a vibrant, intelligent, and articulate candidate. If you write about research you conducted five years ago, you'd better brush up before your interviews. Think about the following:

- What was the purpose of your research? Was it part of a larger research question?
- What benefit came out of your research?
- Is there a relevant history to your research?
- What exactly did you do?
- Whether or not your research was ultimately successful, what did you learn?

While letters of recommendation serve as outside endorsements, the personal statement is your own personal sales pitch. You're up against thousands upon thousands of qualified candidates. You have to make yourself stand out from the crowd. Everyone has a story to tell. The key lies in how you tell your own tale.

## Institutional Action

Admissions committees are very concerned with the moral character of potential physicians. Because of this, the AMCAS application asks whether you've ever been the subject of an institutional action. This question must be answered truthfully and completely in the "personal comments" section of the application. In addition, you may be asked to provide documentation or discuss the incident further in an interview.

Because an institutional action—particularly one resulting from a conduct violation—may say something about a candidate's integrity, medical school admissions committees view it very seriously. However, an institutional action will not necessarily prevent admission. Each situation is considered individually in the context of mitigating factors leading up to and surrounding the incident, insight shown by the applicant into her behavior, and the candidate's perspective on the incident.

## REAL ESSAYS, REAL RESPONSES

Below are three essays that were submitted by three students applying to medical school recently. Following each essay are the comments of two admissions officers from two different medical schools. Each admissions officer was given the essays to critique without the rest of the students' applications. As you read the comments, notice that while each of the admissions officers seems to have an individual slant on what he thinks are the positive and negative points of each essay, they agree on the larger points: that essays should be personal, well written, and convincing and should clearly answer the question "Why medicine?"

## ESSAY 1

Robert F. Kennedy, during a campaign speech for the Presidency of the United States, said that "Tragedy is a tool for the living to gain wisdom, not a guide by which to live." It was a Friday night, on August 28th, 1992, when I was compelled to live that quotation. On the way home from Sabbath services with my parents, two sisters, and brother, our car was struck by a drunk driver, killing my sister Sarah and severely injuring my family. As I lay in the hospital bed, tubes and machines surrounding me, I could only foresee a life of despondency.

Now, five years later, I understand Kennedy's words; my despondency has changed into a strong commitment to help others. Less than a year after the accident, I took a course to become a certified emergency medical technician (EMT), having learned from first-hand experience the importance of basic life-saving skills, I was determined to gain that knowledge. Once in college, I became actively involved with the Brandeis Emergency Medical Corps (BEMCo), an organization of volunteer EMTs who respond to all emergency medical calls on campus.

The summer between my freshman and sophomore year, I worked for a private ambulance service in Los Angeles. I found this experience very valuable because it brought me into the inner-city for the first time. I was exposed to individuals who lived on a daily basis with fear and uncertainty about their health when some of the finest medical technology was just moments away. Intrigued by these issues, I later enrolled in a specialized health, law and medicine program at Brandeis to study possible solutions to the problems I saw.

By the end of my sophomore year, I knew that I wanted to see for myself and learn more about the effects of diseases on the body. As a result, I took an internship at the UCLA Department of Pathology, where I began assisting in autopsies. I was able to apply the textbook description and organ functions that I had previously learned into their clinical aspects. From this experience, I not only acquired a greater appreciation of how the human body functions, but I also learned that bodies are more than just organs and series of chemical reactions.

I have come to realize that there is no deeper way of understanding the human face of medicine than to be a patient or clinician oneself. When I was growing up in France, my family and I had built a deep-rooted relationship with our family physician. Dr. Celan knew each of our personal and medical history, and with love, attention, confidence, and trust cared for us and his other patients. I know from the accident that being alone in an emergency room can be very frightening. I also know that regardless of how may shots of anesthetics I received that night, nothing helped me more and gave me more strength than holding my doctor's hand. A simple human approach can bring significant results.

While no activity I take part in will ever bring my sister back, I can and will forever strive for the strength to take what I have learned from the accident and help others in her memory. I am now starting my fourth year in BEMCo. I have the primary responsibility for our three-person team, and I am one of two supervisors for the Corps. Every time that I respond to an emergency, I look at the patient and see Sarah's beautiful face. I am reminded each time that even if I do not know these patients, they are still as important to someone as Sarah was and is to my family.

### Comments of Admissions Officer 1

Admissions committees rely on the student's essay in the personal statement as one tool to assess the personal qualities that are deemed significant in future medical students and physicians. They seek mature, intelligent, and compassionate individuals who are also positive, articulate, and goal-directed—in essence, individuals who will excel in the art of medicine as well as the science of medicine. Essays are examined with an eye to how successfully the student has achieved the goal of communicating to an admissions committee that he or she will be an asset both to the medical school and the medical profession.

This essay is a pleasure to critique as it embodies the elements that craft a successful personal statement. The student draws upon a compelling personal experience, along with a powerful quotation, to develop the thematic thread that unifies the essay. The introductory section of the essay immediately piques the interest of the reader with its clarity and articulation of purpose. The student's assertion of a "strong commitment to help others" is not merely the words often quoted by premedical students when asked "Why medicine?" This student is able to describe a variety of medically related experiences that support and give credence to his motivation to pursue a medical career. The essay explores the student's logical progression of decisions in his quest to gain an in-depth knowledge of the medical profession. His choice of academic study reflects an individual who is motivated to understand the deeper issues of healthcare and serve as a problem solver.

This well-crafted essay succeeds in presenting the strength of the candidate's personal qualities—his maturity, confidence, intelligence, and compassion. The student presents himself as a winner—someone who stands out from the crowd—and his originality flows naturally through this essay. Given that other factors in the application are competitive, it is likely that an admissions committee would view this student as a potentially strong candidate both for its medical school and the medical profession.

**Comments of Admissions Officer 2**

A quick reading of this personal statement leaves this reviewer with an excellent impression of the applicant, who appears to be the type of person whom you would enjoy interviewing for medical school. The essay is above average in quality; it captures the reader's attention immediately through the description of a personal tragedy and continues with a chronological outline of extracurricular activities to test the applicant's motivation for medicine.

A closer examination of the personal statement indicates that it is written in classical essay style and presents a number of interesting topics that would form the basis of a meaningful discussion with an interviewer. The first paragraph outlines the genesis of the motivation for medicine as a result of the tragic loss of a sister. In the second paragraph, the applicant's motivation for medicine is clearly stated along with a strong statement of social commitment to help people. This is exactly what the experienced admissions committee member is looking for in a future physician and precisely what the present-day changing world of medicine needs. Furthermore, the applicant took the initiative to take an EMT course and participate in emergency medical calls, and he thereby has tested his motivation through a hands-on situation.

More hands-on experience and a learning experience about other cultures makes the third paragraph a powerful statement. The words express a social consciousness and a concern for people of other cultures who are less fortunate than the applicant— traits that would put the applicant in good standing with the admissions committee. Enrolling in the health, law, and medicine program indicates just how motivated the applicant is to learn about the healthcare system.

The fourth and fifth paragraphs present an interesting literary and medical contrast that is rather effective. The applicant has expanded his experience and commented in a cogent manner on two contrasting medical specialties, pathology and family medicine. He demonstrates considerable insight when he comments on the value of "holding (his) doctor's hand." A role model, Dr. Celan, has been identified by the applicant, suggesting that he appreciates that physician's humane characteristics and would administer to patients in a similar fashion.

The final paragraph completes the literary theme, returns to thoughts of the deceased sibling, and reinforces the reason for this applicant's deep motivation for medicine. Mentioning that this is his fourth year as an EMT at school, and that he has prime responsibility for a team, will be noted by an admissions committee. This suggests the presence of several attributes that interviewers look for in applicants: a sense of accomplishment, a commitment to service, and leadership qualities.

This reviewer's summary impression is that this personal statement is above average in quality because the pertinent information is presented with a well-connected motivational theme. One gets the impression that the applicant possesses desirable characteristics for the practice of medicine. The person described is mature, motivated to practice medicine, thoughtful, energetic, and people-oriented, and he understands the human condition.

## ESSAY 2

Last Sunday as I came back from the church buses for the children's ministry, one man asked how it went and I said good. He then commented, "Well, it's different every week. I've been here seven years and it's different every week," which caused me to smile. How fortunate that it is different every week. There will never be a loss of finding something to do, or someone new to meet and listen to.

When volunteering at Cancer Treatment Center on Mondays, I expect the patient visits will be good . . . but I never really know. I do not know if the patient that spoke to me for thirty minutes last week about her daughter will even be conscious enough to recognize my face that day. I do not know if I will encounter hope, hostility, or sadness. I remember one morning I walked into a dim room where a bearded man sat looking into the distance, though looking at a wall. His eyes were somber and completely lost in the knowledge of his condition. He began to ramble about the news his doctor had given him—that he should go home and set his life in order before the cancer totally took him over. He muttered about this place being his last hope and now he would have to fly home that day. As I left the center, I informed my supervisor of the situation and suggested that a chaplain be sent to this man's room. That morning I was brought to face the limitations of medicine, and was glad to discern it from a handicap. Medicine is not a perfect field with the solutions to save the world, but a piece of service to mankind. It addresses those who have hope for physical well-being as well as those who do not.

I find I cannot go back to my high school days when my dreams of being a doctor simulated visions of a clean, tidy office full of cute babies waiting to be examined. Several years ago I spent a summer shadowing my father during his ENT surgeries. It was my pride that kept me concentrating on standing up straight and breathing deep as the sterile surgical smell filled my nostrils and tempted me to collapse at the sight of tonsils scooped out like ice cream. It has been these types of experiences that have injected a shot of realism into my dreams and thus changed my perceptions of how it will be in the lush fields of medicine and how I fit in. I will work with people who have problems entirely real and more threatening than my trivial worries have ever been. These people will be of all ages, professions, and levels of society. They will also need someone in whom to entrust their health—their security. I meet these people every day, and they have no clue that I notice or would like to help. I see the redheaded man who develops my film at the one hour photo has a limp, and wonder if it is a recurring injury or from a recent accident. My hairdresser says she will give birth in just a month and I sit secretly wishing to be there and assist in the miracle. My father begins recovery free from a long month of radiation treatment, and I can only pray and hope to love him enough.

I have asked myself again and again if being a physician is really who I am, or if there is something else. After wrestling with this question, I realized that being a physician is not who I am, though it is an integral part of me. Growing up under the shadow of my father, his example has shaped my ideology to believe that being an instrument in restoring others to health actually changes lives—and this is what I have grown to be a part of and is irrevocably a part of me. It is through this connection with medicine that I see my paradigms of the world shift, and wake up to find that each day is different, new, and challenging.

## Comments of Admissions Officer 2

It is evident that the student did not place a high priority on writing this essay for his personal statement. The essay suffers from several deficiencies; the most obvious is the lack of an organizing theme. A strong statement of purpose in the opening paragraph is essential to give the reader a sense of direction as the essay unfolds. Unfortunately, the student's thoughts are vague and rambling and it is difficult to understand what the student is trying to say. (What is meant when he states that medicine is "a piece of service to mankind" in paragraph two?) The student's language reflects a lack of sophistication that reflects a serious weakness in his written communication skills. The reader can only conclude that the essay was hastily written and without consultation to improve its structure and content.

While the essay lacks strength and cohesiveness, it speaks volumes as to the state of mind of the writer. The student's writing lacks energy, enthusiasm, and self-confidence. His view of medicine is immature and without adequate grounding in reality. In fact, the reference to "growing up under the shadow of my father" leaves the reader with serious concerns about the student's actual motivation to pursue medicine as a career. Is this his decision or his father's? It appears that the student's view of medicine has been adopted, rather than acquired. The student has failed to answer the critical question "Why medicine?" in a way that relates to him, personally. The issue of how to revise this essay is moot in comparison to the larger issue: The student needs to come out from under his father's shadow to mature and develop his own identity. When that is accomplished, he will be able to clearly articulate his motivation for a medical career and convince an admissions committee that he will be an asset to the profession.

### Comments of Admissions Officer 2

A first read of this personal statement left this reviewer with the impression that the various thoughts, some of which are very good, are not well connected because of an awkward style of composition and poor wording. Nevertheless, this applicant from a physician's household demonstrates a nurturing quality complemented by a social commitment and may warrant additional review by an admissions committee.

The first paragraph is poorly composed and detracts from the start of the personal statement. This reviewer's guess is that the writer was attempting to demonstrate that she likes working with children at church and that meeting and talking with people is a natural inclination. These are necessary qualities for a future primary-care physician.

The second paragraph would have made a better opening statement because it demonstrates a testing of the applicant's motivation for medicine and some important personal characteristics for the practice of medicine. Volunteering at the cancer center demonstrates the applicant's motivation and provides "reality testing." The effective part of this paragraph is the applicant's reaction to the depressed, moribund patient.

This is the highlight of the essay. The applicant's recognizing the symptoms, informing the supervisor, and suggesting a course of action is what medicine is all about. These actions suggest that the writer is a sensitive, mature, take-charge, and nurturing individual.

The third paragraph loses its intended impact because of the fragmented writing style. A rewrite or expansion into the major portion of the essay would serve to greatly enhance the impact of the personal statement. However, the paragraph as written conveys a meaningful message. To this reviewer, several attractive traits are conveyed: a long-standing interest in medicine; a realistic view of the field, gained by observing surgical procedures and volunteering; willingness to be a physician to a wide spectrum of society; and an interest in the human condition.

The poor writing at the essay's end diminishes the impact of what could be a revealing, introspective statement. The writer seems to be unclear as to whether she is self-motivated to pursue a medical career or is just following her father's desires. This is a legitimate question for any child of a physician, and it demonstrates maturity, independence, and a reasonable level of introspection. To the applicant's credit, the essay ends with an expression of optimism for the future and a spirit of adventure.

This reviewer's final judgment of this personal statement places it in the below-average range because the desultory composition and rudimentary syntax detract too greatly from the considerable substance that the candidate may have. The apparent first-draft quality of the statement may place the candidate in jeopardy of being overlooked—as you write, so shall you be judged.

# ESSAY 3

The most vivid image I have from this past year is that of a twelve year-old child running up and throwing her arms around her pediatrician and giving him a hug hello. Clinically, Violet was wasted, immunilogically depressed, and had the height of an eight year-old and the weight of a six year-old. The sores in her mouth prevented her from eating normally; she fed herself through a valve known as a "PEG tube" that poked out just northeast of her bellybutton. But now, in the presence of her doctor, she was glowing.

She didn't get along terribly well with her classmates when she was well enough to go to school. Word got out that she was HIV+ and the kids around her taunted her about it until she cried. Her mother wasn't any better. She ignored Violet on her good days, beat her on the bad ones. She told me that she would feed her daughter dog food when she didn't feel like cooking. It seemed as if a dark cloud enveloped Violet when her mother would enter the room. But as soon as Dr. K walked in, that cloud lifted away and was replaced by a sparkling smile that widened her emaciated face. He was her friend.

During the course of my studies at the Tulane University School of Public Health and Tropical Medicine I saw a lot of patients like Violet. Some sicker, some healthier. Some older, some younger. Some richer, some poorer. I studied their charts and, more importantly, I studied them. Whether I was at their bedside in the hospital, at the busy clinic just a stone's throw away from the housing projects, or in a consultation office somewhere in the rural bayous of Louisiana, I learned to listen to patients and absorb what I saw and what they felt. The volumes of charts I examined for my research filled out the blanks in my spreadsheets. My coursework in biostatistics and epidemiology enabled me to analyze the data and look for trends. The numbers told me that, yes, pediatric AIDS patients' nutritional status does improve with aggressive nutritional support and drug therapy despite the fact that there is no uniformly successful treatment for cryptosporidiosis. This research will likely be published. But while my charts and graphs deftly illustrate quantity of life, talking to a patient face to face provoked thoughts about quality of life. I started to think about which was more important: a patient's serum albumin level or his desire to get out of the darn hospital so he can get home and play ball with the neighborhood kids. I didn't come up with any answers, just more questions.

After our visit with Violet, Dr. K told me that a smile like hers made him forget all of the bad things that he'd seen that day, if only for a moment. I believe that the reverse is also true: For a moment, Violet forgot that she was dying. She found comfort in the presence of her doctor. The high quality of care she received came not only from the years of training that her physician completed, but also from the person who dedicated his life to making his patients feel well in every sense of the word.

### Comments of Admissions Officer 1

The writer of this essay succeeds in weaving a compelling story with compassion and sensitivity. The story of "Violet" creates the thematic thread that unifies this student's essay. Within that thematic context, the student presents important details of her own experiences in both the medical and research arenas. These experiences reveal an understanding of the strengths and limitations of medicine, from first-hand experience with the rich and the poor. Her writing style is simple and direct, with an eloquence that speaks to her depth of understanding.

Clearly, this student possesses many of the personal qualities that admissions committees are seeking in candidates—such as maturity, compassion, and intelligence. She has the ability to communicate in an articulate manner and demonstrates a realistic understanding of the medical field from both the clinical and research arenas. What is problematic in this essay is that the student fails to make a direct statement as to *motivation*—why does she want to be a doctor? The conclusion of the essay begs for an articulation of her goals and ambitions in medicine. It is a major omission in an otherwise well-written essay. One of the pitfalls of using another person's story as the focus of an essay is that the writer often becomes secondary to the story. If her essay is to succeed with an admissions committee, it is critical for her to answer the question "Why medicine?" in a personal way.

### Comments of Admissions Officer 2

This is a well-written essay with poignantly described patient situations and perceptive descriptions of the attending physicians. One gains the impression that this individual is either a reapplicant or someone who was recently motivated to apply to medical school while in a graduate public health program. In either case, an explanation of the applicant's motivation for wanting to be a physician would greatly enhance her chances for being considered a highly desirable candidate.

The first paragraph is a splendid way to begin a personal statement in a medical school application, since it will likely evoke a favorable response from everyone on the admissions committee. The writer seems to be highly observant of the condition of the young AIDS patient, as well as of human behavior—good traits for anyone entering medicine. The only detractor is the misspelling of "immunologically"; a graduate student should not make that mistake.

The second paragraph lacks a description of the writer's personal involvement, but the descriptive narrative is touching and indicates sensitivity as an observer. The lengthy third paragraph, in which the writer describes her research, is nicely written and presents the fact that she has experienced patient interactions. It also manifests a personal interest in the patients, but the writer missed a golden opportunity to clearly state that she wants to be a physician so that she can help people like those described. One thinks that perhaps the writer might rather continue in the field of epidemiology.

The final paragraph is well written and follows the pattern of a classic essay by returning to the opening statement and presenting some cogent observations. The comments indicate that the writer is a sensitive individual who has gained considerable insight about the doctor-patient relationship. This would have been the ideal place to clearly state her desire to be a physician such as the one described.

In summary, the writer of this well-written essay demonstrated insight yet remains for the most part a reporter of human drama. Since she fails to declare an interest in medicine, or to even state a desire to help people, the narrative's impact is lessened. Had this been done, the essay would have been above average in quality and certainly would have had an excellent impact on an admissions committee. In the absence of clearly stated goals in the health sciences, the writer may be at a disadvantage in the admissions process of the more clinically oriented schools.

## IN SUMMARY

The personal statement gives you an invaluable opportunity to describe who you are and why you want to be a physician. Use it to your advantage: Start thinking well in advance about what you want to say to the medical schools to which you are applying, and make sure you put great care into honing your essay so that it clearly illuminates your individuality as well as your desire to enter the field of medicine.

# CHAPTER 10

# The Interview

The final step in the evaluation process involves a personal interview. The medical profession is the only profession that requires a personal interview for entry. This fact alone should provide a powerful statement as to the importance admissions committees place on your performance at the interview.

There is a fair amount of mythology surrounding the medical school interview. Much of this stems from the legacy of the "stress interview." One of our favorite tales is this classic passed from one generation of premeds to the next: The interviewer asks the unsuspecting candidate to open a window. As hard as he tries, he can't open it. Why? Because it's nailed shut. (We believe that this story is apocryphal.)

You can rest assured that stress interviews are the rare exception, not the rule. But the interview is an assessment of your composure and maturity. You may be asked a question that makes you uneasy. If something weird or stressful does happen, keep your cool.

## THE INTERVIEW AND ADMISSIONS

Since medical schools are inundated with applications, most admissions committees use the interview as the means for making the final selection. Whereas the first round in the admissions process—reviewing your numbers—may seem impersonal, the interview introduces an element of humanity. Here is where you can let your personality and charm really shine through.

Once you have reached the interview stage, the academic differences among applicants become more subtle. Committees look for patterns of behavior as a means of distinguishing one applicant from the next. They will look at exactly what courses you took to get those As, and they'll ask themselves the following questions:

- Were there any community colleges listed in the official transcript? Why?
- Did you achieve competency in a foreign language? (Studying medical school vocabulary and information requires many of the same skills that learning a language demands.)
- Did you take advanced-level courses or easier ones?
- Did you use AP credits to place out of a subject or to place you into a higher level?
- How many pass-fail classes have you taken? Were these required or elective courses?
- Do you have a pattern of withdrawing from classes?

---

**Bone Up**

It's a good idea to keep a copy of your secondary application with your catalog, so you can review them both the night before your interview.

---

Getting the interview means the school thinks you can do the academic work and that you have something else to offer. As one dean put it, "Brilliance in a doctor doesn't hurt, but we know there are many other attributes that it takes to get through medical school. Persistence, balance, determination: These things are important too."

Schools also tend to have an unwritten "flavor" that their committees try to build. For example, a committee might always tend to favor "niceness" in a class but might attempt in a particular year to accept more students who are interested in surgery or primary care. Or, it might look for students to provide more geographic diversity or minority representation.

## INTERVIEW DAY

Most medical schools still operate fairly formulaic interview systems. Interview days start with an introduction, followed by a tour, after which come one or two interviews. That means that half of the day is dedicated to a tour of the facilities and half to two 45-minute interviews. Schools will tend to schedule between 3 and 20 students per day, and most schedule around 12 to 15. Expect a crowd of other nervous, nametag-wearing applicants gathered in an office or waiting room.

## The Introduction

When you first get to the admissions office, you'll likely be given an introduction to the school. Because this is the first thing, don't panic if you are unavoidably late. All you'll miss is an introduction, so don't let it throw you for the whole day. On the other hand, don't act overly casual about it either, as though you make a habit of being late. Assuming you show the proper amount of concern, no one takes a huge red marker and writes "late" on your application, so if you're poised, your interviewers will never know. That said, there is almost no reasonable excuse for being late, so plan to give yourself plenty of time.

> **Food, Glorious Food**
>
> Most med school interviews break for lunch after the tour and before the first interview. It's usually a free meal at the school cafeteria, often in the company of "host" med students.

## The Tour

Med students who are conducting the tour may be evaluating you as well. If this is the case, it will usually be made clear early in the process. Again, remember to treat every interaction as if it were a part of the interview unless otherwise noted. The medical student is getting a free day off work, so he or she will likely be very happy to chat with you. Find out from him or her, both directly and indirectly, if the medical school is for you. Ask questions like "How does the testing schedule affect your stress level?" "Do people in your class socialize together?" "What's the major hospital like?" "Do you feel safe walking to the parking deck at midnight?" and "What's the best/worst thing about this school?" Don't be aggressive or belligerent. If you've heard the school is not particularly welcoming to minorities, ask the question gently. Keep in mind that med students do tours because they like their school and have some of the same motivations as the volunteering faculty.

You can get a feel for the school by watching the medical students in the hospital portion of the tour. Do they look comfortable? Do they seem well oriented to the wards? How do they walk through the emergency department—do they waltz through or timidly invite you to look through the windows? These sorts of observations can give you hints about the type of clinical training the hospital gives, that is, hands-on or by instruction.

## Advice from the Inside

We asked an admissions committee member for some pointers on interview day. Here's what she told us:

- Be incredibly nice to the school admissions secretary, who can be your best ally or your worst nightmare.
- It's fine to bring in bags if your flight leaves immediately after the interview.
- Most schools offer coffee when you first arrive. Be aware that caffeine can make you nervous.
- Don't try to outdo the competition by comparing stats or name-dropping while waiting in the "greeting" room.
- Don't be vocal about not wanting to go to that school, even casually. "This is my safety" can be a good way to not get an offer.
- Do your homework and be prepared to ask questions.
- Ask the interview coordinator ahead of time whether the interviews are "open" or "closed," about the format of each interview, and about how long each interview should last (more about these issues later).

# PREPARING FOR THE INTERVIEW

Many students go into their first few interviews completely unprepared, hoping to get the hang of it as they go along. This strategy is extremely unwise. You want to be able to anticipate the questions and formulate the key points of your responses. Doing this can help you maximize your potential for success.

## Understanding the Dynamics

The interview experience is multidimensional. Obviously it is a time for the admissions committee to check you out, which means it's also a time for you to "show your stuff." However, you should also approach the interview day as a chance to determine whether or not you would want to attend that particular medical school, assuming you have multiple acceptances.

Given that your primary concern is getting in, it is important to think about the interview from the perspective of the person on the other side of the desk—the interviewer. At most schools, you will have two interviewers: One will usually be given by someone who sits on the committee, while the other will be given by a physician from the community, the residency program, or the faculty. Alternatively, many medical schools utilize med student interviewers, and a few use administrative personnel. Regardless of their affiliation with the medical school, both of your interviewers are volunteering their time—giving up at least an hour of clinical, research, administrative, or study time.

The interviewer's fundamental job is to determine whether or not you have the necessary interpersonal skills and characteristics required of a future physician. These interpersonal skills include, but are not limited to, communication skills, social awareness, empathy, and cultural competency. In the process of the interview, the interviewer will be asking herself, "Do I like this applicant?" and "Can I see myself teaching him as a medical student, consulting with her as a colleague, or referring family members to be his patient?" If the answer is "no," and that opinion is echoed by the second interviewer, it is unlikely that you will be accepted.

Why would interviewers volunteer their time to interview prospective med students? There are a few reasons, most of them altruistic, including the following:

- Quality control over those entering the healthcare profession
- Interest in helping choose the best candidates to better the school's reputation
- Loyalty to the admissions committee's goal of getting the best possible class
- Curiosity about the upcoming batch of future doctors
- Desire to help certain candidate types for personal reasons (minorities, football players, etc.)
- Interest in education
- Feeling of duty toward an alma mater or the profession

### When It Doesn't Click

The overwhelming majority of those interviewing do so out of conviction. Those with really strong convictions join the admissions committee itself, rather than just volunteering to interview on occasion. There may, however, be the occasional community or faculty physician who likes the power dynamic or who wants to find someone like herself, the best tennis-playing biology major from Indiana. If your interviewer asks questions you don't think are appropriate or seems to be biased against you from the start, don't let it rattle you.

**The Interviewer from Hell**

Politics are rampant in all systems; chances are, if you get a weird feeling from the interview, the person conducting the interview is someone whom the committee can't politely refuse. For example, it may be well known that Dr. X is abrasive, but if he is also the head of cardiology, it's possible that the committee couldn't refuse his interest in the interview process.

Many medical schools will end the interview day by asking you to complete a questionnaire concerning your interview experience. If you truly believe your interviewer was inappropriate, you may want to make note of it on your questionnaire. If you do, be specific: Don't say, "Dr. X didn't seem interested in my application," when what you really mean is "After the first time Dr. X referred to me by a wrong name, I corrected him. Unfortunately, this continued throughout the interview. As a result, I was left wondering if he had me confused with another applicant." Alternatively, you may speak with an admissions office staff member regarding your concerns.

### Learning Their Interests

At the beginning of the interview day, you're likely to receive your personal schedule of events, including the names of your interviewers. Some schools try to match you with interviewers who share your interests, but it may not always be possible. If you happen to know your interviewers by research or clinical reputation, great. But if you don't, forgo the temptation to run to the library to look up their publications or where they did their training. Chances are you won't have time; besides, it makes it look like you're trying too hard. Instead, we recommend you mull over these things while you await your interviews:

- Older faculty members/heads of departments probably make up most of the members of the admissions committee itself; however, this isn't always the case, as many schools will also have current medical students as voting members of the committee.

- Researchers are more likely to be interested in and ask questions about your research, or about science.

- Generalists, younger doctors, and medical students are more likely to ask personal questions (see below), questions about how you'll approach the learning part of medical school, or questions about personal "survival" characteristics (how you handle stress, whether you study or play well with others, etc.).

- Administrators may be more likely to ask questions about ethics or your future plans as a doctor.

# TYPICAL AREAS OF ASSESSMENT

The faculty members at each medical school are charged with determining the institutional mission of their particular school and, to that end, the qualities upon which its medical students shall be selected. For this reason, it is impossible to know which characteristics will be assessed in each of your interviews. However, the following are common areas of appraisal:

### Intellectual Curiosity

It should come as no surprise that intellectual ability is an area of assessment throughout the application process. However, by the time you make it to the interview, it is generally recognized that you have the intellectual ability to negotiate the medical school curriculum. Therefore, what is being assessed at the interview is not so much your ability to do the work as the ways in which you approach the unknown. Do you do so openly, with curiosity? How do you organize your thoughts? What is your preferred style of learning? What learning experiences have you had outside of the traditional classroom setting? As a future physician, you will be required to learn continuously from your patients, colleagues, and scientific journals, as well as from the world around you. It is imperative that you enjoy learning, that you have appropriate study habits, and that you have broad intellectual interests.

### Social Awareness and Cultural Competency

As a future physician, your patients will come from backgrounds that are similar to and very different from your own. Therefore, the interview is used to assess the extent to which you have exposed yourself to people whose interests, religion, culture, economics, gender, age, ethnicity, language, education, and race are different from your own. What value do you place on these differences? It is important that for each of your patients, you are able to modify your behavior in such a way as to show respect, inspire confidence, and motivate them to implement whatever changes they need to make to positively affect their health.

### Communication and Interpersonal Skills

Again, the interviewer will be assessing your ability to interact with people who are different from you, whether they be your patients and their families, allied health personnel, or other physicians. Before you interview, it's important that you gain some awareness of yourself as a social being: What is your perception of the impression you make on others? What is your response when others have misunderstood your words or actions? What experiences have you had working or playing on a team? What is your response to criticism? As a future physician, it is imperative that you have the appropriate communication and interpersonal skills to interact successfully with others under dynamic and often emotionally charged conditions.

### *Maturity*

Medicine is a very wonderful, but very difficult, career. It has often been said that it is not so much a profession as a calling. The interview is therefore used to explore your expectations of a medical career as well as assess your maturity, your ability to cope with frustration, and your leadership skills. What efforts have you made to explore a health career? Have you experienced disappointment in your life? What are you most proud of? Under what circumstances do you become frustrated? What is your definition of a leader? In order to be a happy, successful physician, it is important that your expectations be at least somewhat grounded in reality and that you have the necessary personality skills and characteristics required to cope with the challenges and stress of being a doctor.

## TYPES OF INTERVIEWS

There are five types of interviews you're likely to encounter: open, semi-open, closed, group, and multiple mini-interviews.

### *Open*

With these, the interviewer has already reviewed your application and personal statement. She will often begin the interview by referring to the application or a particular section of your personal statement.

### *Semi-Open*

Here, the interviewer has read your personal statement but nothing else. These interviews are likely to begin by relating to whatever event or opinion you put forth in your personal statement. If you didn't explicitly make much of it in your essay, the interview may begin with, "So how did you decide you wanted to be a doctor?"

### Closed

Here, the interviewer has never seen your application folder. He may begin with a very open-ended question, such as "Tell me a little about yourself." The unfortunate side effect of the "closed" interview is that you feel you've put hours and hours into your application, only to have an interviewer ask questions easily answered by the first few sentences. Although you may be tempted to give a sarcastic response to "Tell me about yourself" out of frustration that your masterpiece went unread, avoid the urge. Answer pleasantly and think before you go into an interview about how you'll launch into talking about yourself if the interviewer hasn't read your essay.

Schools that conduct "semi-open" or "closed" interviews often do so to avoid something called the "halo effect." If an interviewer looks at your wonderful scores and grades, she runs the risk of thinking everything you say is wonderful, even if in person you're not that scintillating. On the other hand, if you bombed junior year, your interviewer may write you off without really listening to how you fed your family, went to school, and managed to save enough to do relief work in Uganda over the summer. The downside about the semi-open or closed interview is that the interviewer may not know everything she needs to know about your application in order to represent you adequately before the admissions committee. Remember that one of your interviewer's primary responsibilities is to act as your advocate. If you are granted a semi-open or closed interview, it is up to you to bring to your interviewer's attention anything concerning your application that you believe requires further discussion. That way, the interviewer will be best able to address questions posed by the admissions committee about your application.

### Group

This is the exception. In a group interview, you might have three interviewers and three interviewees in a room. After an introduction and a generic "loosen up" question, each of the interviewers gets to ask questions of each interviewee. Given time constraints, there is usually just time for one question apiece from each of the interviewers, and those questions may not be the same for each interviewee. (For example, Dr. Bob may ask the following questions of different applicants: "John, tell me more about your Space Shuttle experience. Mabel, how do

---

**Tips for Group Interviews**

Etiquette tips for group interviews:

- Don't hog the airtime.
- Refer to others' answers if you get the same question after them.
- Try not to take yourself too seriously.

---

you see your cold fusion experiments relating to medicine?") Group interviews are designed for a school to gauge how well you "play with others" and whether you can share airtime while being charming and eloquent, too.

### Multiple Mini-Interviews (MMI)

A few schools in the United States have adopted a multiple mini-interview (MMI) format. An MMI usually consists of five or more "stations" or "mini-interviews" through which applicants rotate. At each station, the applicants are challenged by a specific question, task, or ethical scenario that requires them to demonstrate something about their problem-solving skills or social and situational awareness. This format provides an opportunity for a larger group of evaluators to provide input on you as an applicant. Generally, there are no "wrong" answers to an MMI scenario, but interviewers/evaluators are interested in seeing your process in working through each situation. MMIs represent a significant departure from traditional interview format, so most schools that employ this interview method will provide detailed information on what to expect prior to your interview.

As was mentioned earlier, a typical traditional interview will last anywhere from 30 to 45 minutes. However, it is not unheard of for a school to schedule interviews of 15 minutes or 90 minutes in length. This is an important piece of information for you to have before you begin the interview, so ask the interview coordinator how long interviews generally last at that particular medical school. How you prioritize the topics you would like to cover during the interview will be very different if you are anticipating that the interview will last 15, 45, or 90 minutes.

## HOW TO PREPARE

As we said before, don't even think about going into your interviews cold. You need to prepare well in advance. You'll need to think about not only what you may encounter—based on the format of the interview and the information provided to you—once you're facing your interviewer, but also when you'll interview, how you'll get there, how you'll behave, and what you'll wear.

Your best resources when preparing for the interview will include your premed adviser, students currently attending the medical school, and the school of medicine's catalog and website.

## Scheduling

Your interview invitations will probably arrive at approximately the same time. Remember, the sooner you have your interview, the sooner you'll be considered for acceptance. Schedule the interviews as early as possible. Many students will try to schedule interviews at less competitive schools earlier, to gain interview experience and overcome early jitters. However, don't postpone your other interviews too long, as it will delay completion of your applications.

Financial reasons may compel you to try to schedule groups of interviews in particular geographical regions. For instance, you may want to set up a West Coast interview tour and visit several schools in the same area during one trip.

If you get one interview in a far-flung region and haven't yet heard from another school in the same place, don't hesitate to give the second school a call. Politely ask, "I'll be in this region on such and such a date interviewing at So and So. If you are planning to interview me, would it be possible to schedule an appointment near that time so I can make only one plane trip?" Schools will usually ask to get back to you, go look at your file, and then tell you yes if they are planning to interview you. If they're already booked for that time, they may offer another time slot.

## Travel and Accommodations

It is at this point that the whole application process can really begin to get expensive. You probably know that you can keep costs down by making airline reservations as far in advance as possible and staying over a Saturday. But did you know that major airlines often offer discounts to applicants for interview travel? Check with your pre-med adviser or premed club for details. It might also be worth your while to check with discount travel agents. They frequently have discounted tickets for sale, even if you have only a few days' notice. One other air travel tip: Carry your luggage with you on the plane. The last thing you want on interview day is to have your luggage sent to the wrong place.

Always do research in advance to find out about parking or the best way to reach the med school from the airport. Usually, your interview offer will include directions to the school and information on accommodations. Many medical schools have programs allowing you to stay with a med student for free. Although a complementary room may be economically enticing, remember that it's important for you to be comfortable. If sleeping on the floor of a medical student's apartment is going to stress you out, you'd be better off staying at the nearest budget motel.

On the other hand, if money is short and you can find a student with an extra bed, it may be a good opportunity to get an inside scoop on the school's personality. Also, just as the medical student showing you around can give you great information and can affect how you view the school, someone you stay with can have an impact on your admission. Since he is doing the admissions office a favor by agreeing to be your host, the office secretary will listen to that person's feedback, such as, "Hey, that last guy was really great! He'd be good to have in the class." It therefore behooves you to treat your host with respect. Remember you are a guest in his home. Don't be demanding, don't expect him to act as a taxi service, don't hog all the hot water for your shower in the morning, and remember to clean up after yourself.

If at all possible, try to arrive the night before the interview in order to familiarize yourself with the area and the school. This allows you to avoid travel delays the day of your interview and will also give you the opportunity to unwind and get a good night's sleep.

## Dress

The interview is not the time to make a fashion statement. Whether you like it or not, your physical appearance will be the first impression you make on the interviewer. You want to be remembered as the self-confident candidate with loads of charm and wit, not the one with the funny hat or braided facial hair.

Men should opt for a dark suit (blue, gray, or black) and an attractive, but not too flashy, tie. Your tie should be a real one, not a clip-on (you don't want it falling off in your lap during the interview), and unless you're already experienced in this area, this is probably not the time to start experimenting with a bow tie. Facial hair should be groomed, and you should probably forgo the earring even if you normally wear one (but it's up to you). Sneakers are definitely out.

Women should wear a suit or dressy coordinates. If you opt for a dress or skirt, watch your hem length. Remember, a short hemline may become inappropriately short when you sit and cross your legs. Your shoes should be closed-toed. You should go easy on the jewelry and makeup, and you should probably forgo the perfume altogether. Stay away from dangling earrings and plunging necklines. If you haven't packed an extra pair of nylons in your purse, it's better to wear a pair that matches your skin tone in case you get a run. Also, dress to tour: Uncomfortable shoes won't help you show yourself at your best. You may want to bring a leather folder or binder for the extra packets of information they give you, but don't bring a briefcase unless you have to.

Be prepared for whatever the weather brings. If it is expected to be hot and humid, wear a blouse or shirt that you wouldn't mind being seen in if you were to take your jacket off. If there is a possibility of rain in the forecast, carry an umbrella and wear a coat. Snow? Opt for a sweater instead of a blouse or shirt, add some gloves, and don't forget your coat.

Finally, one suit or dress is usually enough. You don't have to change outfits for every interview. In fact, when you go to your interviews, you'll begin to recognize certain of your fellow candidates by their interview outfits. It doesn't matter. Remember that you're trying to impress your interviewer, not your competition. If you have a bunch of interviews in a row, make arrangements for dry cleaning your beloved interview outfit.

## SHARPENING YOUR SKILLS

You can get yourself psyched up for the interview by giving yourself a "trial run," anticipating the questions you'll be asked, and understanding what you might encounter on interview day.

### Mock Interviews

Mock interviews are invaluable trial runs. You finally have a chance to answer some of those practice questions. You can have someone evaluate your speaking style, the content of your answers, your body language, and your overall presentation.

Some colleges offer mock interviews. Check the availability of these by consulting your premed adviser or career center. In any case, even if a formal mock interview is not available, you can always have a friend or relative act as the interviewer and evaluate your performance. You may even want to videotape your interview for

---

**Candid Camera**

Trying recording yourself in a mock interview and playing the recording back on fast-forward. Any nervous gestures you display will seem even more obvious (and comical) when they repeat every two seconds.

a more detailed critique. Regardless of which route you take, be sure to wear your interview outfit. As corny as this sounds, you need to practice wearing your professional attire, which unfortunately isn't like wearing your favorite pair of jeans. Not only do you need to get used to the feel of your new clothes, but if you're going to suddenly develop a nervous tic, chances are it will somehow be related to your interview clothes. If this happens, it's better to discover and correct it during your practice interview, not during the real thing.

After your mock interview, be sure to solicit feedback. Only then will you realize if you speak too quickly, should enunciate more clearly, have a tendency to play with your tie or skirt hem when you are nervous, or start every sentence with "like," "umm," or "you know."

## Common Interview Questions

More often than not, the interviewer will base her questions on your personal statement and application. But on occasion, you might be asked to comment on a medically related current event or ethical issue. Since you're planning to become a doctor, these questions are fair game. It's not expected, however, that you'll be an expert on these topics—just that you'll have thought about them and have something reasonably intelligent to share. Read the newspaper and keep up on current events. Go through some back issues of a news magazine and read all the pertinent medically related articles.

Here are some classic interview questions:

### Personal

- Tell me about yourself.
- What do you do for fun?
- Why have you decided to pursue medicine as a career?
- When did you decide that you wanted to be a doctor?
- Do you have any family members who are physicians?
- What is your greatest strength/weakness? Success/failure?
- If you don't get into medical school, what will you do?
- What did you like about college?
- What is your favorite book? What are you reading now?
- What area of medicine are you interested in?

- Where do you see yourself in 10 years? (Hint: Don't say "prison.")
- Where else have you applied? Why do you want to go here?
- What leadership roles have you assumed?
- What clinical experience have you had?

## Ethical

- What are your views on abortion?
- Do you have an opinion on stem-cell research?
- How would you feel about treating a patient infected with HIV?
- What are your views on euthanasia?
- How do you feel about treating uninsured or indigent patients?

## Hypothetical Situations

- You are treating a terminally ill patient who is being kept alive by life support. You feel that he should be taken off the machines. What do you do?
- A pregnant teenager comes to you to discuss her options. She hasn't told her parents about her pregnancy. What do you do?

## Healthcare Issues

- What's the biggest problem facing medicine today?
- What do you think the role of the government should be in healthcare?
- Do you think healthcare is a right or a privilege?
- How do you feel about socialized medicine? The Canadian and British health systems?
- Do you know what an HMO is? A PPO?

Obviously, you won't encounter all of the above questions. Additionally, there may be others that you're asked that aren't on this list. If you take the time to examine these issues, you'll have the confidence to answer most questions that come your way. Practice answering these questions, but do not memorize answers or practice monologues in front of the mirror. An interview is a conversation; you're not auditioning for *Hamlet*. Nothing is worse than answers that sound canned. You must be able to improvise and think on your feet.

## "Illegal" Questions

Medical schools know that questions about your relationships, personal or family history, or future plans for family are strictly illegal; such questions leave schools vulnerable to lawsuits based on sexual discrimination. You will never be asked such questions in writing on either the AMCAS or AACOMAS applications, nor on the secondary applications developed by individual medical schools. Nonetheless, there is the possibility that you will be asked inappropriate questions in an interview, and you should consider how you might respond to them.

### Is It Illegal?

The most common illegal questions are about marriage, family, and childcare plans. Often they are questions that might be appropriate to ask in other situations but that are not relevant to your ability to study and practice medicine. If a question elicits information about your ability to function as a medical student or a medical professional, it probably is reasonable; but if it does not, then it probably is not warranted.

---

**Women and Medicine**

The Council on Graduate Medical Education's Women and Medicine Report delineates five findings related to women in the physician workforce:

- The number of women in the profession is increasing.
- Women remain underrepresented among leaders in medicine.
- Women concentrate in a limited number of specialties.
- Physician gender has little impact on workforce forecasting.
- Barriers to women's equal status remain as obstacles to their advancement.

---

You may be asked if you plan to marry and how you plan to juggle marriage with a demanding career in medicine. You may be asked if you plan to have children; if you have revealed that you have children already, be prepared for questions about how you plan to care for them and what your spouse thinks of your career choice. Some women have reported being asked rather outrageous questions, including those about birth control use, relationship issues, and adequacy of parenting skills.

### How to Respond

First, try to answer the question in a way that is favorable to you without affecting your integrity. For example, if you are asked how you plan to care for your three children while you're in medical school, you can remind the interviewer that you have been successful in your past academic performance and that you expect to continue to be successful in your future performance at their school.

Second, remember that you are not required to answer any question. You can point out to the interviewer that the question being asked is illegal. (However, you probably won't get accepted at that school if you do this blatantly or aggressively.) You could ask the interviewer how the issue in their question relates to your performance as a medical student, but you need do this in an upbeat and nonconfrontational manner if you wish the interviewer to back off and continue the interview.

As a rule, it is rarely to your benefit to offer information about your plans to get married and/or have a family. However, there are situations in which you would want to discuss your personal life, such as if your spouse is applying to medical school at the same time you are, since you will likely want to attend the same school. It's appropriate to discuss with the school how they view both of you attending their school. It is a bit tricky, as rarely are both husband and wife perceived by a school to be at the same competitive level, but if you seek to attend the same school, you need to address this early with admissions personnel. If you are concerned about childcare or spouse or family support groups, don't voice your concerns to your interviewer; instead, check the school catalog or contact the personnel in charge of these services to answer your specific questions.

Bear in mind that it is the rare interviewer who will ask an illegal question with malice intended or with conscious awareness that he is wading into inappropriate territory. It's more likely that your interviewer is a physician who is accustomed to asking his patients scores of personal questions and is not fully aware that he is "trespassing" in the particular context of the interview.

You can, and should, report to the admissions office before you leave campus any discriminatory behavior, illegal questions, inappropriate questions, or poor interview technique (for example, if the interviewer spent only fifteen minutes with you because she was late and had to leave early). You have the right to request another interview, and the school should provide it. If that means you must stay over another day, the school should help you with your arrangements.

## Anticipating the "Why"

Admissions committees don't want to know the "what" of your answers as much as the "why." For example, if you're asked what you're most proud of and the answer is running a marathon, you might want to extrapolate by saying something like "I had never been athletic, but as I researched health and medical school, I realized that exercise really matters. I decided that my future patients would benefit from my

---

<table>
<tr><td>

### Address Your Weaknesses

"If an applicant has anything on his résumé that might raise eyebrows, I would encourage him to write to the admissions committee addressing the apparent weakness. I flunked my chemistry course in college. I retook it after college and got excellent grades, but there was no hiding the F on my undergraduate transcript. I sent out letters addressing this to every school I applied to and was commended for my honesty and maturity in doing so."

—Laura Hodes, Columbia University College of Physicians and Surgeons; adapted from *Newsweek*/Kaplan's *How to Choose a Career and Graduate School*

</td></tr>
</table>

practicing the exercise I'll preach, so I started running. I was also feeling like I needed to prove to myself that I had the discipline for medical school, so I decided to commit to running a marathon."

When you're asked a personal question, make sure your answer is—and sounds—honest. Nothing sounds worse than a corny, altruistic revision of an event. If the "why" of an answer is unrelated to medicine, that's fine.

## MANAGING THE INTERVIEW DAY

You'll probably be more than a little nervous on interview day. Here are some tips to help you make the experience more manageable.

### Before the Interview

- Arrive early if you can. Nothing is worse than being late to an interview, so make sure to give yourself plenty of time to get there. Don't be rushed.

- Don't bring family members or significant others to the interview. Drop them off at the nearest coffee shop. Just don't take them to your interview!

- Be sure to review your application and your personal statement before you arrive. The interviewer may ask you specific questions concerning your application and personal statement. Bring a copy with you as well.

- After arriving at the admissions office, be sure to be polite to the receptionist or other support staff. A rude comment or inappropriate behavior can quickly be passed on to admissions committee members and interviewers.

- Treat every interaction as if it were an integral part of the interview.

### During the Interview

- Acknowledge the interviewer by name ("Hello, Dr. X") and introduce yourself.

- Shake hands (firmly but not bone-crunchingly).

- Maintain eye contact.
- Don't fidget.
- Don't cross your arms.
- Don't touch any items on the interviewer's desk.
- Try not to speak too quickly.
- Smile at appropriate times.
- Avoid being arrogant and dogmatic. Remember you're not a doctor yet. You don't know what medical school or medicine is really like. At the same time, do not compromise your views in order to please the interviewer. Be firm, but flexible.
- If the interviewer is being antagonistic, do not answer in kind. Think before you speak. Do not raise your voice. Speak slowly. Be cool and composed.
- If you don't know the answer to a specific question, don't be afraid to say that you don't know. If you try to make something up, the interviewer will see right through you. This could simply be a composure test. It takes a great deal of maturity to simply say, "I don't know." (Of course, you can't answer "I don't know," if the question is "Tell me about yourself.")

## After the Interview

- Shake hands and say good-bye.
- You will want to write your interviewer a thank-you note. Be sure to obtain the address of the interviewer through the admissions office. A card or short note is appropriate (but no novelty greeting cards, please). Try to mention something specific about your interview.
- You can express your continued interest in the school, but don't grovel. Without being arrogant about it, remember that these med schools will be lucky to have you as a student.
- Most importantly, sort out your impressions of the school and decide if you really want to go there. It's your future, after all!

# CHAPTER 11

# The Admissions Process: An Inside View

As noted earlier, less than half of applicants to medical school get in. For the more competitive schools, the odds are much slimmer. Since so many med students are seemingly qualified—with good GPAs, respectable MCAT scores, and prerequisites in place—how do med schools make the cut? What are the factors that really count?

## INITIAL REVIEW

The first criterion for getting an interview and an offer is "Can the student do the work?" You'll prove you're capable of medical–school–level work primarily with your grades and MCAT scores. Some admissions officers will candidly say they have a formula such as GPA, "school-difficulty conversion factor," and MCAT score. Many have soft cutoffs that differ for in- and out-of-state candidates, and that are mediated by extenuating circumstances described in the personal statement or premed cover letter. Remember, one of the reasons many schools get lots of secondaries is to get the fullest possible point of view on an applicant before making a decision.

The first cut will eliminate those who fall below the school's typical standards for both GPA and MCAT. Left are those who have sufficient proof of their academic ability. The weighting of the GPA and MCAT depends on a number of different things.

# GPA

How your GPA is viewed is colored by where you went to school, the particular classes you took, whether your grades are inflated, and whether there are any other mitigating circumstances.

## Difficulty of the Classes

Princeton University, for example, is known in admissions circles to have a grueling organic chemistry class, for which a C may represent perfectly good work. Especially if you are applying to schools near your undergraduate alma mater, you can expect that the local admissions officers are acquainted with the professors and difficulty of the classes. They can look at individual class grades and interpret how much harder you had to work for the B in P-Chem than for that A in Advanced Anthropological Debates. That said, passing the first-round draft requires that you do have a certain GPA. More of the specific evaluation of your classes occurs after you've gotten past the interviews.

## School Selectivity

One way in which schools can determine the value of your GPA is with the *Comparative Guide to American Colleges,* which ranks schools from "Most Selective" on down. This enables medical committees to view your GPA with regard to how tough your school really was.

## Grade Inflation

The committees also consider grade inflation, which is prevalent at many schools. Committee members usually know which institutions tend to inflate and which don't, and they take that into account when evaluating your GPA.

## Foreign Study

Every year, a few students run into problems because the majority of their undergraduate-equivalent education was not done in this country. English and Irish educational systems, for example, do not curve grades. This means that a student ranked third in a class of 500 at a highly selective institution can have a GPA of 2.3. If you've done your undergrad work outside of the States, have a school official include class rank with the transcript. You can also ask for a letter from the dean—detailing what percentage of students get, for example, a mark equivalent to 70 percent—to show that your 74 percent put you at the top of the class. Finally, make sure your letters of recommendation (in English) mention your performance compared to that of your classmates, and the selectivity of the program.

### Narrative Evaluations

If your school uses narrative course evaluations rather than grades, admissions committee members will convert these evaluations into grades if you're to be considered further. Since this is not always a straightforward process, consider requesting a letter grade instead of an evaluation, particularly for prerequisite courses.

### Trend

Some medical schools consider a positive trend in your GPA over time. If you got off to a slow start but have improved significantly in later semesters, take heart. On the other hand, if your grades have been dropping, you may have a problem. These schools believe that a GPA of 3.5 arrived at by GPAs of 3.0, 3.5, and 4.0 in your freshman, sophomore, and junior years, respectively, differ markedly from a 3.5 earned by a 4.0, 3.5, 3.0 sequence.

## MCAT Scores

Because the GPA is subject to such variability and interpretation, the MCAT score has become increasingly significant in past years. It's quite possible that your MCAT score will be the single most important component of your application. The MCAT score is used to give the admissions committee a nationally standardized view of your science background, reasoning ability, and future potential.

### How They're Used

MCAT scores can be viewed in different ways. Some schools add the three scores (four for MCAT 2015 onward) and consider this as one combined value, while others consider each score separately.

Verbal Reasoning on the pre-2015 MCAT, or Critical Reasoning and Analysis Skills on MCAT 2015, is designed to test your logical ability, thinking skills, and ability to evaluate information, and it is often viewed as a gauge of your overall intelligence and ability to communicate. The science scores are usually seen as measures of your abilities in particular sciences and as a standard for comparison to your grades in those subjects.

### Taking It More Than Once

The AMCAS summary page lists your most recent MCAT score, the second-most recent score, and a reading for the total number of MCATs taken. Taking the test more than once can work in your favor if you improve, but it can work against you if your score goes down, especially if you were an applicant with a potentially competitive score. Most schools will give more, if not all, consideration to your most recent attempt. If your previous score was certainly below that required for admissions, then you have less to risk with a retake. However, if your overall score improves but you still perform poorly in a particular subject more than once, this may reflect negatively on your application. If your first test results indicate a weak area, make sure you prepare well before you take the test a second time.

Officially, you can take the MCAT only three times in a calendar year. However, if extraordinary circumstances exist, AAMC may waive this limit on a case-by-case basis.

## THE SECONDARY REVIEW

As the admissions committee reviews your secondary application, its focus begins to shift from your intellectual abilities to your nonacademic accomplishments. It is at the secondary stage that you may be asked to submit letters of recommendation, a list of your extracurricular activities, a second essay on a designated topic, and any number of additional materials.

## Who Gets a Secondary?

Some medical schools send secondary applications to only a fraction of the applicant pool, while other medical schools send secondary applications to virtually all applicants. What does it mean if you have received a secondary? If the school "prescreens," then you know that you have been found to be academically competitive and are somewhat comparable academically to the other applicants also receiving a secondary. If the school does not prescreen prior to sending out secondaries, the fact that you have received one doesn't tell you much. If you want to determine your statistical chances of receiving an interview after receipt of a secondary application, it is possible to do so by comparing the number of applicants receiving secondary applications to the number of applicants receiving an interview at any given school; you can find this information in the MSAR.

## Understanding the Process

You can learn a great deal about how the admissions process works at an individual medical school by reviewing that school's secondary application, which should be available at your school's premed office. Unlike the AMCAS application, which is a generic application used by most medical schools, the secondary application is the individual medical school's own work, created by that school. Therefore, you are asked to address only issues that are relevant to that particular school's admissions process. For instance, if on its secondary application a particular medical school asks you for a great deal of information concerning your extracurricular activities, it's a pretty safe bet that extracurriculars are counted in its screening process. Conversely, if you aren't asked about your extracurricular activities, they are probably not considered important to that institution. If you are asked whether a relative, no matter how distant, attended their college or university, you can be pretty certain you'll get "brownie points" if you can answer in the affirmative; it's likely that they're looking for family "legacies." Other schools make no mention of family connections because they're not relevant to the process.

## Criminal Convictions

You may be asked on a secondary application if you have a criminal record. The AMCAS application asks about history of felony convictions. Some medical schools limit the type of convictions that applicants must report on the secondary application to felonies, while other medical schools broaden the scope to include traffic violations and misdemeanors. Because criminal behavior says something about a candidate's veracity and integrity (both of which are critically important characteristics in a physician), and potentially the candidate's ability to be licensed to practice medicine, medical school admissions committees view prior criminal convictions very seriously.

Unless the particular state in which a medical school is located prohibits a physician with a conviction for a specific offense from obtaining a license, then conviction for that specific offense, in and of itself, will not prohibit an applicant from gaining acceptance to medical schools in the state. Admissions committees look at each situation on a case-by-case basis and view the behavior holistically, considering mitigating factors leading up to and surrounding the conviction as well as the individual's perspective on the incident. For this reason, two admissions committees may view the same incident or applicant differently, and the same behavior committed by two different applicants may be viewed differently by the same committee.

---

**Tell Them Yourself**

As with all aspects of your medical school application, you should be forthright when discussing prior convictions. Information of all sorts has a mysterious way of falling into the lap of admissions committees. If a committee learns of previous criminal or unethical behavior from a source other than you, your chances for admission are virtually nil.

---

## Secondary Fee

In most cases, you must pay a fee when you submit a secondary application. While a small number of schools do not have a fee, the majority charge between $25 and $100. The MSAR contains information regarding the amount of each medical school's secondary fee. If you are unable to afford the fee, contact the admissions office concerning its fee waiver policy. Some medical schools will waive their secondary fee if you received a fee waiver through the AAMC Fee Assistance Program (FAP), while other medical schools have their own fee waiver policy.

## AFTER THE INTERVIEW

Your application is complete, and you've had a wonderful interview. What happens now?

At this point, both the expertise of the admissions committee and sheer luck come into play. One important element that is beyond your control is whether you are the candidate who fits the profile that a particular medical school needs at that particular moment. If you are, the admissions committee may quickly decide to accept you. If you're not, however, you are on equal footing with many other applicants who are as qualified as you are and who have also had strong interviews. If you have someone on the admissions committee who is particularly taken with you, your chances increase. If you don't have a champion on the committee, or if there is nothing remarkably distinctive in your application, however strong it is, you may be wait-listed—or rejected.

## Importance of the Interview

An invitation to interview at any medical school means you're acceptable on paper. That's the good news. The bad news is, so is everyone else being interviewed. The interview adds the only new piece of information and therefore has the potential to become the deciding factor.

After your interview, your interviewers will present, in written or oral form, to the admissions committee their assessment of your candidacy for medical school in general and for their medical school in particular.

At all medical schools, if you have a poor interview, you will almost certainly be rejected. That is how important the interview is. It is also an indication of how important admissions committees believe personal characteristics are in the making of a great physician.

At most medical schools, a particularly strong interview may ensure your acceptance. However, there are a few medical schools at which the results of the interview come into play only if they are negative. At those schools, as at all others, a negative interview is likely to result in the applicant's rejection. But the results of a positive interview there are not considered, and applicants fall back to their pre-interview rankings. These schools reason that all applicants know they should be on their best behavior and most will be able to behave in a socially appropriate manner for a 30-minute interview. An applicant who cannot pull this off is either completely out of touch with social norms or simply doesn't care. In either case, this is not desirable behavior for a future physician.

## THE ADMISSIONS COMMITTEE

After reviewing the entire application, including the interviewers' comments and recommendations, the committee votes on the candidacy of each applicant. The vote may be a yes/no vote, it may be an immediate accept/wait list/reject vote, or it may be a numerical score indicating each committee member's individual level of support for that applicant. As a result of the committee vote, candidates will either receive an immediate acceptance, will be rejected, or will be placed on the alternate list—otherwise known as the wait list.

## What Is the Admissions Committee?

The Liaison Committee on Medical Education (LCME), the body that accredits medical schools, states that the selection of medical students is the responsibility of the medical school faculty through a duly constituted committee. That committee is commonly referred to as the Admissions Committee. The LCME permits others to assist with the evaluation of applicants but does not permit the final responsibility to be delegated outside of the faculty. In other words, medical schools are required to have a faculty admissions committee that may have nonfaculty members. The schools are given wide latitude in the size and composition of that committee.

### Size and Composition

Admissions committees vary in size from the very small (8–10 members) to the very large (75 or more members). At some schools, especially those with very large committees, there may be a number of subcommittees, each charged with reviewing a segment of the applicant pool. Applications may be distributed alphabetically, by region, or by the undergraduate college the applicants attended. There may be a separate committee or subcommittee to review MSTP or MD/PhD applicants or applicants for other special programs. Another approach is to have an Executive Committee that guides the work of the subcommittees. Some medical schools have separate subcommittees to review minority or disadvantaged applicants.

At most medical schools, the majority of Admissions Committee members are members of the faculty from either clinical or basic science departments, and in some cases, they are nonfaculty administrators. Schools try to balance committee membership by age, gender, departmental affiliation, and ethnic background. Many schools also have one or more medical student members. The student members may have full voting rights or may be advisory to the committee. Some schools include one or more representatives of the affiliated undergraduate college. Representatives of the general public also serve on some schools' admissions committees.

### Duties of an Admissions Committee Member

All admissions committee members share one basic responsibility: the selection of applicants for admission. At many schools, the committee members' duties go well beyond just making final decisions. For example, they may also participate in the initial review of applications to determine which applicants will be asked to submit supplemental materials or which students to invite for interviews. Frequently, admissions committee members conduct admissions interviews, and at some schools, they are the only ones who interview. On the other hand, some schools do not permit admissions committee members to interview any applicants.

### How Admissions Committees Work

With 141 medical schools in the United States, it is likely that there are nearly that many different ways in which admissions committees arrive at their final decisions. There are, however, some relatively common approaches.

In one approach, applications may be discussed during a meeting of the committee. In this model, either a committee member or an admissions office staff member "presents" the application. Details of the application are described by the presenter, with discussion following the presentation. The person who interviewed the applicant may be the presenter or may be present and join in the discussion. A vote may be taken following the discussion, or committee members may assign a score to the application, with the applicants receiving the highest scores being admitted. Advocates of this method believe that the open discussion of applications is essential to arriving at the best decisions. Opponents argue that a particularly vocal committee member can skew the votes of others and have an undue influence on the decision process.

Other schools use a rule-based approach in which committee members review and award points to each part of the application (GPA, MCAT scores, interview, personal comments, recommendations, out-of-class activities, etc.) based on a predetermined scoring system or rule. The applicants with the highest scores are admitted. Advocates of this system point to the inherent fairness of treating each part of the

---

**How Do They Decide?**

Admissions committees most commonly use the following approaches to arrive at their final decisions:

- Open discussion of all candidates, followed by a vote

- Rule-based system in which each section of the application is scored separately

- Holistic system in which the entire application is read and scored as a whole

---

application in the same way for all applicants and reducing the advocacy effect of particularly vocal committee members. Opponents say that it minimizes the judgment each committee member can bring to the process and eliminates valuable discussion between committee members.

Schools using a holistic approach have several members of the committee read and score the application as a whole. Each reader brings his own knowledge, experience, and judgment to the process. Schools using this method believe that because the reader has access to the entire application and the freedom to score the application as a whole, he can judge the file as a whole. The use of multiple readers adds collective judgment to the evaluation of applications. Supporters of this approach cite the value of collective judgment and the opportunity for committee members to weigh the parts of applications differently depending on circumstances and to thoroughly review all parts of the application. Opponents point out the danger of inconsistently weighing criteria and the absence of discussion.

## ALTERNATE LISTS

Applicants have a love-hate relationship with the alternate lists. Learning that they have been placed on the alternate list brings most applicants feelings of relief ("Thank goodness I wasn't rejected"), followed by feelings of disappointment ("What do you mean you aren't accepting me at this time?"), which ultimately culminate in feelings of frustration ("Won't someone tell me what my chances are?"). These feelings are compounded by the fact that medical schools use their alternate lists differently and for the most part are reticent about divulging specific information regarding an applicant's status.

### How the Alternate List Works

There are two basic ways alternate lists may be utilized. In the first, the list is very fluid. Interviewed applicants are constantly added to the list after they clear the admissions committee, while accepted applicants are skimmed off the top. In the second method, the alternate list is used as a large holding category for the applicants who are not accepted with the initial round of acceptees. These two basic methods are further complicated by the fact that some medical schools rank applicants on the alternate list while others do not.

How an individual medical school uses its alternate list is largely influenced by its acceptance policies. All medical schools ultimately need to accept more students than are reflected in the actual class size. This is because many successful applicants receive multiple acceptances and therefore have to turn down all but one school, leaving the "rejected" schools to offer new acceptances. Admissions committees have a perspective based on history as to how many acceptances they must offer to fill the medical school class. Depending on the school's admissions policies, the dean of admissions may send out enough acceptances to initially fill the class and may then wait for withdrawals to occur before sending out additional acceptances. As an example, imagine that medical school "X" has a class size of 100. In the past, this school has made between 230–250 offers of acceptance to fill each class. In this admissions scenario, the first 100 acceptances would be sent out. Further acceptances are not sent until a position is declined by one of the originally accepted applicants. Then, and only then, would an additional offer of acceptance be sent. This process would continue until the class matriculated in the fall. Under this process, movement on the alternate list is fluid, with applicants constantly being drawn from the pool to fill openings as they occur. As a result, alternates may begin receiving acceptances as early as the spring.

Alternatively, the dean of admissions may decide to accept most if not all of those applicants that the admissions committee finds to be immediately acceptable, even if it results in the potential overfilling of the class. Imagine that the admissions committee of medical school "X" found 200 applicants to be immediately acceptable. The dean of admissions would send all of them acceptances, knowing that it generally takes 230–250 offers of acceptance to fill a 100-person class. She therefore feels comfortable sending out 200 acceptances right off the bat, knowing that she is still under the total number of acceptances ultimately sent in any given year to fill the class. Now, the dean waits for an opening to occur before new offers of acceptance are made to people on the alternate list. But at this point, 101 accepted applicants must withdraw before the first opening is created and the first alternate is accepted. Under this scenario, alternates do not typically hear about an acceptance until shortly before the class matriculates.

Unfortunately, most medical schools are somewhat reluctant to discuss an applicant's chances of being accepted from the alternate list. This may be because the alternate list is unranked or because no one really knows how many applicants will be accepted from the alternate list in any given year.

## Making Your Case

If you're placed on a school's waiting list, you still have a chance to make your case. You might submit an additional letter of recommendation or updated transcripts.

The letter might give the admissions committee additional information that can swing the balance; besides, the fact that you've sent something extra indicates that you're really interested in that particular medical school.

## IMPORTANT DATES IN THE WAITING GAME

With the exception of Early Decision Programs, AMCAS schools do not offer acceptances prior to October 15 of the application year. This is the earliest date for acceptances; many schools do not offer acceptances before December or even January.

By March 15, AMCAS medical schools are supposed to have offered a number of acceptances equal to the size of their entering class. This would mean that med school "X" must have offered 100 acceptances (its class size) by March 15.

AMCAS recommends that applicants be allowed to hold multiple acceptances prior to May 15. But AMCAS schools adhering to these guidelines are, in the words of the MSAR, "free to apply appropriate rules for dealing with accepted applicants who, without adequate explanation, hold one or more places in other schools." This means that without specific permission of the individual medical schools to which an applicant is holding multiple acceptances, the affected medical school(s) may individually choose to rescind their offer of acceptance.

If you find yourself unable to make a decision between your schools prior to May 15, contact the schools at which you've been accepted and ask for a deadline extension. It is entirely within their prerogative to approve, or disapprove, such an extension. Ignore the May 15 date at your own risk.

Because AMCAS medical schools are theoretically filled by March 15 and applicants are free to hold multiple acceptances until May 15, the interim two months is a very slow period for new acceptances. With the passage of May 15, a significant number of positions become available. The acceptance process continues throughout the summer as openings occur.

Applicants may continue to receive new acceptances after May 15. When this happens, they must decide between the acceptances they are currently holding and the new acceptance just received. New acceptances may be received up until the time the applicant matriculates in medical school.

# CHAPTER 12

# What If You Get Rejected?

In 2012–2013, 48,014 applicants competed for the nation's first-year medical school positions; 20,055 matriculated. Put another way, more than 58 percent of the applicants were not accepted. Rejection was undoubtedly painful. However, if you have been rejected from medical school, that shouldn't stop you from applying at least a second time.

## WHAT WENT WRONG?

Despite the promising statistics concerning acceptance rates of reapplicants, you shouldn't be lulled into thinking that all you need to do is reapply. You don't get points for perseverance. One of three broad areas must change in order for you to be successful in your reapplication efforts:

- Your application credentials must improve.
- The applicant pool must become less competitive.
- The profile of the applicant being sought by a particular medical school must change to fit your application.

> **Don't Give Up**
>
> "If you think this is what you want to do, you might meet a lot of obstacles, but don't give up. If you want it badly enough, you will find a way to make it work. And it will be worth it."
>
> —University of Alabama med student

## IMPROVING YOUR APPLICATION CREDENTIALS

The only one of these things you have any control over is your application. Therefore, before investing the time, energy, and money it takes to reapply, you need to identify those areas of your application that need improving. This involves the following steps:

### Talk to Your Premedical Adviser

Your adviser is the person most likely to have a good sense of your credentials and how they compare to those of applicants from your college who have been successful in getting into med school in the past. He may also be able to suggest reapplication strategies that other students have used successfully.

### Check with the Medical Schools That Rejected You

Many medical schools will give you the opportunity to talk to someone from the admissions office about your application. You should particularly try to talk to schools that interviewed you to find out if they will discuss aspects of your application that the admissions committee found to be weak. You don't need to talk to the dean; most members of the admissions staff will be able to discuss their school's needs for their class and how your application fits into the big picture.

> **Rely on the Experts**
>
> Be wary of well-meaning but uninformed advice from those who have no connection to the medical school admissions process. This includes medical students who may be associated with a medical school but who have not had direct involvement in the review of applications.

After getting feedback from the schools you applied to, summarize their comments. Be careful not to get caught up in the minutiae. Keep your perspective. There is no governing body that stands over all the medical schools and dictates admissions policies. Rather, the faculty at each institution determines the qualities and characteristics they look for when selecting the student body. Therefore, it is entirely possible that what one admissions committee is looking for in a potential medical student is entirely the opposite of what another medical school is selecting for. You need to see the big picture. Your premed adviser will probably be able to help in this regard. Look for those aspects of your application that most medical schools believed needed strengthening. Disregard comments that were made by only one or two people.

### Conduct a Thorough Self-Analysis

Examine each element of your application in the same way that an admissions committee member would. Start with your academic record. How does it compare to those of applicants admitted recently? In 2013, the average GPA of admitted applicants was 3.69, with a standard deviation of 0.25. Only about 13 percent of acceptees between 2011 and 2013 had GPAs below 3.4. If your overall and/or science GPA is below the 3.4 level, it is likely that your academic record needs improvement. Remember, though, that this is the national average and that the range of acceptable grades varies widely from school to school.

**Grades.** Look at the trend in your grades over time. Have your grades been steady, improving, or dropping? An improving trend over time may be a sign that some additional strong coursework will be helpful, while a sharply dropping trend may be a sign of a more serious problem.

**MCAT Scores.** Take a hard look at your MCAT scores. Avoid summing the scores from the multiple-choice sections. Rather, look at each section separately to identify areas that need improvement, if any. Averages for students admitted in 2013 were: Physical Sciences, 10.6; Verbal Reasoning, 10.0; and Biological Sciences, 10.8. As with grades, the range of acceptable MCAT scores varies widely from school to school. Read the section on retaking the MCAT that appears later in this chapter to help determine whether you should sit for the test again.

**Extracurricular Activities.** Do your extracurricular activities reflect your interest in healthcare? Remember that admissions officers identify knowledge of healthcare and healthcare experience as among the most important factors considered in admissions. Do your activities show that you are the kind of multifaceted person that medical schools seek? As one admissions officer put it, "I look at what the applicant did when nobody was making him or her do anything, when nobody was looking." Medical schools are looking for more than good students. They want a wide variety of interesting people in their classes.

On the other hand, does your record of out-of-class activities indicate that you were overextended? Any claim that your relatively low grades should be excused because you had too many activities will generally fall on deaf ears. Admissions committee members will likely conclude that you exercised poor judgment in setting your priorities.

**Personal Statement.** We discussed the personal statement in chapter 9. Read that chapter again and then look at your personal statement with a critical eye. Are you comfortable that an admissions committee member reading your statement would get to know something about you as a person and why you want to be a physician? What kind of picture of yourself did you paint?

**Letters of Recommendation.** Letters of recommendation can be hard to assess because you have not seen them. If you followed the advice given in chapter 7 and discussed your request for a letter with those writing your letters, the chances are that those letters were supportive. If your premedical committee submitted a letter on your behalf, you may be able to get some sense of its level of support when you meet with your premedical adviser. Be open to constructive feedback. This is not the time for confrontation.

**Interview.** Were you invited for any interviews? If not, this may be an indication that your application did not pass the academic/MCAT screen. Another possibility is that you applied to the wrong schools. If you did get some interviews, how did they go? Were you prepared? Were you able to answer the interviewer's questions and participate in an engaging dialogue? How did you feel after the interview was completed? Although it is hard to judge for yourself how you did in an interview, if you felt uneasy afterward, that may be an indication that it did not go well.

---

### Alternative Life Plan

"I think it's important to have an alternative life plan when considering becoming a doctor. As a faculty member, I've seen many superb, well-qualified candidates who have not been accepted, and I don't know in some cases if I could tell you why one person got in over another. Keep in mind that the thing that you've chosen may not choose you."

—MD, Johns Hopkins University

---

**Application.** How did you approach the application process? Did you treat it as one of the most important activities in your life? Were you professional? Did you apply early, follow instructions carefully, respond to requests from schools promptly, and treat admissions office staff with courtesy? Were your AMCAS application and any supplemental applications completed neatly and clearly? Remember that the approach that you took with these matters will certainly be perceived in your paperwork. While a neat, professional, well-timed application will not make up for a lack of strong academic and personal credentials, a sloppy and unprofessional one can be your undoing.

### Consider the Alternatives

As you already know, getting into med school is not easy. Each year, many well-qualified applicants are denied admission. As mentioned earlier, the statistics for reapplicants are encouraging, with about one-third being admitted on their second attempt. Success rates fall off after the third and subsequent applications, although each year some of these applicants are admitted. Still, especially if you have been turned down more than once, it may be time to think about other options.

Begin by assessing your reasons for wanting a career in medicine. What drew you to the idea of becoming a physician? Was it a desire to help people? A love of science and problem solving? The intellectual challenge? Or something else? Knowing the answer to these questions can help you to start investigating other professions that may provide you with the same rewards and challenges. Do you want a career in the health professions, or will another area, such as research or teaching, meet your needs?

### Develop a Plan of Action

After you have sought feedback from the medical schools and your adviser, conducted a self-analysis, and considered the alternatives, you are ready to develop a plan of action. There is no magic formula. It stands to reason that medical schools will be looking at what you have done to strengthen your credentials for this application. By now, you should have a pretty good idea of your strengths and weaknesses as an applicant, and you should be ready to do what you can to improve your chances for success.

Remember to attack your weaknesses. If your grades are low, you can't fix that by doing research. If you have a GPA of 4.0 but low MCAT scores, you won't help yourself by taking more courses and getting As. The same goes for other parts of your application. Remember that your personal and academic record were not made in one day, and it may take some time for you to show improvement. The following are some ways to improve your chances for admission:

**Retake Courses.** If your science grades were too low, or if the college you attended wasn't viewed as competitive enough, take harder or different science courses. If you got straight As in night school at a community college, you may need to prove you can do the same full-time at a four-year university. Even though it's a sacrifice to take a full-time course load, nothing proves you can handle the work of full-time science classes like taking full-time science classes.

| |
|---|
| **Improving Your Chances** |
| To improve your chances of acceptance the second time around do the following: |
| • Retake courses. |
| • Retake the MCAT. |
| • Reconsider your timing. |
| • Rethink your school selection. |

**Retake the MCAT.** If you did poorly or at an average level on your MCAT, you need to decide whether to retake it or not. In trying to answer this question, ask yourself if you gave it everything you had to give. Did you take a prep course for the MCAT? Yes, we really do think you need to take one, and not just because we're in the business. Most people don't have the time, the resources, or the discipline to study on their own. Students who take a prep course benefit from the structure, study plan, instruction, and feedback that a course provides. If you took a course and didn't like it, take a different one. If you did take a course, did you follow all of the advice given by your MCAT instructor, or did you pick and choose which advice to act upon? Did you study for several hours a day over four or five months? Or did you give it a few hours a day for four or five weeks?

If you can really say you gave it your all, then you probably shouldn't retake the MCAT, even if you were disappointed with your scores—because your scores are probably "real." However, if you did not put the time and energy into studying as hard as you should have (be honest, now), then it may be worth your while to retake it. Just remember that admissions committees don't give you points for perseverance, so if you're going to go through the effort of retaking the MCAT, make it count!

**Reconsider Your Timing.** If you applied late and interviewed in mid-spring, it's likely that your rejection was related to poor timing. Reapply the next chance you get, making sure everything is pristine and ready to go by June 1.

**Rethink School Selection.** It's also possible that you didn't get accepted because you applied to the wrong schools. Go over your list with your adviser to be sure you are applying to those schools that will look at your application in the most positive light.

## POSTBACCALAUREATE PROGRAMS

Postbaccalaureate programs are academic programs specifically designed to help applicants improve their chances of gaining admission to medical school. Individual admissions committees differ in the value they attribute to postbac work.

## Types of Postbac Programs

There are three types of postbac programs, designed to meet the needs of three different types of applicants. The first type, which is geared for individuals making a career change, is discussed in detail in chapters 2 and 14.

The second type of program is designed to increase the number of underrepresented students (defined as African American, Mexican American, Native American or Native Hawaiian, mainland Puerto Rican, and applicants who come from socioeconomically or educationally deprived backgrounds) currently entering the health professions. Many of these programs are designed for applicants who have applied unsuccessfully to medical school. Programs of this nature are generally funded by the state or federal government and range in length from several months to two years.

Unlike the other two types of postbac programs, the third type results in a graduate degree in the biological sciences. These programs are typically associated with a particular medical school. During these one-year programs, postbac students take classes alongside medical students, thereby giving future applicants the chance to "show their stuff." Typically, applicants from the postbac program are the first candidates to be considered for the upcoming medical school class by that particular medical school's admissions committee.

---

**Pros and Cons of Postbac Programs**

Pros:

- You don't need any prior experience or preparation.
- You don't need to give up your former life completely. Flexible course schedules allow you to work full or part time.
- Your fellow students will be more diverse, with greater life experience than typical undergraduates.
- Many programs claim that postbac students make exceptionally good med school candidates.

Cons:

- You may have to fork over big bucks.
- You'll have to work very hard.
- While your friends are working 9 to 5 jobs, you'll be stuck at home doing homework.
- You'll have to get good grades.

---

## Is Postbac for You?

Whether or not a postbac program is right for you depends on which aspect of your application you need to strengthen. In general, postbac programs are designed to strengthen academic performance. Could you design a program yourself that would allow you to strengthen your academic preparation and performance? Maybe.

But most would-be applicants do better with the structure and resources that a postbac program offers. Additionally, many postbac programs have feeder-school relationships with particular medical schools. As a result, the most successful programs have acceptance rates approaching 90 percent. The downside of postbac programs is that many of them are located at private institutions, are rather costly, and do not guarantee that you will receive an acceptance to medical school. Therefore, make your decision about whether or not to attend a postbac program only after you have realistically assessed what it can offer you. Check out AAMC's website at http://services.aamc.org/postbac for a listing of selected programs.

## GRADUATE SCHOOL

Many med school applicants consider earning a graduate degree as a means of enhancing their medical school application. If you are considering graduate school because you believe that it will give you breadth and depth as an applicant, then graduate school may be right for you. If, however, you are hoping that your academic performance in graduate school will make you a more attractive candidate, think again. Many medical schools do not consider graduate school grades when they are reviewing an applicant's academic history. There are a couple of reasons for this.

First, when reviewing an applicant's GPA, admissions committees generally take into consideration the institution from which it was earned. Admissions committees know (as you do) that grading standards vary tremendously, and while they have a great deal of information on the relative difficulty of one undergraduate institution compared to the next, they have very little information on the relative difficulty of the numerous graduate programs throughout the country.

The second reason many medical schools do not give great weight to graduate degrees is that a graduate education does not necessarily make a candidate more attractive. Assuming an applicant is planning a clinical career, the admissions committee will look to see that she is broadly educated, has the necessary interpersonal skills, and has demonstrated an aptitude for the sciences. It is not required, nor is it necessarily preferred, that a candidate have advanced studies in any particular area, much less the sciences.

There are a few exceptions to the above rule. As discussed above, there are a few medical schools that specifically use their graduate biological science programs as feeder schools into their medical school. These medical schools' admissions committees will be particularly interested in applicants from their own university's graduate programs. Also, if you are considering a Medical Scientist Training Program (MSTP), another MD/PhD program, or a career in academic or research medicine, getting graduate training in biology may be advantageous. Finally, there are some admissions committees that do consider graduate school grades in the evaluation process, and to the extent that an applicant's record is strong, it will be viewed positively.

In summary, while there is nothing wrong with going to graduate school, you should not do so because you believe it will help you get into medical school. Rather, your decision should be based on the fact that you are fascinated by the subject matter, are considering it as a career option, or believe your graduate education will augment your medical education.

## FOREIGN MEDICAL SCHOOLS

You probably shouldn't consider a foreign medical school until you've been rejected from American or Canadian schools at least twice (if not three times). Then you should speak to your premed adviser and do extensive research on the quality of the schools that you are considering.

In summary, if you attend a foreign medical school, there is a real possibility that you will be unable to obtain a US license (either because you'll fail the licensing exams or will be unable to obtain a US residency position). Therefore, you should only consider this route if it is all right with you that you may be ultimately limited to practicing (and living) outside of the United States. If this is acceptable to you, then a foreign medical education may be a viable option. But if it's not, don't do it.

## OSTEOPATHIC MEDICINE

Osteopathic medicine should not be thought of as a fallback position if you don't get into an allopathic medical school, because osteopathic physicians have the same rights, privileges, and responsibilities as allopathic physicians. However, some students do stumble onto their true calling in osteopathic medicine after being rejected from allopathic medical schools. This is an option that you also might want to consider.

---

### Turning Failure into Success

"I was rejected from most of the schools to which I applied. Osteopathy was an alternative path, and I decided that I wanted to try doing it. I have no regrets about going straight into osteopathic school rather than reapplying to allopathic schools the following year. Now I am where I wanted to be; I was heavily recruited when going through the process of choosing a residency."

—DO, University of New England

---

For more information on applying to osteopathic medical schools, see chapter 4.

## CHOOSING OTHER PATHS

As you think about your professional goals, you may decide that for whatever reason—length of study, financial strain, etc.—medical school is not for you. There are a number of fields in healthcare that may suit your needs better. Here are a few closely related professions. In all of them, practitioners do the following:

- Give primary and secondary care to patients
- Make diagnoses
- Have a decision-making role in the care of the patient
- Are well compensated

### Physician Assistant

More than 170 US schools offer Physician Assistants programs. The programs average three years, ranging from 12 to 48 months. In many, clinical rotations are done side by side with third- and fourth-year medical students. PAs typically get their clinical training in many different locations, based on which electives interest them. On completion of the program, PAs must pass the accreditation exam, given by the National Commission on Certification of PAs, to practice as "PA-C."

---

### Less Pain, Pure Gain

"I realized I wanted to be doing primary care work, and I had no desire to spend seven years in school. I got out in three years, and now I'm working at a women's health clinic doing exactly what I wanted."

—Physician assistant

---

PAs can act independently in a clinical setting under a physician, or they can bridge the gap in a hospital between the nurses and doctors. States differ on the degree to which PAs can prescribe medicine or sign for in-hospital treatments. The majority of PAs practice in a private-practice setting, while others practice in hospitals.

Many students choose to become physician assistants rather than physicians because of the shorter length of study and the less burdensome expense. Some realize that what they really want is to provide primary care, and they aren't as concerned about commanding the prestige that doctors generally hold.

One potential downside of the profession is the somewhat limited choice that the PA faces after graduating. Generally, PAs choose a specialty during school, such as pediatric surgery or clinical gynecology, and will continue to specialize in that field after graduation.

For more information and a directory of programs, contact:

> Physician Assistant Education Association
> 300 North Washington Street, Suite 710
> Alexandria, VA 22314
> (703) 548-5538
> Fax: (703) 548-5539
> Email: info@PAEAonline.org
> Website: www.PAEAonline.org

## Nurse Practitioner

Advanced practice nurses—nurse practitioners, midwives, and clinical specialists—have gained significant recognition and legislative practice authority as quality providers of primary healthcare, with a special emphasis on patient education. Nurse practitioners can act in approximately the same capacity as physician assistants, although they must always act under an MD or DO when prescribing medicine. Nurse practitioners can function as primary care givers in both private-practice offices and health clinics. There is always a connection with an MD in case the necessity arises to admit the patient to a hospital or to get a second opinion, but many patients may be entirely cared for by an NP.

Nurse practitioners usually earn an MS or MSN (Master of Science in Nursing) degree. Both degrees generally take two years of full-time study but can usually be pursued part-time. Many graduate nursing programs require the BSN (Bachelor's of Science in Nursing) for entry, but an increasing number of programs admit students with other college degrees.

**Not for Women Only**

Although only 10 percent of nursing students today are male, more and more men are entering the field, often as a second career.

For more information on becoming a Nurse Practitioner, contact:

National Organization of Nurse Practitioner Faculties
1615 M Street, NW, Suite 270
Washington, DC 20036
(202) 289-8044
Fax: (202) 289-8046
Email: nonpf@nonpf.org
Website: www.nonpf.com

## FINAL THOUGHTS

When it comes to advising the unsuccessful medical school applicant, there is another school of thought that cautions against considering alternative careers in allied health. Adherents to this perspective urge applicants to consider the reasons they were attracted to medicine as a career. Do you like being in a position of authority and responsibility? Do you want respect within your community? Do you want to achieve a high standard of living? If these are the things that attracted you to the notion of becoming a physician, then you may not find a fulfilling, satisfying career in healthcare if you cannot become a physician. If, after careful consideration and some soul searching, you realize that some of the above motivations are yours, consider investigating other high-powered, intense, dynamic professions. Talk to your career counselor. Talk to family and friends. Pick up a book in the library or bookstore on making career choices based on your personality profile. Your ultimate goal should be to find a career that is well suited to you, whether or not it is in medicine.

# CHAPTER 13

# What Medical Students Have to Say

Kaplan MCAT faculty include current medical students and recent graduates. We asked them to reflect on some of their own experiences while in medical school. Here's what they shared.

## THE MCAT

**Christopher Traner, University of Toledo College of Medicine, Class of 2016:** To prepare for the MCAT, I did a lot of self-study using the Kaplan materials that I had purchased separately from the class. I thought that I was disciplined enough to study on my own. In retrospect, I really should have taken the more structured approach that is offered by a prep course. Especially as an undergraduate studying for the MCAT, you are juggling so much: undergraduate courses, studying for the MCAT, extracurriculars, volunteer opportunities, and even possibly a job. It's hard after a long day of class to sit down and really focus. I found myself putting off studying many nights simply because I saw it as just a simple review of classes I thought I remembered.

**Maurice F. Joyce, MD, EdM, Anesthesiology Resident, Tufts Medical Center:** I prepared for the MCAT during the winter/spring prior to the year in which I took the exam, and I still use many of the test-taking techniques that I learned in the class (and now teach) when I take exams to this day. With regard to how my MCAT score influenced my competitiveness as an applicant, I believe it was just one component of my "balanced application" (solid MCAT, solid GPA, good EC's/leadership, volunteering, shadowing, etc.).

**Kareem Hassan, University of Arizona College of Medicine, Class of 2015:** The MCAT was really my opportunity to show medical schools that I could succeed. I had a lower GPA due to being uncertain of my career path early in college. I ended up scoring well and receiving multiple interviews and admissions. A large part of this, I believe, was due to my MCAT. To prepare for the MCAT, I took the Kaplan MCAT course. If I were to study for the MCAT again, I would prepare with more practice questions. One of the highest-yield methods of studying is to answer practice questions and then review the questions you were stuck on or that you got wrong. If you are able to both understand the correct choice *and* understand why the incorrect choices are wrong, then you have a good foundation of the concept being tested.

**Kerranna Williamson, MBA, Medical University of South Carolina:** If you think the MCAT and the preparation for the MCAT are grueling, keep in mind that you haven't seen anything when it comes to how demanding and challenging *medical school* is. One of the reasons students should learn how to effectively study for the MCAT is simply that medical school itself significantly steps up the game when it comes to challenging academic study.

I took a free practice test that was offered on my college campus during my sophomore year. I wanted a good idea of what I was going to be getting myself into before starting a study plan. It was a good reality check! At first, I decided to study for the MCAT on my own, dedicating time on the weekends solely to the exam. I mostly studied content on Saturdays and tried to fit in a practice exam every two weekends. I continued with this approach for about 4 months.

At the time, I was busy with school and other exams, so I failed to put the appropriate amount of pressure on my MCAT studying. Regrettably, I didn't even have a clear goal for what I needed to accomplish before Test Day. I naively thought that as long as I was spending some time on MCAT study, I would miraculously arrive at a place where I could score well. The real reality check came when I received my scores back on that first MCAT exam. I didn't do terribly, but I did not score high enough to feel confident or competitive for med school applications. One of the best things I did was take this first exam with ample time to really get myself in gear and test again.

The biggest regret I have is that I didn't focus properly the first time around and was forced to do the process all over again. Nobody wants to study for and take the MCAT more times than necessary. So after the first testing, I decided to really analyze how to build a bulletproof study plan. I decided to take the Kaplan class for the sake of structure and to have access to the plethora of prep materials. I made short-term goals that fit into a long-term plan, focusing on studying smarter versus just studying more.

Being organized and setting realistic goals were the keys to my study success. When I could tell that I was not getting the most out of a study session, I would step away or change something up. I also kept track of my time spent and goals met, and I celebrated my progress by doing non-MCAT things. And I always put a "prize" at the end of each short-term goal—for example, if I managed to get everything done that I planned for over a period of two weeks, then I would take a weekend off and have a mini road trip planned with friends. It motivated me to have things to look forward to along the way.

**Jeffrey Tompson, MS, Drexel University College of Medicine, Class of 2017:** I took the MCAT just once, fortunately. Your score on the MCAT is a large factor for the schools that you can get into. To open as many doors as possible and to make yourself a competitive candidate, you want to get the highest score possible. You should probably plan to devote five to six months of your life preparing for this exam and to be able to achieve your dreams of going to medical school.

**John R. Zade, New York Medical College, Class of 2016:** I studied for the MCAT the same way I studied for any major test or final as an undergrad: I read night and day and took notes on what I was reading. I think the most important part of studying for the MCAT is not to change the way you study drastically; you got to this point in your academic career with a method. If you learn best in classrooms, sign up for a class! If you learn best in groups, find a study partner! Just remember that your studying will need to be ramped up a few notches, even if you use the same methods. Be open-minded and adjust your style as needed for success. You'll likely be using the same approach for medical school and the USMLE—only turned up a few notches!

## The Personal Statement

**CT:** I spent a long time thinking about how I wanted to approach my personal statement. I reviewed my résumé multiple times and tried to reflect on all my experiences. Once I had decided on the direction, the actual writing did not take particularly long. Then, once I had finished, I enlisted all kinds of people to read my writing. I had English teachers from college and high school assist me with proofreading. I also asked all my recommenders to read it. Finally, many of my friends and family members read it as well. The more eyes that look at the statement, the stronger it will become. Of course, then the challenge is deciding whose advice to take, since not everyone will give you the same feedback.

**KH:** I'm a slow writer, so I started early. I got feedback from my adviser and mentor on content and theme. From my grandmother (a retired English teacher), I got tips on grammar and style, etc. The latter is very important, as schools will use your personal statement as a means of evaluating your ability to communicate in written form.

**MJ:** At first I wrote a philosophical piece that I thought was great and would really impress the medical school committees. I sent it to a few people, and they ripped it apart. It just didn't give you an image of who I was and why I wanted to go into medicine. After some denial and hesitation, I changed my essay completely, and instead of trying to impress the committee, I just tried to explain my story and why I chose medicine.

**JT:** While writing my personal statement, I sent it out to everyone that I knew: family, friends, residents, attendings, high school teachers, my Kaplan manager (I was teaching at the time), and professors. All of these people knew me in a different context and were able to give me their opinion on my piece. With their feedback, I was able to mold my personal statement into something that really defined me from my own perspective and the perspectives of other people.

## RECOMMENDATION LETTERS

**CT:** This area was particularly hard for me. One of the reasons was that I hadn't asked many people for letters when applying to be an undergrad. That being said, I am a big proponent of putting the onus on the people you are asking to think about whether they would be good recommenders. What I mean by that is as follows:

1) Be very clear when you meet with them how important it is or how strong your desire is to go to medical school. Feel free to give them details as to why you want to go to medical school so much, whether it be a personal story or some experience.

2) Phrase the question correctly. Don't simply ask, "Can you write me a letter?" Instead, phrase it as "Given my strong desire to go to medical school and the extremely competitive nature of the application process, do you feel comfortable writing me a strong letter of recommendation?" This really makes people think about your relationship, your experiences together, and how well they really know you as a student and as a person. Only if they feel really strongly about you will they agree when you pose the question this way. This will help you know that you will get the absolute best letter.

3) Finally, thank them and always offer to support their writing by supplying a copy of your résumé, a draft of your personal statement, or a list of awards and accomplishments so that they have all the information they could possibly need.

**JZ:** The key is to be very up-front with letter writers and ask them if they'll be able to "write [you] a strong letter of recommendation." Be sure that you know the letter writers beyond "just [being] a student in their class." If possible, try to obtain at least one letter from an MD, though only if this person knows you well enough to comment on you both personally and academically.

**JT:** I chose professors who I would frequently visit in office hours and had a good relationship with. It is always helpful to choose professors whose courses you have done well in, so that they can attest to your academic abilities. To give medical committees a better idea of who I was, I chose to provide a letter from someone familiar with my volunteer work and my extracurricular activities at my university.

**MJ:** If possible, it is a good idea to get a letter from a physician whom you have shadowed. I always tell premeds who ask me for advice to try to shadow a physician as early and often as possible. For one thing, the experience will provide you with genuine insight into the field of medicine and tell you if this is the right career path for you. It will also show medical committees that you have been exposed to the medical field and are interested in applying to medical school. A physician who can support your interest and dedication to medicine, as well as comment on how you interact with others in a professional manner, can really set your application apart. Finally, getting a letter from a research mentor would be a good idea for students who are interested in schools with a heavy emphasis on academic medicine.

**KH:** I went to a school where science lectures frequently had 400 students in attendance. This made it difficult to get a good letter of recommendation from science professors. The usual advice is to go to office hours, etc. However, I had the most success simply asking a few professors whose courses I did well in to meet with me for coffee and discuss why I wanted to go to medical school. Some professors were open to the idea, and others weren't. In the end, I received more personal letters from my professors than from others at my school. Remember to ask for letters early. Professors are busy, and they're doing you a favor. Some of my letters took over three months to receive!

**KW:** I asked people who knew me on multiple levels (academically, professionally, and personally) to write my recommendation letters. Your letters should attest to your character and personality. They shouldn't just be a list of skills and competencies. I also asked my recommenders what I could do to make the process easier for them. For example, I offered to share my CV and my personal statement, along with sample letters and templates. Your recommenders are busy enough with their own jobs and lives; I found it went a long way to offer support.

## APPLYING

**CT:** I applied directly from college and started medical school in the fall right after I had graduated. People tell you this is the "normal" pathway to medical school. Honestly, if I could start over, I might have taken a year off; many people do. At the beginning of school, it was sometimes hard to keep at the studying; it was easy to get burned out from being in the "student" role for so long. Many students worry that if they take a year or two off, then they will be "old" when they start and finish medical school. But the important thing is to arrive at medical school energized and prepared to learn a lot. It's a great experience and there is fun along the way, but it is a lot of work, too.

**KW:** I took a year off before medical school and taught high school English in France. I had studied abroad in France as an undergrad and knew that I wanted to experience living abroad again. I wanted to truly immerse myself in the language and culture—the challenge seemed exciting, and I knew that I needed to take such an opportunity while I had the chance. I really believe that this year abroad was crucial to my personal development. It was good for me to step away from the books and to allow myself a chance to evolve and grow in a completely different environment from what I knew before.

**KH:** I applied to around 20 schools. I chose schools by stratifying them into three categories: dream, realistic, and safety. I determined these categories by comparing the schools' average MCAT and GPA to my own. The majority (around 10) of my applications went to schools that were in the realistic category (i.e., they were very close in GPA and MCAT to mine). The other important thing I considered was whether I would go to each school—and city—if I was accepted. Medical school is four years of your life, and if you hate a certain type of weather or environment, don't apply there!

**MJ:** Keep in mind that applications and the interview process are expensive! Applications, traveling, hotels, etc. add up quickly. Be realistic and prepared when you send out applications. Finally, be patient. Sometimes it takes a *very* long time for schools to get back to you regarding interviews or decisions.

**CT:** I applied to 15 schools total (5 in state and 10 out of state). Although that sounds like a lot, I'd say that number is fairly typical, given the competitiveness of the process. Besides, if your desire is strong to get into medical school, you want to maximize your chances to get into schools. I interviewed at 8 of the 15 schools to which I applied.

**JZ:** I spent a year off after college working in the HealthCorps division of AmeriCorps and teaching MCAT classes. Taking that year was great. It gave me a chance to do something and gain an experience I probably won't get at any other time of my life. And it also gave me a much-needed break from school. By the time I was done with the year, I was itching to get back to studying.

**MJ:** The most important thing is to do things that you are passionate about. Obviously, clinical experience is essential to getting into medical school. But volunteering or working at a certain place just to get into medical school is the wrong approach. It is usually clear when someone is doing things simply to "check off requirements." You also want to find ways to stand out. If you are passionate about politics, get involved with your local representative. If you love sports, play intramural sports or try out for a local team. The bottom line is medical schools want someone who is passionate and involved, even if their passion isn't always related to medicine.

**JZ:** I felt that my premed adviser prepared me very well. The one thing that I *definitely* recommend is to not be afraid to ask questions. This is your dream and probably (for some of you) the end product of a lifelong journey. Do not rely on secondhand information when it comes to your application. Ask your adviser questions and even ask some of your professors. Ask people at your school for a list of students who have gone to medical school before you. Your predecessors can be a wealth of information (and may even house you for interviews!).

**CT:** Take the process one day at a time. It's a long journey from MCAT Test Day to the first day of M1. Medical schools get thousands of applications, so there is no need to call every day (and some people do) to check on the status of your application. Once you get that first acceptance, then you can breathe a big sigh of relief. From there on out, you at least know that no matter what happens with the other schools, you will be going to medical school!

**KW:** I definitely felt like the application process was lengthy and at times very arduous. I'm sure I put more pressure on myself than I should have. While it's definitely good to have people from inside and outside the world of medical applications review your application, remember to take their advice with a grain of salt. Try to strike a balance among all of the different points of view that people share with you.

## ADMISSIONS PROCESS

**KW:** The thing that helped me the most with medical school applications was the relationship I built with the admissions office. I reached out early on in the process (about one year before I applied). I took the time to schedule a meeting in person with the office and asked questions about the specifics of the admissions process (the algorithms and selection methods used to sort applicants). This helped me eliminate any unknowns in the process and focus my efforts when putting together my application, etc. It also gave me the opportunity to connect with people involved in admissions. I followed up every couple of months with the people I had met. On Interview Day, it was such a relief to have familiar faces when I arrived and to not go into the process cold.

**CT:** I took my MCAT at the end of April, and I submitted to AMCAS on June 1st. My first interview was the first weekend in October, but I got at least one interview each month until my last one occurred in late February. My first acceptance came around the middle of November, and I definitely will never forget that day!

**KH:** Going through the admissions process was grueling, but exciting, too. It was fun to get an opportunity to see new cities and new schools. Even if I didn't get into these schools, it was a chance to explore. Looking back at my applications, I wish I'd known that applying to medical school is unpredictable. Having been involved in admissions and seen the results of it, I now realize that a lot of thought goes into deciding who gets in. There are things that an applicant simply cannot control when a committee is constructing a cohesive class. Relax and be yourself; the rest is out of your hands.

**JT:** I applied soon after AMCAS opened. Earlier is never harmful. Keep in mind that there are more interview spots earlier in the cycle.

## INTERVIEWS

**CT:** All but one of my interviews were conducted one-on-one. Most of my interviews consisted of two 1-hour sessions with different interviewers. From school to school, there was some variation in interviewers. Typically, my first interviewer was a clinician, and the second interviewer was a student, another clinician, or a basic scientist.

**JT:** Several types of questions came up frequently in my interviews. Medical students like to ask how you work in teams, how you relate to others, and what qualities you possess as a person. It seemed like they were trying to get a feel for how I may or may not "fit in" with the "typical" student or student mentality at that school. Basic scientists asked about my research. If you have done research, be prepared to answer questions (and specific ones!) regarding what you have done. Many times, the basic scientist had a copy of a paper from the lab in which I had worked and was familiar with the research. Clinicians tended to ask about ethical scenarios and really delve into my desire to become a doctor. Additionally, they will ask for your thoughts about current issues going on in the world of medicine.

**KH:** In preparing for interviews, keep up on current topics in healthcare. You don't have to be an expert, but at least be aware of headlines and big changes. Being an economics major, I was frequently asked about my thoughts regarding healthcare reform from a business perspective. Also be prepared to relate *any* experience you have had to medicine or how it could potentially make you a better physician. On my application (as my final activity spot on AMCAS), I listed that I had spent a summer working at an amusement park as an undergrad. I was not expecting it, but nearly every interviewer asked me about this experience. So really reflect on everything you have done, especially activities that are listed on your application.

**JZ:** Some schools had interviews with only faculty members, while others had interviews with both faculty members and current students. For the most part, my interviews were conversational, and the bulk of the time was spent discussing aspects of my application in detail. If you list research on your application, be prepared to discuss it extensively. Do your homework on the school and be prepared to ask questions about unique aspects of a school's curriculum or student experience. It is *never* a good idea to answer "Do you have any questions?" with "No." While interviews are very important, remember, one bad interview will not kill your chances. My worst interview happened to be at the school I ended up attending.

**MJ:** Be prepared, but don't sound *rehearsed*. Make sure you've thought about tough topics (end-of-life care, healthcare reform) and have an opinion—you'll likely be asked (and pushed) about your thoughts on these topics. If your school offers an opportunity to do a "practice" interview, definitely do it. Practice interviews help you pick up on things you wouldn't otherwise. When I became an interviewer myself, I observed many bizarre and distracting behaviors from applicants.

**CT:** One school at which I interviewed used the multiple mini-interview format. There were multiple 10-minute interviews about a variety of subjects. I didn't care for this style of interview. I really had no idea how to prepare differently for it, so I treated it in the same way that I treated other interviews.

**KW:** The interview was by far my favorite part of the application process. Naturally, I was nervous, but I was determined to enjoy Interview Day. It helped a lot that I had already been in touch with the admissions staff. When I showed up on the morning of Interview Day, the familiarity of a few faces and the ease of quick small talk with these people helped remove any jitters I had.

My advice: Be comfortable. Wear clothes that you feel great in and that you know well—there is nothing worse than a wardrobe malfunction or being uncomfortable. Be friendly to everyone, especially the admissions staff and those helping organize the interview day. Small efforts of kindness go a long way, even with the people that you may not think are the decision makers for your acceptance. Connect with people on a human level. If you can, step beyond the medical school stuff and find a way to connect with people on common areas of interest. You will enjoy the conversation more yourself, and the interviewer will remember you more because of this. Be honest. If you don't know how to answer a specific question, don't hesitate to say that. It is better to be upfront than to get yourself in a hole. You can prove your competencies and intelligence in answering other questions.

## Dual-Degree Programs

**CT:** I did not apply to any MD/PhD programs. However, I was extremely interested in an MD/MBA degree when I was applying. It wasn't a requirement for me, so I didn't let it influence where I applied, but I did pay close attention to whether that degree program was offered. If you are thinking of applying for that joint degree, I'd really recommend giving some thought as to why you believe that the extra degree will help you in your ultimate career aspirations. What ultimately caused me to decide against enrolling in that program was the realization that the MBA wouldn't really do anything for my career. My desire to be an academic practicing clinician would not really be enhanced by obtaining the MBA. Examine the rationale for the extra degree to make sure you're not just taking classwork for the sake of having a few extra letters after your name.

**MJ:** I did not apply to a dual-degree program, but I have since obtained a Masters of Education during my residency. There is an increasing realization that there is a major need for "physician-educators," just as there is a need for "physician-scientists." I used my One-year EdM program to study educational theory, pedagogical techniques (e.g., teaching by the case method), and medical-simulation education. I plan to work in an academic center after residency and hope to spend a significant portion of my career in teaching/curriculum development (medical school, residency) and possibly medical school administration.

# AFTER YOU'RE ACCEPTED

**JZ:** It is important to weigh a lot of factors when you are considering where to go. Consider how comfortable you felt at the interviews. Make sure you ask questions of current and former students when you have the chance. Find out what they like and dislike about their schools. When you are interviewing, think about whether you see yourself fitting into the student body and whether you like the feel of the school. Medical school classes are usually between 100 and 200 people. It's almost like high school all over again. You'll be spending all of your time with these people, so you want to make sure that you'll fit in with the people who seem to gravitate to that school.

**CT:** Definitely think about cost. Unfortunately, medical school is extremely expensive, and many times all of it will be paid for with loans. Since there are not a lot of scholarships available to medical students, you should look at the total cost for four years of going to that school, not just the first year. Sometimes there can be a large difference between those numbers. I ultimately decided to stay at an in-state school because the cost difference turned into at least $125,000 of savings over the four years. While going to a new place may be exciting, you don't necessarily want it to add another 5–10 years of loan payments to your life.

**JT:** Make sure to find out how successful the students are at the schools to which you've been accepted. If it's not provided, ask the school for its first-time Step 1 pass rate and find out where its graduates match. Even though the rate might be 93 percent pass for Step 1, why do 7 percent fail? This is especially important since medical students are supposed to be some of the brightest students on campus. Do students match at competitive places? Do a high number of students not match?

**MJ:** As you deliberate over what school to attend, consider cost, reputation, curriculum, location, and your gut feeling. Talk it over with your family/significant other. You will be spending an enormous amount of time at your chosen school for four years, so make sure you'll be happy. Think realistically about cost—it's a huge investment.

**KH:** I decided to go to my state school simply due to cost. I may have had "better" (in terms of rank or prestige) options, but by and large, medical education is similar across the board, and I was looking to save myself from as much debt as possible. Looking back, the only thing that I neglected was the status of certain programs within my school. If I had known I wanted to go into a certain field (especially if it is a competitive one), I would have made sure the school I decided to go to had a residency program in good reputation in that field. Your home school can often be a "safety" when applying to residencies, and more prestigious programs at your institution will usually come with more meaningful letters of recommendation.

**JZ:** After being accepted, I spent time working, saving money, and carefully choosing a place to live for the next four years.

**KH:** After I graduated, I returned home with my parents and mostly relaxed. Medical school is a lot of work, so you definitely do not want to burn out the summer before you start because you took a stressful job or did some incredibly detailed research. Spend some time getting to know your classmates via Facebook. I found my future roommates this way. Also, look at setting up housing near school soon so that you have the best options.

**CT:** I just relaxed and spent time with my friends and family. One thing that I cannot tell enough premeds is to not spend your summer before medical school studying. This is the last summer you have when you really don't have many responsibilities.

**MJ:** I did not spend any time studying prior to starting classes. You'll spend plenty of time studying in medical school, so enjoy yourself!

## WHAT'S THE FIRST YEAR OF MEDICAL SCHOOL LIKE?

**CT:** At first, I think that all of us in my class were very overwhelmed. The volume of material you cover and the speed at which you cover it can be extremely challenging. During the first nine weeks of class, we covered almost 75 percent of the material for the biochemistry major that I spent four years working on in undergrad. The workload is manageable, but it is definitely an adjustment for a lot of students. Time management is key. Additionally, you have to be disciplined. You're in medical school, so you might not be able to do as many activities or watch as much TV as you did as an undergrad. You'll definitely have free time, but you just have to be smart about your schedule. Medical school can be a drag sometimes, and at times, you'll question exactly why you are putting yourself through this. During those times, I'd walk into the hospital or sit down and think to remind myself what a rewarding career being a physician is. Our profession is a noble one, and we all work to help and provide the best care and quality of life we can to each patient. Those thoughts get me through late-night studying and keep me pressing on through.

**KH:** The biggest surprise about medical school is the sheer volume of material and the quick pace at which the material is covered. Something that is covered over a period of several months in undergrad is covered in several weeks in medical school. It is important to develop a study schedule and really stick to it. Find a study method that works for you. It is also important to make connections between subjects—find ways to integrate the histology of the kidney with the physiology of the kidney. This approach will allow you to more thoroughly understand the material, and it will also allow you to better appreciate pathophysiology. It also happens to be the best approach to learning during your clinical years.

**JZ:** The hardest part about MS1 is the transition into medical school. Weekends become more of a concept than a reality, and you come to cherish the free time you have. Once you get into a study routine and define your expectations, medical school becomes more manageable.

**JT:** To succeed in medical school, you need to have a strong daily work ethic and build yourself a routine to follow each day. Being around others who are studying is helpful for motivation, but only if it is at a place where others can't easily distract you. Although isolated studying may not be the most enjoyable, it is the most productive. When you are learning the material for the first time, you should avoid study groups.

**MJ:** MS1 was a fun year, especially getting to know your class. The most important thing to remember in the first year of medical school is that you are now surrounded by an incredibly intelligent group of colleagues. People coming into medical school frequently have been used to excelling at everything they do. It is important to realize that there is a 50 percent chance you will be below average in medical school, and that's OK. Struggling a little bit and being flexible by learning new study techniques is just part of the process. Medical school is hard, but it's definitely doable. You'll have plenty of time to yourself to do whatever you want. This is especially true for the first two years of medical school.

## LIFE OUTSIDE OF MEDICAL SCHOOL

**JZ:** You can definitely make the time to see friends, family, and your significant other. As long as you are organized and plan for your free time, you'll do just fine. The only caution I will give is to be judicious when volunteering for activities; avoid becoming overcommitted by always keeping in mind the amount of work you'll have to do to learn the current material.

**MJ:** During my freshman year of college, I started dating the woman who would become my wife, and she has travelled the medical school and residency journey with me. We got married during my fourth year of medical school. I've been on call or had to study for exams during some birthdays/anniversaries, but I've always tried to maintain a good work-life balance. It is so important to have some type of support system (family, significant other, close friends) during this training process, as you will encounter difficult situations on nearly a daily basis.

**CT:** It's difficult, and you may lose touch with some of your friends who you were not really close with. Always try to keep in touch with your family, close friends, and significant other. A strong support network is a great thing to have in medical school and reminds you of why you entered medical school in the first place.

**KH:** Becoming a physician is a huge investment that involves a lot of hard work and sacrifice, both personally and financially, but it is also incredibly rewarding. Patients are often coming to you at their most vulnerable moments, and you have an opportunity to make a significant impact on their lives. While the pace of the hospital/clinic sometimes doesn't allow you to really sit down and talk with your patients, when you do have the opportunity, seize it! Patients will often be your best "textbooks." I have learned a significant amount about medicine and life in general through my conversations with patients.

# PART FIVE

# Special Considerations

# CHAPTER 14

# Nontraditional Applicants

by Cynthia Lewis

The majority of applicants to medical school apply directly after completing an undergraduate degree, typically in a science major. However, countless others take a less traditional route to the medical profession. Some people have an interest in becoming physicians when they are young, but for one or more reasons, they do not pursue that interest. For other students, it may take years for their interest in medicine or for their self-confidence to develop.

If you are a "nontraditional" applicant, you're not alone. In recent years, more people from diverse backgrounds, often older people with rich life experiences, have been entering the medical profession. For the 2011–2012 entering class, 9 percent were at least 29 years old.

## WHO ARE NONTRADITIONAL APPLICANTS?

Nontraditional applicants often fall into the following categories:

### Postbaccalaureate Students

Many students have earned degrees in areas that have not prepared them for medical school, such as the humanities or social sciences. These students may enroll in postbaccalaureate programs. Other postbaccalaureate students have completed their premedical course requirements but have earned marginal grades in the sciences and need to strengthen their academic record.

### Re-entry Students

Some students never finished their undergraduate degrees, for a multitude of reasons, and they now need to complete their coursework in order to reach their goal of a career in medicine. For example, some women took several years to raise families and deferred their own education; some people entered the military and deferred a career in medicine.

### Career Changers

Some people apply to med school as the result of a career change. They may have entered a career in an effort to support a family, to meet expectations, or because the career was appealing at a certain stage in their lives. At some point in time, they may discover a repressed desire to pursue medicine, or they may even develop one after experiencing a family member's struggle with illness. Still others wish to change careers in order to make a more significant impact in the world. If you find yourself highly motivated to become a doctor for positive reasons—that is, not simply because you need a change from your present career—you may be on the right track.

---

**The Postbac Advantage**

"If you enroll in a postbac program, you may have a greater chance of getting into med school. The jury is still out on this one, but postbac students stand out from the general crowd of undergraduates; they often have life experiences that make them stand apart from other applicants. Furthermore, admissions committees may feel that the extra effort postbac students put in reflects particularly strong drive and dedication."

—Postbac student, Columbia University

---

You may fit into more than one of the above three categories, or your motivation for applying to medical school may be unique. Most medical schools do not single out nontraditional applicants. But, of course, your nontraditional qualities can shine in your application, so it is up to you, and perhaps a trusted adviser, to assess your strengths and to make certain that they are clearly seen and heard.

## PREPARING TO APPLY

Nontraditional applicants often ask what they need to do to prepare to apply to medical school. If you're trying to carve out a preparation plan, your first step should be to make an initial assessment of how much time you can devote to preparation, how supportive your immediate family is, and how much you have set aside in financial resources to develop your application. Rarely is it clear and easy to work out the appropriate strategy; you may find it helpful to share your background and concerns with someone who has worked with many nontraditional applicants and to enlist his or her help to develop your personal strategy.

That said, below are some ways to prepare to apply:

### Formal Postbaccalaureate Programs at Private Colleges

If you have a strong academic record in a nonscience degree and are changing careers, consider this sort of program. Generally, you will need to quit working and put full-time effort into being premedical in order to take this route. This may work best if you have ample funds and wish to complete preparation quickly. The benefits of this type of program are that you interact regularly with a small group of pre-medical peers, you will likely have access to an advising program, and you can complete your premed requirements in a compact one- or two-year academic sequence. MCAT preparation may or may not be included in the package. You may get more individual treatment in this type of program.

A few medical schools offer a subset of this type of program, where you take courses with the school's medical students. You may earn a master's degree upon completion of the program. If you earn top grades in competition with the medical students, you may have an edge in admissions at that school, or you may be offered a guaranteed interview or acceptance into that school's medical program.

---

**The Postbac Challenge**

"Postbac programs are especially tough for students who are a bit rusty. The attrition rate at many programs is quite high and the challenge of the material can be quite a shock–it and sometimes makes people remember why they never studied this stuff before . . . and why they shouldn't in the future.

Admissions committees know that postbac students do not have to balance the same kind of academic load undergraduates do, so GPA for the classes taken in the postbac program, usually over two years, is extremely important."

–Postbac student, Columbia University

---

### Inexpensive Postbaccalaureate Programs

Some private and public colleges offer free or inexpensive postbaccalaureate programs, primarily for underrepresented minority students who need to improve their academic records. Some schools offer programs with one or two years of upper-division science courses such as molecular biology, embryology, and immunology, as well as clinical experience, research opportunity, and MCAT preparation. Eligibility requirements vary tremendously; some schools require that applicants have previously applied to, but not been accepted to, med school, while others have minimum GPA or MCAT scores. The duration of these programs varies, as does the cost of tuition and how much financial aid is provided. In addition, such programs may require that you reside in a particular state.

### Informal Coursework

Like many nontraditional students, you may need to continue working full-time, so taking premedical coursework at night or on weekends at a local college may be your only option. This route, though, has its drawbacks. Many allopathic medical schools view academic credentials from community colleges as less rigorous than those from four-year institutions. (Osteopathic schools seem not to distinguish between records from two-year and four-year colleges.) Some four-year colleges provide weekend or evening schedules to meet the needs of older, working students. However, extension courses are probably not the best way to prepare: Medical school admissions committees may have difficulty evaluating extension courses and may not want to "take a chance" on someone who is an unknown quantity. Your best bet is to call the schools where you will apply to verify how they view these academic venues.

> ### Grad Grade Boost
>
> "I was absolutely amazed when I got into med school. My freshman year of undergraduate school had been academically poor, and I thought that it would be a major obstacle. But I think my dismal undergraduate performance was countered by how well I did during my graduate career in biomedical engineering and on my MCATs."
>
> —Med student, University of California at Davis

If you are going to take the premedical requirements on your own, you can do so as a second baccalaureate student (and you may be eligible to receive some financial aid). You may not need to complete that second degree in order to apply to medical school; you may just need some of the coursework from it. Or, you may register as an unclassified postbaccalaureate student, which means you can select exactly those courses that you need for your premedical requirements. The downside is that you may not be eligible to receive financial aid with this option. And, you may be totally without an adviser, which makes navigating the admissions process all the more difficult.

### Graduate School

If your undergraduate grades in the sciences were not strong, you may need at least two years of science coursework to prove to admissions committees that you can handle medical school and to prepare yourself to do well on the MCAT exam. One way to do this coursework is to complete a graduate program. You'll need to assess exactly where your undergraduate weaknesses lie; it helps to have an adviser assist you. Then, select your degree in an area that will showcase your refined strength in previously weak areas. Suggestions include earning a master's degree in biology, applied life sciences such as ecology or molecular biology, exercise physiology, nutritional sciences, public health, chemistry, and so on. One important note: If you do not ultimately attend medical school, for whatever reason, make certain that this degree is one you enjoy and one upon which you can build another career.

## HOW YOU'LL BE ASSESSED

Older applicants are expected to bring some interesting and fulfilling life experiences to the application table. From the perspective of admissions personnel, older applicants should have more insight, maturity, and self-knowledge than younger applicants. It's fairly certain that you'll be asked, "Why are you applying to medical school *now*?" Admissions folks expect you to have learned something from your earlier career(s) that may be applicable to your possible new career in medicine.

Generally, medical schools pool all applicants for screening and do not separate out nontraditional or older applicants. So, as long as you can reasonably and convincingly explain why you are applying to medical school now, your application stands a good chance.

Many older students wonder if age matters in the decision-making process. By law, medical schools cannot discriminate against you because of your age. While they can't outright ask you for your age, they can easily calculate it from your date of birth or high school graduation. Generally, students who apply by their mid-thirties stand an excellent chance if their applications are strong. You may have to be really exceptional for schools to consider you seriously if you apply in your 40s or later, however. And there have been a few applicants in their 50s who have been accepted into medical school.

### Academic Background

If you took few or no science courses as an undergraduate, you are not necessarily at a disadvantage. You'll need to start reviewing, taking, or retaking basic material and then adding other science courses in the required sequence. Most people take two years to complete the required sciences; some take three years, while a few can complete everything in one or one and a half years. Remember that having a nonscience major may work to your advantage: Since only a small percentage of all applicants are nonscience majors, your background may make you more interesting to admissions committees. Make sure you describe why you selected that major and, if applicable, how you developed it into a career.

### Undergraduate and Postbaccalaureate GPAs

Schools vary as to how they consider your undergrad and postbac GPAs. Some schools consider recent strong academic records (from postbaccalaureate and graduate work) coupled with strong MCAT scores a sufficient indication that you are a solid candidate. Others look at undergraduate coursework (usually in the sciences), the trend from year to year, and the MCAT scores; although they consider the postbac or graduate GPA, the latter may not outweigh poor undergraduate grades. Your best bet: Call the schools you are most interested in to hear how these factors are weighed.

### Will You Be Taken Seriously?

Some nontraditional students fear that their career change will not be seen in a positive light. It's important that you tell your individual story—why you are switching careers, re-entering college after a long hiatus, etc.—on your application and in your interview, so be prepared. Describe why you decided to go into the military, have children, or become a teacher. For example, "I joined the military directly out of high school because I was not sure I could handle college. I didn't have any role models in my family who attended college," or "My family expected that I would enter the family business when I graduated from high school." Then, explain why you would like to become a doctor now.

Medical schools want to know that you have clearly considered why you want to pursue a career in medicine. If you are a nontraditional applicant, this issue may be even more important. You'll need significant medical, community, service, and leadership experiences that substantiate your claim to your new career. If you have been developing these things for several years, then you already have a track record. If you have not taken opportunities to develop these aspects of your background, you must begin to do so now. It will take at least a year or longer to do this.

## FINDING AN ADVISER

A premed adviser can help you plan the courses you need to take and the steps required to prepare for your medical school application. Finding an adviser may actually be the most important decision for a nontraditional student. You may be an expert in your present career, or you may have mastered the balancing act between family obligations and your work life up to now, but this is a whole new ball game—juggling family, college, work, and medical experience. A trusted adviser—someone who has experience working with nontraditional students—can help you set

| **Get Help** |
|---|
| "As a graduate student, I needed an adviser who understood how to assess my undergraduate and graduate record and to help me devise a good strategy. I needed a sounding board to verify that I was doing the appropriate activities and taking the correct courses, and that I was handling the application process to my best advantage." |
| –Medical student |

schedules and priorities, as well as find appropriate opportunities for you. Building an application strategy is as important as earning As.

A premedical adviser who has worked with nontraditional students can also help you connect to faculty mentors who understand the needs of nontraditional or postbac students.

## ADJUSTING TO COLLEGE

If you've been out of college for a while, you may be daunted by the thought of returning, and you may wonder about how you'll adjust and how you'll be treated by other students and faculty members. One way to help is to join—or form— a postbaccalaureate support group. At one college, such a group has a monthly meeting at a cheap, local restaurant or at a student's home. Their stated purpose is to "address specific circumstances unique to nontraditional students; to unify, to become acquainted with peers, to provide an atmosphere of academic and social support; to share and build ties to the academic and professional community; and to increase awareness of opportunities that are related to our career plans." If your college does not have such a group, start one. Knowing that there are other students with similar goals and backgrounds can make the postbac experience more pleasant and rewarding.

## THE JUGGLING ACT

Preparing for medical school is hard work, whether you're fresh out of college or have another career under your belt. But if you are trying to balance going to school full-time, working part-time, getting clinical experience, and spending time with your family, your task will become even more challenging. In fact, if you're juggling work, school, and family life, it will probably take you longer to complete the premedical course requirements than it will a full-time college student. The goal here is to maintain the highest grades you can while keeping sane at home and still sleeping, eating, and having some social existence. Here, too, an adviser whose perspective lies outside of your narrow focus may be able to help you develop a reasonable schedule.

Admissions personnel will take into account that you are working full-time while juggling part-time college and raising a family, but you must make this perfectly clear in your written application, secondary application, and interview. Make sure you explicitly state the number of hours per week you have been working, name the jobs you have had, and explain whom you are supporting.

## ADVANTAGES OF BEING NONTRADITIONAL

Nontraditional applicants are often the most interesting premedical candidates because they have a broad perspective on life, as well as high levels of motivation and focus. Lawyers, corporate executives, engineers, and stockbrokers don't wish to become doctors to gain prestige and large salaries. In fact, they will certainly lose earning power for many years and may never earn as a doctor an amount equal to their previous salary.

Usually, nontraditional applicants give careful consideration to their motivations before making a leap into another lifestyle or career. One student said, "I feel like one advantage I have being an older, re-entry student is that I really am certain about my desire to pursue a medical career. Moreover, I believe that I was able to convey this to most interviewers, which helped me tremendously."

## FOR MORE INFORMATION

To get information on postbac programs, visit the AAMC website: http://services.aamc.org/postbac.

# CHAPTER 15

# Groups Underrepresented in Medicine

by Will Ross, MD

At the 1996 annual meeting of the Association of American Medical Colleges (AAMC), the association's president showed a picture of his 1965 residency class at Harvard University School of Medicine. They were all white men. Harvard's class reflected a time when de facto segregation restricted access to medical education for African Americans, Mexican Americans, mainland Puerto Ricans, and Native Americans.

Until recently, enrollment of underrepresented minorities in US medical schools had increased steadily. The AAMC re-energized the national effort to boost minority medical school enrollment in 1991 with the launching of "Project 3000 by 2000," an effort to increase yearly matriculation of underrepresented students to 3,000 students by the year 2000. In the early 1990s, underrepresented student enrollment continued to grow, increasing to 12 percent of medical students.

Yet the "diversity bridge" is sagging. In 1995, the University of California Board of Regents passed resolutions prohibiting the use of race or ethnicity as a criterion for admission to the UC system, a resolution that was later codified by voters of California as Proposition 209. And in 1996, the Fifth Circuit Court of Appeals, in a reversal of 1978's Bakke Decision, rejected any consideration of race or ethnicity as a factor in admission to the University of Texas Law School, "even for the purpose of correcting perceived racial imbalances in the student body." After the US Supreme Court refused to hear an appeal, the ruling became law in Texas, Mississippi, and Louisiana.

In 2003, two US Supreme Court decisions in cases involving the University of Michigan reversed the 1996 Fifth Circuit ruling but narrowed the acceptable methods by which race and ethnicity may be applied as admissions criteria. The Supreme Court ruled that while race can be a factor in shaping admissions decisions, point systems that give members of minority groups a quantifiable advantage in the admissions process violate the Equal Protection Clause of the 14th Amendment of the US Constitution. The AAMC formally supported the consideration of race and ethnicity in a brief filed with the Supreme Court. These decisions signified that universities could continue to use race and ethnicity as factors in their admissions decisions but would have to use less definitive methods in doing so. The two Michigan cases only relate legally to public institutions that are funded by tax dollars. However, private schools will likely follow their example in order to maintain a sense of fairness and consistency in the admissions process.

During the same week of the 2003 Supreme Court decisions, the AAMC decided to drop its use of the term *underrepresented minorities* (URM) in favor of the term *underrepresented in medicine*. The term *URM* at the time included only African Americans, Mexican Americans, Native Americans, and mainland Puerto Ricans. The AAMC sought to broaden its definition of an underrepresented student group by defining the term as follows: "'Underrepresented in medicine' means those racial and ethnic populations that are underrepresented in the medical profession relative to their numbers in the general population."

As a result of the 2003 Supreme Court decisions, in 2004 the AAMC clarified its definition of the term "underrepresented in medicine" to exclude the goal of racial balancing in medical school admissions, and instead to consider race and ethnicity with the goal of increasing diversity in medical schools for its educational benefits of "improving the cultural competence of the physicians our schools educate and improving access to healthcare for underserved populations."

While minorities represent close to 30 percent of the US population, underrepresented minorities constituted less than 17 percent of the medical school matriculants in 2012.

The need for minority medical student training continues to grow. Minority health providers have provided, and will likely continue to provide, disproportionately more care to the rapidly growing minority populations in the United States (estimated to grow to 40 percent of the national population by the year 2035). Studies show that minority patients tend to trust the healthcare system more when they are under the care of physicians who share their ethnic background. Furthermore, underrepresented students graduating from medical school are far more likely to serve in underserved areas than are their nonunderrepresented counterparts. Finally, a recent medical report concluded that African-American physicians care for more patients with Medicaid, and Hispanic physicians care for more patients without health insurance, than do physicians not from groups underrepresented in medicine. For all these reasons, it is imperative that medical schools train more minority physicians to attend to the healthcare needs of an increasingly diverse patient population.

There is evidence that efforts to increase applications from groups underrepresented in medicine are working. The number of medical school applications from Hispanic students rose by almost 37 percent between 2005 and 2012. Likewise, the number of African-American applicants rose by nearly 17 percent between 2005 and 2012. These trends are likely to continue in the future.

## CHOOSING A SCHOOL

While there are numerous factors to consider when deciding which schools to apply to, minority students often have unique concerns. According to one AAMC study, factors such as curriculum, financial aid, and the availability of minority programs and faculty mentors are of greater concern to underrepresented minority students than to nonminorities.

A valuable resource to make sure you get your hands on is the publication *Minority Student Opportunities in United States Medical Schools*. This biennial publication provides information from individual medical schools about recruitment, admissions, academic support programs, enrichment programs, student financial assistance, educational partnerships, and other important topics. The data published show the number of minority applicants, the number offered an acceptance, the number of matriculants, and the number of graduates by gender and racial/ethnic group. To learn more about this important adjunct to the MSAR and to order it, visit the AAMC website at www.aamc.org/students/minorities/.

Another excellent source of applicant and matriculant data—including information on minority applicants, accepted applicants, matriculants, enrollment, and faculty—can be found on the AAMC website at www.aamc.org/data/facts/applicantmatriculant.

## Opportunities in Primary Care and Community Medicine

Underrepresented candidates are more likely to pursue schools that offer community-based learning experiences, family medicine clerkships, ambulatory and primary care opportunities, and classes in medical ethics. If that describes you, you can find out more about these programs and opportunities by looking at a school's published bulletins, talking with current medical students, and visiting the medical school's Web page.

## Financial Aid

Financial aid is often the limiting factor affecting minority students' choice in medical schools. However, aid is available, as well as help with financial planning for educational debt. There are minority merit scholarships available, as well as numerous loans, so speak to the school's financial aid officer and visit AAMC's website at www.aamc.org. You might also inquire about programs that offer loan forgiveness for future practice in medically underserved areas. For more information on financial aid, including scholarships, grants, and loans, see chapters 20 and 21.

## Programs for Underrepresented Students

You can get a good sense of a school's attitude toward recruitment and retention of minority students by checking to see what minority programs it offers. Special programs may include prematriculation programs offering refresher courses, mentoring programs in which students are paired with minority community physicians, board preparation courses, and academic assistance. Several schools have expanded summer programs that encompass academic enrichment, basic or clinical research, and clinical medicine exposure. These programs often start in middle school or high school. You can find out more about programs like these by contacting the minority affairs office at the medical school, talking to your premed adviser, or contacting the AAMC.

In addition, most medical schools have active chapters of the Student National Medical Association (SNMA) a student branch of the National Medical Association, a prominent national organization of minority physicians and educators. The SNMA offers peer support, academic enrichment programs, and practical approaches to succeeding in med school. It also offers a Big Brother/Big Sister mentoring program for incoming students. As one medical student said, "The medical school experience can be grueling, but it's a lot less stressful when you share your experiences, good and bad, with your classmates. The important thing is to try not to do it alone." For more information, contact SNMA:

Student National Medical Association
5113 Georgia Avenue NW
Washington, DC 20011
(202) 882-2881
Fax: (202) 882-2886
Email: operations@snma.org
Website: snma.org

## APPLYING TO SCHOOLS

Underrepresented minority students share many of the concerns faced by all medical school applicants throughout the entire application process. But there are a number of special concerns faced by URMs.

### Self-Designation on the Application

On the AMCAS form, you are asked to designate your race/ethnicity. Most medical schools accept the designations at face value. However, once an applicant designates himself as an underrepresented minority, his application may be reviewed for the degree of cultural immersion or cultural identity with the specified ethnic group. Applicants may be asked specific questions about cultural identity during the interview. A complete lack of affiliation with the designated group may indicate frank dishonesty to an admissions officer—and dishonesty is not a good policy in any part of the application process—but it may also reveal assimilation into mainstream culture, which admissions officers tend to tolerate.

An increasing number of students identify themselves on their applications as biracial or multiracial, a designation that poses challenging questions to admissions committees, most of whom will assume that these students have maintained a cultural identity with the designated minority group and are not using the designation for secondary gain.

The AMCAS application also asks whether you consider yourself to be a disadvantaged applicant. This is a difficult question to answer because, while medical schools have different definitions of disadvantage, they will try to consider the effects of disadvantage on an applicant's later performance. In general, if you feel that you were socially, economically, or educationally disadvantaged during your early years, you may want to consider answering yes to the question. If you do answer yes, be prepared to explain your reasons later in the admissions process.

## Medical Minority Applicant Registry (Med-MAR)

As an underrepresented minority or financially disadvantaged student, you can participate in the Medical Minority Applicant Registry by indicating your willingness to participate on your MCAT form. This free service provides your biographical information and MCAT scores to minority affairs and admissions offices of all U.S. medical schools. You will then receive information directly from them. See www.aamc.org/students/minorities/medmar.htm for more information.

## Minority Candidates and the Application Process

Admissions committees do not formally have a separate process for minority candidates; however, minority faculty members are commonly sought out to participate on the admissions team. At some medical schools, in fact, applications from minority or disadvantaged applicants are handled by an entirely separate admissions subcommittee, a practice that might expand in the light of recent affirmative action rulings.

Remember that it is essential that you submit your application early in the year. Don't wait until the last minute to apply. June or July is not too early. That will allow plenty of time for you to complete supplemental application materials requested by individual schools and give the admissions committee adequate time to review your file. Some medical schools begin interviewing applicants as early as October. Your file should be complete when the schools are ready to begin interviews.

## Minority Score Cutoffs

Few admissions officers will offer statistics on minority MCAT and GPA scores. Disparities do exist between the scores of underrepresented matriculants and others, but it is not clear how much of the disparity may be due to academic preparedness and how much to any inherent bias in the MCAT exam and educational system. With all applicants, but especially with underrepresented students, admissions officers consider qualities such as leadership ability, determination, compassion, maturity, and communication skills in assessing the candidates' suitability for med school and the practice of medicine. The goal of the admissions committee is to recognize the contribution that underrepresented candidates bring to medical school by way of their varying personal experiences and to interpret GPA and MCAT scores in concert with these personal, experiential traits.

## THE MEDICAL SCHOOL EXPERIENCE

It goes without saying that getting into medical school is challenging. But excelling in med school is a challenge as well. For underrepresented med students, medical school has its own hurdles. The most successful underrepresented students are the ones who choose faculty mentors early. Having a strong support system of other minority students and faculty can help you deal with racially insensitive comments and overt racism, and it can also make it easier to deal with any family or personal problems that may arise during your med school years.

# CHAPTER 16

# Students with Family Planning Concerns

by Cynthia Lewis

The number of women applicants and matriculants into medical school has been steadily increasing over the last 40 years. In 1970, women constituted only about 7 percent of all practicing physicians. In 2010, the figure was just over 30 percent. Moreover, there is evidence that the gender gap in medicine is closing rapidly. In 2013, 22,250 women applied to allopathic medical school, and women made up about 47 percent of the entering class. Judging by these trends, it is a distinct possibility that before too long, the percentage of female physicians will reflect the fact that women make up over half the US population.

While there is no such thing as a "typical" female medical student or applicant, there are certainly concerns that many women share. Women medical students often report they are concerned with gender bias, sexual harassment, societal expectations that they will be the primary childcare provider, the need for adequate childcare, and barriers to equal participation of women in some medical specialties and subspecialties. In addition, although family planning considerations are shared by men and women, these concerns tend to weigh more heavily on women.

## THE IMPORTANCE OF ROLE MODELS

Even with the strides made by women in the medical field, it's important to keep your commitment firm. Seek a role model, a mentor, or an adviser who can nurture your potential to fruition. If your instincts say, "Give up," they may not represent a realistic appraisal of your potential. Check with a neutral source of information—not your uncle, the doctor, your sister, or your roommate, but someone who has a good perspective about what it takes to get into medical school. A trusted premedical adviser or faculty member may be that person for you.

## CHOOSING A MEDICAL SCHOOL

While the reality is that most medical school applicants are happy to get accepted anywhere, you should nonetheless assess the characteristics that are most important to you in a school. What are some of the characteristics that women, in particular, look for in a medical school? What is important to you? Here are some characteristics numerous women premedical students have looked for:

- A school at which students help each other. One student said, "By helping each other, we can learn more about different people and how they like to be treated."
- A school with an ethics elective and courses that focus on the art of dealing with people
- A school that provides clinical experience early in training
- A school at which the faculty take time to talk with students
- A school with a representative number of female faculty and advisers
- A school that offers childcare

## WOMEN AS MEDICAL SCHOOL APPLICANTS

As a woman, you probably share with many other female applicants some concerns regarding how you'll be viewed as a medical school candidate.

Many women are concerned that they will be taken less seriously than male applicants by admissions personnel. Administrators and physicians involved in the admissions process are routinely cautioned not to allow gender bias to influence admissions decisions, but that is not to say it does not exist.

One premedical student put it this way: "Throughout my undergraduate years, I never labeled myself as a female student. I have been surprised by comments such as, 'It's great that you are president of such and such group, especially because you are a woman.' Frankly, my concerns lie with the future of all physicians." This is probably the best attitude to have and to reflect as you go through the application process.

Women students also worry about being perceived as more emotional than men. It's pretty unlikely that you'll be seen that way simply based on your gender, unless you give the school or interviewer reason to believe this by having an emotional outburst or displaying other behavior inappropriate to any medical school applicant. For example, if you answer an interview question asking about your personal strengths by stating your empathy toward humans in stressful or painful situations, and if you illustrate that statement with good examples in medical or nonmedical circumstances, that would not be taken as a "sign of being an emotional female."

## BALANCING FAMILY WITH A MEDICAL CAREER

It's not just medical students or physicians who find it difficult to juggle caring for a family and devoting time to a career. Despite advances in gender equality, the lion's share of childrearing still falls on women in our society, although men are taking on more family responsibilities. Physicians and medical students with families have a particularly demanding professional load and have specific concerns regarding the juggling act. Many such medical students and physicians have managed to have both satisfying work and family lives; still, as a parent or spouse considering a medical career, you may have to make some difficult choices and compromises.

Your spouse or partner may face days where you come home at odd hours, only to crash for a few hours. You may need to consider schools that provide adequate childcare or flexible class schedules. Here's one example: A single-parent applicant with two children agonized over whether to select a less expensive public institution that provided a traditional curriculum during a 40-hour curricular week or a competitive and more expensive private

---

### Goals of Some Women Premedical Students

- "To find a satisfying balance between the hard work involved in medicine and my personal interests and relationships."

- "To find a spouse who is willing to accept a nontraditional relationship and who understands and accepts my commitment to medicine."

institution that had flexible class hours, a problem-based curriculum, a small-group setting, and early clinical experience. She selected the private institution because it allowed her to attend classes all morning, return home to two teenage sons in mid-afternoon, spend time with them at dinner, help them with their homework, and then to do her own homework in the evening. In short, she found a comfortable way to integrate her family life into her medical education with a minimum of stress. She was very happy with her choice. This student is completing a surgical residency now; she learned how to balance her family and medical-training time requirements before entering a stressful residency.

## The Single Parent as Applicant

If you are a single parent, you probably have particular concerns related to how you will be perceived and how you will juggle caring for your children and studying. You'll also likely have concerns about financial issues.

First of all, you needn't reveal that you are a single parent. Admissions personnel are not allowed to ask your marital status; even if it is revealed, admissions decisions are made without regard to it. The financial aid office will have your dependent information if you apply for grants, loans, or scholarships, as most students do, but this should not be used in making admissions decisions. (If you find out that it *was* a consideration for denying you admission to a school, you might have cause to charge-discrimination.)

## A "Right Time" for Childbearing?

On entry to medical school, 7 percent of women and men have children; by graduation, 12 percent of women and 17 percent of men have at least one child. Most medical schools do not have formal policies dealing with parental leave; some are flexible, and others are not. Many schools allow a one-semester to one-year leave of absence for childbearing. Certainly, the case can be made that if students can take a leave of absence to do research, do special clinical work in another country, or earn an MPH or an MBA, why shouldn't they be able to take a leave of absence to have children? With good planning and support, you can survive pregnancy and childbirth at any time during medical school. Of course, it probably won't be easy, but the same can be said for the childbearing and rearing decisions made by any professional in just about any job.

The advice from women physicians who have had children during their training varies. Most suggest avoiding having children during the third year of medical school and the intern year, since these are the most time-intensive and stressful training periods. To lessen stress, some women suggest planning pregnancies between the second and third year of medical school, during the fourth year (when electives can be scheduled), during the last year of residency (not surgical), during a year off, or after residency.

One student said, "I plan to delay marriage and childbearing until after medical school, after or toward the end of residency." Another medical student had her first child between the second year (the last basic-science year) and the third year (the first clinical year); her second child was born during the second year of her internal medicine residency, which was creatively split into six months on and six months off with another woman resident; her third child was born after she joined a group practice.

Here's another student's story: "I discovered I was pregnant the same day I received my first request to interview at a medical school on the opposite coast. The next three months were hectic, as I adjusted to my pregnancy, attended classes, and flew all over the country interviewing. The day I was accepted was one of the happiest and most fulfilling times of my life . . . and so was finding out I was pregnant. Both events were planned and anticipated, but the inherent conflict represented therein is perhaps my area of greatest concern. One moment I am ecstatic and confident about the prospect of 'having it all,' and the next, I am panic-stricken at the enormity of what lies ahead."

Clearly, there are many issues you need to take into consideration if you plan to have children during your training. Perhaps most important is that you need to have supportive family and friends to help you manage during this demanding time.

## OTHER ISSUES FACING WOMEN STUDENTS

### Choosing a Specialty

Some medical specialties are still male dominated. Most medical schools and premedical advisers can, of course, tell you about specific cases of women who have entered surgical and other male-dominated specialties and prospered. Women may wish to spend time asking questions of these women pioneers to get a better idea of what trails they may be blazing and whether those trails still beckon after they understand some of the trade-offs they may need to make.

| Number and Percentage of Female ACGME Residents/Fellows by Specialty—2010 | | | |
|---|---|---|---|
| Specialty | Number of Residents in the Specialty | Percentage (%) That Are Female | % of All Female Residents |
| Internal Medicine | 22,009 | 44.7% | 19.3% |
| Pediatrics | 8,106 | 72.7 | 11.5 |
| Family Practice | 9,588 | 55.3 | 10.4 |
| Obstetrics and Gynecology | 4,862 | 81.4 | 7.7 |
| Psychiatry | 4,947 | 54.5 | 5.3 |
| General Surgery | 7,559 | 36.2 | 5.3 |
| Anesthesiology | 5,443 | 37.1 | 3.9 |
| Radiology-Diagnostic | 4,531 | 27.6 | 2.4 |
| Plastic Surgery | 6,960 | 26.3 | 0.4 |
| Dermatology | 1,154 | 63.8 | 1.4 |

Source: *AAMC*

## The Continuing Gender Gap . . .

While women are making huge strides in medicine, attrition among female medical students remains a problem, and for the female doctor, a continuing disparity between male and female physician incomes exists.

| Income/Total by Year | | | | | | |
|---|---|---|---|---|---|---|
| | 1982 | 1984 | 1993 | 1995 | 1998 | 2000 |
| All Physicians | $82,000 | $92,000 | $157,000 | $160,000 | $160,000 | $175,000 |
| Male | $85,000 | $96,000 | $170,000 | $170,000 | $180,000 | $195,000 |
| Female | $55,000 | $61,000 | $110,000 | $124,000 | $120,000 | $120,000 |

Source: American Medical Association for Health Policy Research, Chicago, IL.

So if you think the "pioneers" have done it all, don't worry: there are plenty of challenges left!

Women have an additional component of responsibility: They must be teachers and role models for younger men and women. Male physicians are required only to survive the initiation process; then they become part of the club. Has medicine changed? Most women physicians and medical students would probably say "Yes, to some degree." As more women join the profession, perhaps we will reach equity in leadership roles for women in the professional organizations governing physicians; such equity can only help change some of the attitudes and unwritten rules that challenge women who seek to practice medicine.

# CHAPTER 17

# Students with Disabilities

by Chris Rosa

Thanks to trailblazing efforts of physicians with disabilities and the opportunities created by the Americans with Disabilities Act, people with disabilities are applying to medical schools in greater numbers than ever before. This chapter will attempt to guide students with disabilities through the unique constellation of factors that impact their medical school decisions.

## ARE YOU READY?

The access-enhancing mandates of the Americans with Disabilities Act, coupled with the promise of assistive technology to provide greater access to curricula, offers people with disabilities greater opportunity than ever before to succeed in medical school. However, the decision to go to medical school and become a doctor involves committing to an intellectually, physically, and emotionally demanding course of study, including 4 years of rigorous medical school study and 3 to 12 years of equally demanding residency and fellowship. The decision involves a major commitment of time, financial resources, energy, and investment in the development of a professional sense of self. It is an enormous commitment for any individual, but especially for individuals with disabilities.

In choosing to go to medical school, people with disabilities not only commit the same personal resources that all students devote to the endeavor but must also realign all of the access resources they rely on for independence. This reallocation of independent-living resources to support study in medical school often significantly diminishes their quality of life in other domains.

If you are a candidate with disabilities and you are truly ready for a career in medicine, these sacrifices are surely worth it. However, in order to avoid regrettable decisions, you need to understand what it takes to be ready academically, logistically, physically, and emotionally for the rigors of medical school. You should then be willing to look at yourself critically and ask, "Am I really ready for this?"

## EXPLORING THE LIMITS OF REASONABLE ACCOMMODATIONS

Title II of the Americans with Disabilities Act guarantees curricular and programmatic access for individuals with disabilities in medical schools. The ADA requires that medical schools provide students with disabilities with the reasonable accommodations necessary for them to have equal access and opportunity to succeed in all aspects of the medical school experience. However, with this in mind, medical schools often require things of their students that may be difficult for some students with disabilities to accomplish, with or without reasonable accommodations. The current use of computers and other technologies in medical school instruction has certainly enhanced educational opportunities for students with physical disabilities; aspects of the curriculum that once could only be learned through physical manipulation can now be learned with the assistance of computers.

While the development of these technologies has certainly improved didactic instruction, there remain critical aspects of clinical instruction that still must be performed physically by the physicians themselves. For example, a machine cannot teach someone to perform an abdominal or breast examination. In fact, physicians are legally required to know what certain medical conditions actually feel like to an examining physician when making diagnoses. Similarly, the voluminous amount of reading and memorization invariably required by medical schools may pose difficulties for students with learning and other cognitive disabilities. These demands are important considerations when individuals with disabilities assess whether or not they are willing and able to meet the rigors of medical school.

# THE RIGHT STUFF: GETTING IN

Like all candidates for medical school, students with disabilities must meet the criteria for admission to the schools to which they apply. In constructing applicant profiles, people with disabilities should consider disability issues that will affect their presentation of self as candidates for admission.

## Undergraduate Performance

Candidate performance in undergraduate courses is one of the most significant factors in medical school admissions. Because the medical school admissions process is so competitive, good grades, especially in the courses required for admission, are important to your chances of getting in. If your undergraduate performance was affected by a disability issue (for example, an undergraduate institution's failure to adequately meet your needs for reasonable accommodation, or a learning disability that went undiagnosed throughout most of a college career), you might consider using other aspects of your candidate profile—your personal statement, letters of reference, and/or admissions committee interviews—to "explain away" a lower grade point average. While such disability-related explanations may improve your chances for admission, they often do so at the cost of disclosing your identity as a candidate with a disability.

## To Tell or Not to Tell: Disclosing a Disability

While your personal statement, letters of reference, MCAT scores, and interviews with admissions committees offer you the opportunity to demonstrate the richness of your background and strengths as an applicant, these dimensions of the candidate profile are fraught with opportunities for others to learn about your status as a candidate with a disability. If you are concerned about disability disclosure, these aspects of your candidate profile must be carefully managed. The following are some tips to successfully handle disability disclosure in the admissions process:

- The decision of whether or not to disclose a disability in a personal statement is a very difficult, very personal one. This decision pits people's pride in their disability identity against their concerns that lingering cultural biases against those who disclose their disabilities will cause them to be perceived as somehow less viable by admissions committees.

- Speak to those providing you with letters of reference and let them know how you feel about disability disclosure so that they do not unwittingly disclose information that you're uncomfortable with.

- If you are concerned with the implications of disability disclosure, don't volunteer any information about your disability during admissions interviews. Asking a question like "Do you have a disability?" is illegal in most admissions contexts. However, if you are asked such an inappropriate question during an interview, asserting your Americans with Disabilities Act right to confidentiality will probably not help your admissions chances. Instead, consider simply and honestly informing the interviewer that you have a disability that, with the necessary reasonable accommodations, in no way limits your ability to be successful in medical school. Answering such questions openly and honestly may actually help your interview performance by demonstrating a level of maturity and comfort around disability and illness issues that sets you apart from your peers.

---

### When in Doubt . . .

If you are at all concerned about disability disclosure, unless it is central to your personal statement's thesis or to your ability to explain a subpar undergraduate performance, follow this general rule: When in doubt, leave it out!

---

## Technical Standards

To standardize the technical requirements for admission to medical school, the AAMC in 1979 published *The Report of the Special Advisory Panel on Technical Standards for Medical School Admission*. As a result of this report, most medical schools have adopted a set of Technical Standards, described below, that the medical schools feel are necessary for a candidate to function independently as both a physician and a medical student:

I. Observation: The candidate must be able to actively attend and complete basic science courses. A candidate must be able to examine a patient thoroughly, using the senses of sight and touch, and enhanced by the senses of hearing and smell.

II. Communication: A candidate must be able to perceive both verbal and nonverbal communication when examining patients. Moreover, the candidate must be able to communicate effectively, in both oral and written form, with patients, patients' families, and other members of the medical team.

III. Motor: The candidate should have the ability to examine patients by percussion, auscultation, and other diagnostic procedures. The candidate should also be able to conduct motor activities necessary to deliver general care, to diagnose patients, and to participate in emergency medical care.

IV. Intellectual-Conceptual, Integrative, and Quantitative Abilities: The candidate's problem-solving capabilities must include measurement, calculation, reasoning, analysis, and synthesis. These abilities are required for the candidate to be able to understand medical histories or files, interpret key diagnostic data from individual patients, formulate a differential diagnosis, and remember information necessary for the delivery of adequate patient care. The candidate must possess good judgment and be able to incorporate new information when forming diagnostic and treatment plans.

## TAKING THE MCAT UNDER ACCOMMODATIVE CONDITIONS

The MCAT Program Office outlines a rather thorough process through which people with disabilities may request reasonable accommodations for the MCAT. To receive reasonable accommodations in the exam setting for the MCAT, a formal request for accommodations must be made to the MCAT Program Office no later than the registration receipt deadline. This formal request should be made as early as possible, since certain test centers may not be able to meet your accommodation needs; in addition, the MCAT Program Office may choose to consult with your physician or licensed professional to verify the nature of your accommodation needs. A formal request includes the following:

1. A letter from you that describes in detail your disability accommodation needs.
2. A letter, on office letterhead, from your physician or other specialist who is certified to diagnose and treat your disability. This letter should document the following:
   - A professional diagnosis of your disability (no more than three years old)
   - The treatment provided
   - The credentials of the physician or specialist in question
   - A detailed description of your limitations due to your disability
   - The last date of treatment or consultation
   - An explanation of the need for the requested accommodations

- A detailed statement from you, or documentation from an appropriate authority, regarding any recent testing accommodations provided in the college or university setting or secondary or primary school

If you have not received testing accommodations in the past, your letter should explain why you are requesting testing accommodations at this time (for example, the nature of your disability has changed, there is a specific feature of the MCAT exam format that necessitates accommodation, etc.).

3. If you require additional exam time, your letter should specify the exact amount of time needed and the disability-related basis for this request. Standard AAMC policy permits up to twice the normal testing time with the appropriate documentation.

4. For those with cognitive disabilities, documentation should include a neuropsychological or psychoeducational evaluation from a certified professional using reliable, valid, standardized, and age-appropriate tests. The diagnostician must provide a specific diagnosis and show evidence that alternative diagnoses can be ruled out.

For detailed instructions on the components of an accommodations request, see the AAMC website. It is important to consider that if your scores were earned under accommodative conditions, the fact that the exam was taken under accommodative conditions will be noted in your score report. Scores reported in this manner may serve as a red flag to admissions committee members, alerting them to your disability status. Even though reasonable exam accommodations do not provide testers with disabilities a distinct advantage over standard exam takers, this distinction may cause even the highest MCAT scores to be considered less valid. Thus, if you are concerned about the issues of disability disclosure, you should weigh the potential costs of disclosing your disability to admissions committees against the potential benefits of taking the exam in the most accessible setting.

---

**Red Flag**

If your score report shows that you took your MCAT exam under accommodative conditions, admissions committee members will be alerted to your disability status. If you do not wish to disclose your disability to them, beware of opting to take the test under these conditions.

---

## YOUR PREMED ADVISER: FRIEND OR FOE?

While most premed advisers are generally supportive of otherwise qualified students with disabilities, a small number have been reluctant to support the candidacy of individuals with disabilities. Premed advisers are extremely busy and may attempt to dissuade individuals who are not perceived as viable candidates from applying. If premed advisers have preconceived notions about the viability of qualified individuals with disabilities as candidates for medical school, they may, knowingly or unwittingly, attempt to weed out people with disabilities from the applicant pool.

If you are otherwise qualified for admission, have realistically determined that you are able to meet the physical and intellectual demands of medical school, and are still getting resistance from your premed adviser, you may consider asking your college's coordinator for services for students with disabilities or ADA compliance officer to intervene on your behalf. Your alternative is to go it alone, without the full support of your premed office.

## EVALUATING MEDICAL SCHOOLS

Once you have taken the necessary steps to ensure that you are prepared for medical school and have sufficiently honed your candidate profile, you are ready to make a list of factors to consider when evaluating your fit with a medical school. Besides the factors covered in this book that pertain to all prospective medical school candidates, the following are some issues of particular relevance to candidates with disabilities.

### Home or Away?

Limiting their choices of medical schools to those available locally offers medical students with disabilities the opportunity to draw upon the support of a familiar network of resources to meet the very rigorous demands of medical study. However, by limiting your choices in this manner, you might exclude yourself from programs in other regions that would represent a better fit for you academically and professionally. What's more, given the keen competition in the medical school admissions process, limiting your choices in any way may ultimately hurt your chances of getting into any medical school.

## Sunbelt or Snowbelt?

There are distinctive benefits for people with disabilities to attend medical school in different regions of the country. For example, medical students have found that when they have moved to the Northeast and Midwest, they often enjoy a comparatively higher rate of disability benefits than those available in many Southern and Western states. They also often find that medical schools located in Northeastern and Midwestern cities are more likely to be located near accessible mass transit than many Southern and Western cities. However, medical schools in the Northeast and Midwest are also frequently situated in cold and snowy climates and on hilly terrain that tends to undermine access for individuals with physical disabilities. Schools in the South and West are more likely to have newer, more accessible facilities; to be situated in places that are warm, flat, and dry; and to be near off-campus accessible housing units than those in the Northeast and Midwest.

## Traditional or Problem-Based Curriculum?

Students with learning disabilities may find that the applied problem-based approach to learning makes the medical school curriculum much more accessible to them than traditional discipline-based or system-based learning approaches. Indeed, the problem-based curriculum's emphasis on collaborative learning among colleagues and self-study techniques is often much more amenable to the education of students with learning disabilities than are the high-pressure atmosphere and didactic emphasis of the traditional approach. However, the drawback to choosing a school featuring the problem-based curriculum for students with learning disabilities is that such students may need additional instruction and direction in study in order to pass the first part of the national boards.

## Undergraduate Institutional Affiliation

Medical schools affiliated with undergraduate institutions offer medical students the advantage of utilizing these institutions' comparatively vast access-providing resources in order to gain equal access to all aspects of medical student life. These undergraduate institutions often have offices of services for students with disabilities that can assist in working out the logistics of curricular accommodations and reasonable academic adjustments, auxiliary aids and services (including personal assistance services and sign-language interpreter services), and accessible housing.

# ASSESSING ACCESSIBILITY

Once you've narrowed the field and have a short list of medical schools you're interested in, you'll have to make some tough choices. But before doing that, there's more work to be done. Here are the main factors to consider in judging how accessible your target schools are to people with disabilities.

## Physical Access

The architectural and technological accessibility of medical schools should play a significant role in your evaluation of these programs. The following questions will help you to evaluate the physical accessibility of a school:

- What is the campus terrain like? Is it hilly or flat?
- What is the campus infrastructure like? Are walkways and roadways well-paved or littered with cracks and potholes?
- Are all the buildings accessible to students with mobility-related disabilities? If not, what is the school's policy regarding moving classes and other student activities to accessible sites?
- Are the medical school's laboratory facilities and technologies accessible?
- How accessible is the medical library?
- Are the assistive technologies that you need available?
- Are the academic computing facilities accessible to students with disabilities?
- How accessible is the teaching hospital where you'll be doing your clinical rotations? Is accessible mass transportation available? Does the hospital have the necessary assistive technologies that you'll need to work there effectively?

## Programmatic Access

For all students with disabilities, but particularly for students with learning, sensory, and psychiatric disabilities, the programmatic accessibility of medical schools will significantly affect their choice of schools. When assessing the programmatic access of medical schools and their programs, keep the following questions in mind:

- Most medical schools demand large volumes of assigned and unassigned reading. What are the institution's policies regarding the provision of reading and other course materials in accessible formats?

- What are the institution's policies on the provision of reader, note taker, and sign-language interpreter services?
- What are the institution's policies on accommodative testing?
- Where does the institution keep confidential student disability documentation? It should not store such records in your medical school student files. This file is a quasiprofessional one to which faculty may have access; it is not appropriate for disability documentation to be kept in this file.
- Who has been designated by the medical school to provide reasonable accommodations to medical students with disabilities? In undergraduate institution–affiliated medical schools, is it the office of services for students with disabilities? Is it a member of the medical school's administration or a faculty member? The individual or entity responsible will serve as a key resource in students with disabilities' efforts to succeed in medical school.

---

**See It for Yourself**

The best way to get a feel for how accessible and welcoming a medical school really is to students with disabilities is to visit the school and to speak with faculty, administration, and students with and without disabilities.

---

## Accessible Alternatives

While the physical demands of internal medicine may pose significant barriers to prospective physicians with disabilities, other areas of specialization—such as radiology, psychiatry, pathology, microbiology, pharmacology, medical administration, and public health administration—may be more accessible to doctors with physical disabilities.

## DOCTORS WITH DISABILITIES: PEERS OR PATIENTS?

Because of the impact of the Americans with Disabilities Act and the stereotype-shattering progress of doctors with disabilities, the medical profession has generally become more accepting of people with disabilities in its ranks. However, according to some doctors with disabilities, there are still significant pockets of resistance. According to one doctor, a physician with a disability confounds traditional roles of doctor and patient: He or she challenges some essential elements of the doctor-patient relationship. To some, doctors with disabilities look like patients; some physicians treat doctors with disabilities like patients rather than peers. This physician further suggests that this differential perception of doctors with disabilities is institutionalized within the medical profession through "Committees for Physicians with Physical Limitations" that exist in several states' medical boards and that serve to marginalize physicians with disabilities as a class. While not all doctors with disabilities share this perception, this cultural dimension is helpful in understanding some of the barriers candidates with disabilities may face.

Despite the obstacles that they may encounter, individuals with disabilities often bring unique insight to the role of physician. They offer firsthand experience of living with disability and illness, which may help them to build a better rapport with their patients and enable them to explain the implications of illness and medical interventions in very real terms.

# CHAPTER 18

# Lesbian and Gay Students

## by Allen Maniker, MD

As a gay or lesbian person in medicine, you can be sure that there are many contributions you can make to caring for the health of the population. Nonetheless, homophobia is a fact of life that you may encounter during your medical education and career. As much as you might view physicians as enlightened individuals, there still exist physicians and other health practitioners who disdain, or even hate, people with a sexual orientation different from their own. People with these prejudices may end up being your classmates, your teachers, or your patients.

Throughout the course of your medical education, as well as your career, you will be called upon to assess the source and target of any biases you encounter and to find appropriate responses to them. In any given situation, you'll have to consider factors such as care of and consideration for your patients, damage to your career, compromise of your political standing, and insult to your sense of justice. You may feel so strongly offended that you are willing to pursue official redress for some comment or action, or you may just not feel like fighting on that day. The choices will not always be easy, and each individual must decide for himself or herself how to handle each particular situation—there are no right or wrong answers.

On the other hand, the gay and lesbian community has made enormous strides in the last 15 years toward acceptance and understanding by the larger heterosexual community. You may be pleasantly surprised at the acceptance and the "nonevent" that coming out and being openly gay or lesbian may be, even in such traditionally conservative professions as medicine. The advent of AIDS made the gay and lesbian community much more visible to the medical community, and subsequently, reactions to homosexuals and their particular medical issues have changed significantly. Situations that you might have encountered in 1981, at the start of the AIDS epidemic, are very different from those you might face now.

## GAY-FRIENDLY SCHOOLS

While there are medical schools that may be more "gay friendly" than others, it's not likely that you'll be able to identify them during the interview or overall admissions process. In large urban areas where familiarity with openly gay people is greater, you may find the environment more open and therefore more comfortable. Schools in cities with large gay populations, such as San Francisco or New York, may have even greater outreach to gay and lesbian students. On the other hand, medical schools with religious affiliations may look less favorably on gay and lesbian students, although this, too, is not a given. Yet whatever the location or affiliation, medical schools and academic medical institutions are composed of so many people that the attitude toward gay and lesbian students might differ vastly from one part of the hospital or school to another. All in all, although being open with your fellow students and teachers is nice and even desirable during what will be a stressful period of your life, most gay students don't make finding a "gay-friendly" school a major objective in their choice of schools.

---

**Out or Not?**

Unless you choose to talk about it, your sexual orientation should not be a topic of discussion during your med school interview.

---

## THE INTERVIEW

A school's policy toward sexual orientation in general, and your orientation in particular, should not come up during the interview process unless you as the applicant make it a topic of discussion. Whether you take a direct approach or one that's more discreet is up to you, based on your personal views and the "vibe" in the interview room. Unless you are very sure of your footing, the wisdom of bringing up your sexual orientation is questionable, since doing so risks alienating the interviewer. While taking a less confrontational approach or avoiding the issue completely may compromise your "out and proud" feelings, at the end of the day, the goal is to gain acceptance into medical school and become a physician. This should be your major focus during an admission interview.

There are approaches that can clue you in to a school's policies and attitudes without risking an unfavorable reaction from the interviewer. Before the interview, you should visit the school's website or ask for a student handbook regarding curriculum and policy. Then do the following:

- Check to see if the school has a nondiscrimination policy or provides domestic partner benefits.
- Find out if the school has a human sexuality program in the curriculum. One that does may be more committed to presenting a balanced picture of the range of human sexual expression and may encourage tolerance.
- Take a walk around the campus and observe the other students and their surroundings. Do these look like students with whom you would want to spend time? Could you be comfortable with them in a working environment? Does the whole atmosphere of the institution make you comfortable? You may want to sit in on a class or two to see firsthand the interactions between students and between students and teachers.

## THE MEDICAL SCHOOL EXPERIENCE

Once in medical school, your opportunities for being more open are greater and more in your control. At your school, there may be a group of gay and lesbian students who participate in an organization such as Lesbian, Gay, Bisexual, and Transgender People in Medicine (LGBPTM), which is sponsored by the American Medical Student Association. The Gay and Lesbian Medical Association (GLMA), which publishes *The Journal of the Gay and Lesbian Medical Association,* also has chapters at many medical schools. Organizations like this provide social life, support, and advocacy, but they may maintain a very low profile. If there's no such organization at the school you'll be attending, you may want to consider forming one. The Office of Student Affairs in your school may be able to advise you on how to initiate such a group.

You'll also find in medical school that certain subspecialties may be more gay friendly than others. For example, psychiatry has a tradition of openness toward gay and lesbian people, while surgery and its subspecialties tend to be less accepting. Chalk it up to the "macho man" image of surgeons; nonetheless, this intolerance persists, and one should be prepared accordingly. Intolerance by other physicians should not by any means deter you from pursuing any area of medicine.

While you're in med school, you may be subjected to homophobic comments, both overt and covert. Depending on the seriousness of the comment and the situation in which it is presented, you may choose to confront the offender or educate or ignore him or her. Often, educating offenders is more fruitful than confronting them, since they might not even be aware that they've said something offensive. If a student or faculty member's comments begin to interfere with your work or education, you should consider taking official recourse through the Dean of Student Affairs or ombudsperson.

It's more difficult to deal with homophobia on the part of patients. While it should rarely, if ever, become an issue, you should always maintain a professional attitude in dealing with patients and try to avoid confrontation. Many times a disease process may cause inappropriate behavior or disinhibition. An offensive comment may be a result of a disease process, so to confront a patient would not only be unproductive but also inappropriate. Considering this, it's better just to walk away from an offensive patient. If you feel that taking care of a particular patient is really intolerable, you can always speak with your resident or faculty member and ask to be assigned to another patient. But remember that your patients' health concerns must remain the primary focus.

## RESIDENCY AND BEYOND

Pursuing a specialty requires a residency position and therefore another round of interviews. As with medical school interviews, your approach to the interview must be individualized. Keep your eye on the goal of obtaining training in the specialty of your choice in a location or institution that you desire.

As you progress along the course of becoming a physician, the freedom you'll have for individual expression will become much greater. Once you are an attending physician or faculty member, your decisions regarding your openness about your sexual orientation will be more your own and less dictated by the fear of alienating someone else. Even though medicine is one of the most conservative professions, it is certainly possible to be "out and proud" and maintain a productive and fulfilling professional life. Becoming a physician entails a long, arduous, but ultimately very satisfying journey, and it is one that is most definitely inclusive of gay and lesbian people.

# PART SIX

# Financing Your Degree

# CHAPTER 19

# Figuring Out Costs

By almost anyone's standards, a medical school education is expensive: The total cost can exceed $250,000. The cost is high for a couple of reasons. First, the number of faculty members at medical schools is often two to three times the number of students. Second, faculty members command generous salaries from universities, which must compete with the incomes physicians would make in private practice. Third, schools must budget for state-of-the-art equipment and facilities to provide you with the quality of education you need to enter the field.

Although the costs of a medical education are daunting, don't despair. If you can demonstrate the determination it takes to make it past the hurdles of being admitted to medical school, financing your education should not stand in your way. Financial planning now will mean greater freedom to make choices about the many financial decisions that will follow medical school.

## TRUE COSTS

The first step in charting a financial path is knowing what all of the real costs are. Only then can you develop a strategy for meeting them.

## Tuition and Fees

The most natural place to start assessing medical school costs is by looking at tuition and fees. Be aware that these will probably go up by approximately 5 percent each year. If you're still an undergrad, you'll also need to factor in the years until you graduate plus your four years in medical school when estimating the tuition and fee increases.

> **Going Up . . .**
>
> Expect medical school tuition and fees to rise by about 5 percent each year!

Tuition and fees vary widely from region to region and between public and private institutions. For example, at the public University of North Carolina, annual tuition/fees for in-state residents were $19,499 in 2013–2014. But at the University of Vermont, also public, tuition/fees for in-state residents were $32,897. For private schools, a first-year student could pay $45,502 annually at Howard University or $53,186 at Boston University.

### Public Schools and Residency

Public colleges are almost always less expensive if you are a resident of the state they are located in because the costs are partially subsidized by state tax revenue. However, attractive low rates for residents may mean that admissions standards are more competitive.

If you are a nonresident of the state, very often the added tuition will make your bill look much like that of most private schools. Out-of-state med students at the low-cost University of North Carolina, for example, pay $46,378 in tuition and fees. And out-of-state students at the University of Vermont pay a whopping $56,117 just for tuition and fees! That's more than most private colleges.

### Residency Requirements

While residency requirements vary from state to state, you may be able to gain residency status by living in the state for a year preceding your attendance at the school. But if you're planning to attend as a resident of a public institution outside your current state, make sure you check the residency requirements carefully. The time it takes to establish residency, varies tremendously from state to state. In general, though, to establish residency, you'll need to show evidence such as a state driver's license, a state voter registration card, proof that you paid taxes in the state in the prior year, or even a utility bill that establishes the date you began living in the state. Check with the staff of the medical school itself or with your premed adviser for specifics.

# THE BUDGET

Tuition and fee costs are not the only considerations in the final price tag for medical school. Two other factors can make an institution with low or moderate tuition into a high-ticket item. In assessing total costs, you need to consider the following:

- Total budget
- How much scholarship, fellowship, and grant money you receive

## What It Includes

Calculated by the school's financial aid office, the total budget includes all of the standard required costs associated with spending an academic year at the medical school. In addition to tuition and fees, the standard student budget may include costs for the following:

- Books and supplies
- Room and board
- Transportation (car maintenance or public transit)
- Miscellaneous personal expenses
- Equipment purchases (stethoscope, otoscope, ophthalmoscope, etc.)
- Medical exams
- Licensing exams
- Curriculum-related travel
- Computer and/or tablet (required by most schools)

Budgets, like expenses, vary depending on your year in school. The budgets published by financial aid offices are well researched and based on real or surveyed costs. When financial aid administrators develop the budget, they try to create one that is modest enough to prevent students from overborrowing and yet adequate enough to recognize realistic costs.

Two points are especially important to remember about the budget.

**Average Costs.** Most of the indirect (or discretionary) components of the budget—such as living costs, transportation, and miscellaneous personal expenses—are average costs based on the specific locale of the school and the particular costs of the students at that school. The concept of "average costs" in a budget is important for two reasons.

First, it lets you know what a full year of costs are for the average student and gives you some guidelines for what to expect for expenses such as rent and food in that area. Second, because it is an average, it provides you with a benchmark against which to gauge and work your individual expenses.

**Financial Aid Awards.** The budget is a financial aid budget. It is constructed by the financial aid office and is used to make financial aid awards. Whether you apply for aid or not, you can use these average costs to work out a budget from which you can estimate your monthly projected expenses.

## What's Not in the Budget

Although the budget is created by each school's financial aid office, it is also governed by federal regulations. There are a number of items that the government does not allow a school to include.

**Family Expenses.** The budget can include only costs for the student, not for the student's spouse/partner or children. (It can, however, include childcare expenses.)

**Optional Equipment.** The budget can't include equipment costs (for the purchase of surgical instruments, let's say) unless the equipment is required for all medical students, in the school or in a specific program within the school.

**Car Purchase.** Budgets can't be adjusted for the purchase of a car, even though a car may be required at some point in the program in order for you to travel to clerkships or internships.

**Relocation.** Unless you have the good fortune to attend a medical school in the place you currently live, you will have relocation expenses. Since expenses that are incurred before your actual enrollment can't be considered as educational expenses for the purpose of creating a financial aid budget, your moving costs will be completely your responsibility. Moving across the country can add thousands of dollars to your first-year expenses; these costs cannot be covered with financial aid.

**Debt.** Consumer indebtedness is another source of anguish for students who have lingering balances on credit cards from their pre-medical-school lives. Consumer debts are often the most expensive debts around, especially from credit cards. If at all possible, pay off what you can before you start medical school.

**Residency Interviews.** Even though these interviews normally occur within the fourth year of your program, they are actually related to activity after your enrollment. This means that these costs cannot be included in a financial aid budget and must be planned for separately. (There are special loan programs administered outside the financial aid office that will provide funds for this expense.)

Beyond those kinds of specifics, aid administrators may also limit or expand budgets in particular ways based on their experience with students at your school. If, for example, your school is located in an urban area with good public transportation, the transportation component of your budget may be based on the assumption that you will use public transportation, which may be significantly less expensive than maintaining your own car. If the school has sufficient on-campus housing, the basic budget may assume that all students will live on campus.

In high-cost urban areas such as New York, Washington, DC, Boston, San Francisco, and Los Angeles, the living component of your budget may assume you share housing if you're single.

## COMPARING MEDICAL SCHOOL COSTS

Once you understand the basics of what costs are involved in medical school, you can start to make comparisons between what you will actually have to pay to attend particular schools.

Try to calculate what you may be allowed for monthly living and other nondirect costs at the medical schools you're considering. Subtract the tuition, fees, books, and supplies from the total and divide by the number of months in the academic year (usually nine). This figure can help you estimate what the financial aid office may determine to be a modest monthly allowance for living while attending the school.

## NEXT STEPS: CALCULATING AID

Once you've figured your costs, the next step is to determine how much funding a school may provide in scholarship and grant aid. The real issue is not the actual cost but how much you are going to have to pay. Although private medical schools may seem prohibitive because of hefty tuition charges, some private institutions have endowed awards in the form of grants, scholarships, and low-interest loans. These awards offset their higher costs.

Some medical schools will publish the maximum amount of grant and scholarship funding in their financial aid handbook. Of course, your particular financial circumstances will determine the amount you're awarded. In chapters 20, 21, and 22, we'll detail the financial aid process as a whole and discuss eligibility for various programs, as well as how to apply for each.

# CHAPTER 20

# Applying for Financial Aid

Financial aid application procedures can vary more from school to school than do the procedures for admissions. This chapter will outline the general application requirements and discuss some of the documentation required.

## GET THE FORMS!

The first step: Get the admissions materials and read them thoroughly. Usually, general financial aid information, including the financial aid deadlines, appear in this application. These deadlines drive the rest of the process for you. The admissions application deadline may be earlier or later than the financial aid application deadline. In addition, sometimes there is more than one financial aid deadline. In the case of multiple financial aid deadlines, the first one may be for students interested in scholarship and fellowship assistance. A later deadline may be set for those students who are only interested in federal loans.

### Key Materials

The most common financial aid application is the Free Application for Federal Student Aid (FAFSA).

### FAFSA

The FAFSA form is always required to request any federal financial aid. This form is used for "need analysis," the calculation of what you should be able to contribute toward the cost of your education. The detailed financial information you provide on the FAFSA form is then run through a federal formula to arrive at a contribution figure. The calculations are explained in detail later in this chapter.

You may apply for federal financial aid using the FAFSA on the Web. To do so, go to the US Department of Education website at www.fafsa.ed.gov and follow the step-by-step directions. Carefully read the major sections, "Before Beginning a FAFSA," "Filling out a FAFSA," and "FAFSA Follow-up." Everything you need to know about the electronic FAFSA is explained here. Although you may still complete a paper FAFSA, the online process is far more efficient and less time-consuming.

### Additional Forms

Many medical schools are not satisfied with the information you report on the FAFSA when it comes to determining your eligibility for the school's own money. They want to know more about you and your family's financial situation, and they will ask you to fill out a separate application. Contact the school's financial aid office to determine if such a form is required.

In addition to the above, required forms may include (but are not limited to) the following:

- Separate school financial aid application
- Your prior year's IRS 1040 forms
- Divorced/separated parent statement
- Verification of number of family members in college
- Scholarship and outside award documentation
- Federal verification form

Since some financial aid application deadlines are earlier than April 15, you may not have completed your federal tax form before the deadline. Most schools recommend that you estimate the numbers and then correct them once you get your taxes filed. Others want you to wait until you have all the actual numbers. Read the school's financial aid application or check with its financial aid office to find out the policy about estimating tax figures.

Even though you should be careful on your financial aid application forms, don't work yourself into a panic about them. Mistakes happen, and financial aid officers don't expect you to be perfect. It's usually better to estimate a number than to miss a deadline while you're trying to verify it. You can always submit the actual figure to the financial aid officer when you have completed your tax form.

## FORMS: ROUND TWO

Once you've submitted all the required forms, you may have to wait a while before anything else happens regarding your financial aid. The amount of waiting time will depend on the time of year the forms are submitted, the types of forms required, and the specific application procedures at each medical school.

Meanwhile, the federal processor, a number-crunching center for the government, is crunching away on the information you provided on your FAFSA. Its calculations result in a determination of how much you will be expected to contribute toward your educational expenses for the upcoming school year. Depending on how you submit and process your FAFSA, you will receive either a Student Aid Report (SAR) in the mail or a SAR Information Acknowledgement if you applied electronically. Follow instructions on the SAR or on the FAFSA website carefully.

Remember, if you need money to attend school, it is just as important to stay on top of the process of applying for financial aid as it is to manage all the steps required for getting admitted.

## CALCULATING YOUR NEED

The calculation of how much a student (and family) can contribute toward medical school always seems the most incomprehensible part of the financial aid process. However, it is actually quite straightforward once you know the guidelines and rules.

### Basic Guidelines

The first concept to understand is financial need. Think of it as simple subtraction:

Cost of Attendance – Family Contribution = Financial Need

As we discussed previously, the cost of attendance is determined by the school and consists of the tuition and fees, room and board, books and supplies, transportation, and personal expenses. The family contribution is determined through use of a federal formula called *Federal Methodology* (FM). The FAFSA form that you file gives enough information to the federal processor to run your figures through this formula and produce a family contribution. The federal processor is a selected firm under US government contract that uses the methodology approved by Congress to calculate your contribution.

## Dependent or Independent?

For all programs that receive funding through the US Department of Education, all medical students are considered independent. This means that your parents' financial information is not used in determining your *Expected Family Contribution* (EFC) and is not used to determine your "need" for federal programs offered by the US Department of Education

However, for some programs funded by the US Department of Health and Human Services, and for many institutional funds, students are considered dependent. This means no matter how old you are or how many years it's been since your parents contributed to your support, or even whether or not you have a family of your own, your parents' income and asset information will be required to determine your EFC and need for those programs. In some cases, even information about a natural parent who has been absent for most of your life or your stepparents' financial data may be required.

---

**Federal Methodology (FM)**

A need-analysis method developed by Congress is used to calculate the Family Contribution (FC). The FM determines eligibility for federal student aid programs.

---

Many medical schools do, however, allow students the option of not providing parental information on the application. At first blush, this may seem like a viable alternative. But beware! Many medical schools award their institutional grant, scholarship, and low-interest loan funds based on both student and parental financial information. Before you opt for supplying just your own information as an independent student, find out what you'll be missing out on. For some schools, especially those in the highest price categories, institutional awards may be significant.

## What's Considered

Some of the components reviewed in assessing the federal Expected Family Contribution for an independent student include the following:

- Total family income from the previous calendar year (base-year income)
- Net value of any assets (excluding home equity)
- Taxes paid (federal, state, and local)
- Asset protection allowance
- Number of family members
- Social Security tax allowance
- Income protection allowance

Before you start calculating, you need to understand the components listed above and why they are used in the Federal Methodology.

**Base-Year Income.** The formula in Federal Methodology requires the use of the prior calendar-year income to determine your contribution. This means that if you enroll in fall 2014, you will be asked to provide your calendar-year 2013 income. For the majority of the population, the best predictor of current-year income is prior-year income.

> **Family Affairs**
>
> Federal health-professions programs for which you will be considered dependent are as follows:
>
> - Scholarships for Disadvantaged Students (SDS)
> - Loans for Disadvantaged Students (LDS)
> - Primary Care Loans (PCL)

**Income-Protection Allowance (IPA).** This allowance provides for basic living expenses not included in the standard student expense budget. It will vary according to the number of family members and the number in college at least half-time.

**Asset-Protection Allowance.** The formula includes an allowance for protection of assets depending on your age. This means that a portion of your assets will not be considered in the calculation because they are protected for purposes other than education, such as emergencies or retirement. The older you are, the more your assets are protected.

> **Independence**
>
> Programs for which you are automatically considered independent are as follows:
>
> - Federal Stafford Loans
> - William T. Ford Direct Loans
> - Federal Perkins Loans
> - Federal Work-Study

**Social Security Tax Allowance.** The calculation of Social Security tax is based on existing federal rates applied to income earned from work and may never be less than zero.

## FEDERAL METHODOLOGY (FM)

The formula used in need analysis to determine an applicant's eligibility for most federal financial aid programs has been written into law by the US Congress. Congress reviews this formula every several years and recommends changes to it. The federal formula was established to set objective standards that would be uniformly applied to all applicants.

Broadly, FM takes the income that is received by the members of the student's household, subtracts the taxes paid and the cost of maintaining the members of the family other than the student, adds in a portion of the assets, and then takes a percentage of the result to produce a family contribution. Although this formula may not take into account all aspects of an individual student's situation, it produces generally comparable data on all students applying for financial aid.

## APPLICATION RESULTS

Once the financial aid office has all the forms and data that it needs, it will often wait for the admissions decision before reviewing your application. During this waiting period, it's a good idea to check with the schools to make sure that everything is complete and ready for processing once the admissions decision has been made.

When the financial aid office finds out that you have been accepted, it will make an offer of financial aid. This offer is called a financial aid package. The financial aid package may include scholarships and grants, a Federal Perkins Loan, a Federal Stafford or a Federal Direct Loan, and private loans.

Now you need to review the financial aid packages and decide where you'll attend school. Your choice may not be the school that offered you the largest scholarship. You need to weigh the merits of the financial aid package against the desirability of the school itself.

You need to look at more than just the amount of scholarship funds included in the financial aid package:

- What is your contribution expected to be?
- How much will you be expected to borrow?
- What kinds of loans are offered? Do they feature attractive rates and repayment terms?
- Will you have to work while you are attending school (if allowed by the school)?

> **My Heart Was Set**
>
> A top med school and a lesser-known school may accept you. What do you do? Many applicants have their heart set on going to top-flight schools but accept offers from others that are more generous with their aid packages. Be prepared to weigh all offers based on many factors—including cost.

You should answer these questions before you make your admissions decision.

## NEXT STEPS

To make an informed decision regarding the value of the financial aid package, you need to understand all the awards being offered. Chapters 21 and 22 will explain the various programs in detail, starting with "free" money—grants and scholarships.

# CHAPTER 21

# Finding Free Money

It's every student's dream: Getting "free money"—money you don't have to pay back—to pay for your medical school education. Free money can come from a variety of sources, including federal and state governments, schools themselves, and private donors.

## FEDERAL FUNDS

Both the US Department of Education and the Department of Health and Human Services allocate funds yearly for medical education. For some programs, participating schools also contribute money. Eligibility for federal programs is based on financial need, as well as other factors.

### Scholarships for Disadvantaged Students (SDS)

This scholarship is awarded to full-time, financially needy students from disadvantaged backgrounds enrolled in health-professions programs. For more information on the definitions of "financial need" and "disadvantaged" for this specific program, contact the financial aid office.

Scholarships may not exceed the cost of attendance—that is, tuition, reasonable educational expenses, and reasonable living expenses.

## STATE FUNDS

Some states have grant programs, often based on financial need as well as other criteria such as state residency, that are available to medical students. You should contact the financial aid office to determine if such programs exist in your state.

## INSTITUTIONAL FUNDS

Some medical schools to which you apply will have a pool of funding they call institutional grants or scholarships. While some of this funding may be reserved for awards made strictly on the basis of merit, for the most part, this is the money schools direct toward students based on need in order to equalize grant and loan awards. Other than the small pot administered through the Department of Health and Human Services that is designated for students with need from disadvantaged backgrounds, these are the only "free money" types of aid the institution has discretion in awarding. And you can bet the aid office goes through some pretty amazing calculations to determine who receives these funds.

Some schools use grants or scholarships to reduce or "discount" the amount of tuition students with high need must pay. Others aim to provide a certain level of grant aid for all applicants. Still others award grants as a way of filling the gap after certain other types of aid are awarded. Parental information may be required to determine eligibility for institutional grants and scholarships, and it will be evaluated carefully before awards are made from these funds.

Most medical schools also have scholarships that are awarded from endowed funds donated by an individual or organization and named for an individual. These are also free dollars. Often they are awarded based on the donor's eligibility criteria and can require some form of communication with the donor. The aid office will often let you know if any of these programs are appropriate for you.

Awards can range from hundreds to thousands of dollars. Each dollar you receive as a grant or scholarship from these sources could equal at least two dollars you won't have to repay to a loan program.

# SCHOLARSHIPS FOR SERVICE

Service awards are not exactly "free money": You've got to give back what you get, although not exactly in kind. These programs provide scholarships for students who are willing to practice for a given amount of time in an underserved area, with a particular population.

## National Health Service Corps (NHSC)

The National Health Service Corps provides scholarships to individuals interested in practicing in primary care professions. It also has a loan repayment program for medical students who decide to practice at an approved NHSC Loan Repayment Service Site.

Priority for funds is given to prior NHSC scholarship recipients, to prior recipients of Exceptional Financial Need Scholarships, to students from rural backgrounds who want to return to practice in underserved rural areas, and to applicants who participated in or would have been eligible to participate in federal programs for disadvantaged students.

NHSC scholarships pay full tuition and fees plus a monthly stipend. Recipients are required to practice in federally designated Health Manpower Shortage Areas one year for each year of support they receive from NHSC. (The minimum service period is two years.)

## Armed Forces Health Professions Scholarships

These programs require an application directly to the service branch of the Army, Navy, or Air Force.

While still in school, medical students are required to spend 45 days on active duty training in a hospital with pay, as well as housing and food allowances. Recipients are also required to serve one year of active duty as medical officers (after completing their residencies) for each year of program funding received. Three years of active-duty service is the minimum required. Separate programs with different benefits and service requirements are offered through the Army National Guard.

Scholarships pay tuition, fees, and medical insurance, as well as a monthly stipend. These scholarships also provide reimbursement for books and equipment costs. Because the funding basically covers most educational costs, you may not qualify for other need-based aid. Since these programs are very competitive, if you're applying for an Armed Forces scholarship, you should also apply for financial aid as a contingency.

## Scholarships for Native Americans

These scholarships are available only for Native American and Native Alaskan students. Preference is given to applicants who provide documentation of tribal membership as children or grandchildren of tribal members. Scholarship recipients have a service obligation of two years minimum.

### Award Amount

Students are provided tuition, fees, selected incidentals, tutorial services, equipment, and a monthly stipend. For more information, contact the Indian Health Service Scholarship Program by phoning (301) 443-6394 or going to their website at www. ihs.gov/scholarship.

## PRIVATE-DONOR FUNDING

There are private scholarships, fellowships, and grants for medical school funded by individuals, corporations, and civic or charitable organizations. Beyond being designated for medical students, these gifts are usually specific to the individual characteristics of the student. Eligibility may be based on any of the following:

- County of residence
- College attendance
- Ethnicity
- Gender
- Religious affiliation
- Practice specialty

Make sure you leave yourself with enough lead time (preferably a year) to do research, obtain applications, and complete them by the published deadlines. The trick is to manage the information gathering and application completion, since these scholarships don't have any coordinated deadlines.

## Scholarship Search Services

You've probably seen ads for scholarship search services in the newspaper. These services often charge you a fee to access a database that contains information also contained in grant and scholarship directories.

The search service has you complete an application providing specific information about yourself, which is then fed into the database to find potential scholarships based on your specific characteristics.

## Using the Internet

Surfing the Internet can be a convenient way of looking for money. Although you may have to spend lots of your time searching here, you won't have to shell out any bucks. Since websites are constantly being added and deleted, you may find new sites when you search.

### Search Service Scams

Many students who subscribe to scholarship search services are disappointed with the results. Often the services provide obvious sources. In addition, waiting for the results often means wasting valuable time you could have spent researching for yourself. Be wary of potentially fraudulent scholarship search services.

Keep in mind that these "free" scholarship searches will be useful only if someone is maintaining the database. And, perhaps more important, you still have to apply for the funds. You may have 100 potential sources of private aid. For each, you'll probably have to complete a detailed application and possibly write an essay. Before you actually spend the time applying, check to see that the award amount is commensurate with the time you have to put into applying.

# CHAPTER 22

# Borrowing the Money

Student loans are an important source of support for medical students. Medical schools expect the majority of students with financial need to borrow at least part of their educational costs; you should research loan possibilities early in the aid application process. This chapter provides you with the information you need to decide which loan programs fit your particular situation.

It may take many weeks from the date you applied to receive the loan proceeds, so planning is essential. Also, since the rules and regulations for borrowing through each of these programs differ, you should read each section carefully.

> **Huge Debt Loads**
>
> With tuition at big-name schools now exceeding $50,000 a year, six-figure debt loads have become appallingly commonplace.

## FEDERAL LOAN PROGRAMS

The two federal loan programs available to medical students are generally considered the core loan programs, since they carry certain attractive features defined by law. These features include a low interest rate, low fees, and defined deferment provisions. The two programs are as follows:

- Federal Stafford Student Loan Program (part of the Federal Family Education Loan Program)
- William D. Ford Federal Direct Student Loan Program

The terms of these two loan programs are similar. The eligibility criteria, interest rates, grace period, deferment and cancellation provisions, and other terms are all basically the same. There are, however, some minor differences in the application process and repayment options.

The key difference lies in who provides the loan funds. The Federal Stafford Student Loan is part of the Federal Family Education Loan Program (FFELP), through which loans are made by a private lender (such as a bank, a savings and loan association, or a credit union) and are insured by a state or private guarantee agency sponsored by the federal government. Under the William D. Ford Federal Direct Student Loan Program, the federal government is the lender.

---

**Taxing Details**

Schools may require you to submit additional documentation such as your most recent federal tax form.

---

Most schools participate in the Stafford program, but only some participate in the Ford Direct program. The school you attend will determine which of these two loans you can apply for.

Eligibility for either of these programs is the same. You must meet all of the following criteria:

- Be a citizen, permanent resident, or eligible noncitizen of the United States
- Be enrolled at least half-time
- Be in good academic standing, making satisfactory progress toward the degree (as defined by the school)
- Not be in default of any previous loans without being in an approved repayment program
- Show financial need based on the information provided on your FAFSA in order to qualify for the interest subsidy

## Federal Stafford Student Loans

The Federal Stafford Student Loan Program is an unsubsidized loan. You may defer payments of principal and interest until you graduate or drop below half-time enrollment. Depending on when you first borrowed, there's a grace period of six or nine months before you'll have to start repayment.

The Federal Stafford Loan Program evolved from the Guaranteed Student Loan Program (GSL). The concept of a federal loan program originated in 1965 with the Federally Insured Student Loan Program (FISL). The Federal Stafford Loan Program has the same purpose as these previous financial aid programs—to make loan funds available for students to attend postsecondary school—but the amounts available, interest rates, and deferment provisions have been modified.

### Borrowing Limits

The Federal Unsubsidized Stafford Loan Program allows an eligible medical student to borrow his or her demonstrated need, up to $40,500 per year. The total cumulative maximum is $224,000 (including the Federal Subsidized Stafford Loan and all Stafford borrowing prior to entering medical school). Not more than $65,000 of this amount may be in subsidized loans.

### Interest Rate

If you have a Federal Unsubsidized Stafford Loan, you're responsible for the interest while you're in school, but most lenders will allow you to defer the interest and not pay it until you leave school. During this time, the interest may be capitalized. Capitalization means that the interest accrues while you're still in school and is added to the principal at a predetermined time (often at the point of repayment). In August, 2013, changes in how student loan interest rates are determined were instituted. Interest rates on new federal education loans made on or after July 1, 2013 are linked to the 10-year Treasury rate, plus a fixed margin. The interest rates on new loans are still fixed for the life of the loan; however, each year's new loans will have different fixed rates, based on current market rates. Applications and information about current interest rates and repayment schedules are available at participating lending institutions and on appropriate websites and in the financial aid office.

### Fees

There may be fees associated with this program. They may vary from lender to lender. It is important to consult your lender and financial aid office for an explanation of these fees.

### Sources of Federal Stafford Student Loans

Federal Stafford Student Loans are made primarily through participating banks, savings and loan associations, and credit unions. Contact the financial aid office for recommendations on Stafford Student Loan providers.

### Application Procedures

The process used to apply for a Federal Stafford Loan has changed significantly at many schools. What was once a paper process has at many schools become automated. It is important to determine the specific process used at the school you will attend. Give yourself ample lead time so your loan funds arrive in time to satisfy the deadline for payment of tuition and fees. Even though the process in some schools is automated, it still may take a week or two to receive your funds. Paper-driven, manual processes will take longer.

### Repayment

The amount of your monthly payment will depend on the total amount you borrowed, the number of months in the repayment schedule, the type of repayment schedule, and whether you elected to pay interest on the unsubsidized portion of the loan while in school. A typical repayment period is 10 years. You'll have a shorter repayment term if you borrow a small amount, since there's a minimum monthly installment of $50. Lenders are required to offer the option of standard, graduated, or income-sensitive repayment to new borrowers. A new borrower is defined as someone who has no outstanding balance on a Federal Stafford Loan on or after July 1, 1993.

---

**Promissory Notes**

Terms of repayment are explained in your promissory note. Be sure that you understand them. Keep the promissory note; it's your contract with the lender.

---

If you don't meet the repayment terms of the loan, you'll go into default and the entire balance of the loan will become due. If your loan goes into default, the lender may refuse to allow you to borrow again until the entire debt is satisfied. Check with your lender to explore repayment plan options. Lenders are trying to make it possible for you to stay in good standing with your repayments, and they're willing to work with you to help you manage your debt.

### Deferments

Under certain circumstances, you may be able to defer—that is, postpone—the payments of your Federal Stafford Loan. Deferments are not automatic; you must apply for them.

### Forbearance

You can request forbearance in situations that aren't covered by normal deferments. Forbearance means the lender agrees to grant you a temporary suspension of payments, reduced payments, or an extension of the time for your payments.

### Cancellations

You can get a portion of your loans canceled in special circumstances. Once again, read your promissory note for details.

## William D. Ford Federal Direct Loan

The Ford Federal Direct Loan Program was authorized by the US Congress in 1993. In this program, the federal government is the lender. Individual schools, rather than banks or other financial institutions, originate the loans. This program includes two types of loans: the Federal Direct Stafford/Ford Loan and the Federal Direct Unsubsidized Stafford/Ford Loan.

The eligibility criteria, borrowing limits, interest rate, grace period, and deferment and cancellation provisions for this program are the same as for the Federal Stafford Loan Program. The Ford Federal Direct Loan Program has different application procedures and its own repayment options.

### Application Procedures

The FAFSA and the other required documents that were discussed earlier must be completed. Usually, the Ford Federal Direct Loan will be offered as part of your financial aid package. Once you accept the loan as part of the package, the financial aid officer creates a Loan Origination Record and electronically transmits it to the federal servicer for approval. The approval is transmitted back to the school, and the school produces a promissory note for you to sign. Once the promissory note is signed, the school can disburse the first portion of the loan to your student account. Any funds remaining after any unpaid balance you have with the institution will be refunded to you. The entire process can take less than a week to complete from the point of loan certification to disbursement of the check. Depending on mailing time and the school's schedule for loan disbursements, it could take longer.

---

**Don't Be Surprised**

Procedures for the Ford Federal Direct Loan Program may vary from school to school.

---

### Repayment

Most of the conditions of repayment are the same as for the Federal Stafford Loan Program. Students who participate in the Ford Federal Direct Loan Program have three repayment options in addition to the standard: the extended repayment plan, the income-contingent repayment plan, and the graduated repayment plan.

**Option 1: Extended Repayment.** This option is similar to the standard repayment plan, but it allows the student to repay a fixed amount over a period of up to 25 years.

**Option 2: Income-based Repayment.** You pay a percentage of your salary no matter how much you have borrowed. If you have a high debt, this option could require many more years of repayment than the standard 10 years. As your salary increases, so would your loan repayments. The drawback to this option is that the longer you stay in repayment, the more interest you pay on the loan. Indeed, if your payment does not cover current interest due, unpaid interest will be capitalized, increasing the amount of principal you owe.

**Option 3: Graduated Repayment.** This allows you to opt for lower payments at the beginning of the repayment cycle, when your salary is lower. The payments automatically increase as the years progress. The repayment term may be extended beyond 10 years, but the payments are more manageable in the beginning, when you probably have a lower salary.

No matter which repayment option you select, the plan will be explained in the promissory note you sign. Repayments will be made to a federal loan servicer contracted by the US Department of Education.

## Federal Perkins Student Loan

Administered by colleges and universities, the Federal Perkins Loan Program is made possible through a combination of resources: an annual allocation from the US Department of Education, a contribution from the participating educational institution, and repayments by previous borrowers. The program was originally called the National Defense Student Loan Program when it was instituted by the federal government more than 30 years ago. The program was one of the first financial aid programs instituted by the federal government.

> **Maybe/Maybe Not**
>
> Not all schools allocate Federal Perkins Loan funds to graduate and professional students.

### Eligibility

The school determines eligibility for Federal Perkins Loans based on your financial need (calculated through the FAFSA) and the availability of funds. Besides demonstrating financial need, you have to be enrolled at least half-time and maintain satisfactory progress toward a degree. Keep in mind that Federal Perkins Loans are reserved for the neediest students.

### Borrowing Limits

Federal policy allows a maximum annual loan of $8,000 per graduate-level student. However, many schools lack the funds to allocate this much to any one student. A graduate student may borrow up to a cumulative total of $60,000, including all outstanding undergraduate and graduate Federal Perkins Loans.

### Interest Rate

The terms are very good. The annual interest rate is currently 5 percent. Interest does not accrue while the borrower remains enrolled at least half-time.

### Fees

Another perk of the Federal Perkins Loan Program: no fees.

### Application Procedures

Usually, you're automatically considered for this loan when you apply for financial aid. If you've been offered and have accepted a Federal Perkins Loan, you'll sign a promissory note. The promissory note lists the amount of the loan and states your rights and responsibilities as a borrower. When the signed note is received, your account will most likely be credited for one semester's portion of the loan.

### Grace Period

Federal Perkins Loans have an initial nine-month grace period after you graduate or drop below half-time attendance. During this period, no repayment is required and no interest accrues.

### Repayment

Borrowers under the Federal Perkins Loan program repay the school, although there may be a middleman: Many schools contract with outside agencies for billing and collection. Repayment may extend up to 10 years, beginning 9 months (your grace period) after you cease to be enrolled at least half-time. The amount of the monthly payment and the maximum number of months allowed for repayment are based on the total amount borrowed. The federal government has set the minimum monthly payment at $40. Under some special circumstances, borrowers may make arrangements to repay a lower amount or to extend the repayment period. There is no prepayment penalty.

### Deferments

You can defer payments of your Federal Perkins Loan until you graduate or drop below half-time. This deferment is not automatic; you must request the deferment forms from either your school or from the billing agency where you are repaying the loan.

### Cancellations

This might not make you jump for joy, but it's good to know. The entirety of your Federal Perkins Loan will be canceled if you become permanently disabled—or die. You can get a portion of your loans canceled in less drastic circumstances, if you do any of the following:

- Teach handicapped children
- Teach in a designated elementary or secondary school that serves low-income students
- Work in a specified Head Start program or serve as a VISTA or Peace Corps volunteer

Check your promissory note. Your loan may have additional cancellation provisions. Also, if you have "old" Federal Perkins, there may be some different conditions depending on when the original loan was made. Check with your previous school for any special circumstances.

## FEDERAL LOAN CONSOLIDATION

Federal Loan Consolidation allows students with substantial debt to combine several federal loans into one larger loan with a longer repayment schedule. The new loan has an interest rate based on the weighted average of the rates of the consolidated loans. Stafford Loans, Federal Insured Student Loans (FISLs), Federal Perkins Loans, PLUS loans to students, parent PLUS Loans made after 1986, SLS, Health Professions Student Loans, Health Education Assistance Loans, and Nursing Student Loan Program loans may be consolidated only by lenders that have an agreement with the Department or a guaranty agency for that purpose.

To qualify for federal loan consolidation, you must be in the grace period or in repayment status on all loans being consolidated; if in default, you must have made satisfactory arrangements to repay the defaulted loan. To consolidate a defaulted loan, you must make three consecutive reasonable and affordable monthly payments. A borrower in default can qualify for a Federal Consolidation Loan without having to make three required payments if the borrower agrees to repay the loan under the income-sensitive repayment plan.

Furthermore, a borrower in default must not have another consolidation loan application pending, must agree to notify the loan holder of any address changes, and must certify that the lender holds the borrower's outstanding loan that is being consolidated or that the borrower has unsuccessfully sought a loan from the holders of the outstanding loans and was unable to secure a Consolidation Loan from the holder.

If you are unable to obtain a Federal Consolidation Loan from a lender eligible to make such loans, you may apply through the US Department of Education for a Federal Direct Consolidation Loan. You must certify that you have been unable to obtain from an eligible lender a Federal Consolidation Loan or a Federal Consolidation Loan with income-sensitive repayment terms acceptable to the borrower.

You have the option of consolidating all eligible loans or only some of your loans. No fees are charged to participate in this program.

If you consolidate your loans, you have the option of choosing the most appropriate repayment plan for you and your circumstances. These options include level repayment, graduated repayment, or income-sensitive repayment. You should consult one of the websites noted at the end of this chapter for detailed information on loan consolidation.

# FOR MEDICAL STUDENTS

The federal Department of Health and Human Services has a few loan programs designed specifically for students in certain health professions. Contact your school's financial aid office to determine if it participates in the loan programs that follow.

## Loans for Disadvantaged Students (LDS)

Funds for this low-interest loan program are directed toward students who have exceptional need and come from disadvantaged backgrounds. Interest on the loan is 5 percent and begins to accrue one year after you complete medical school. LDS does not have a primary-care practice requirement. For more information, contact your school's financial aid office.

## Primary Care Loans (PCL)

These low-interest loans are specifically for students intending to practice in a primary care field. Interest on the loans is 5 percent, beginning 9 months after the month you complete medical school.

If you receive a Primary Care Loan and agree to select a primary care residency and practice in a primary care specialty until the loan is paid in full, you pay only

5 percent. But if you do not complete your agreement, your 5 percent interest will rise significantly. Before taking out this loan, be prepared to meet your commitment.

## Defaulting on Loans

Defaulting health professionals received a lot of negative press several years ago. This led the Department of Health and Human Services to beef up the measures it takes when a borrower defaults on an HHS loan. Now, if you default on an HHS loan, HHS may do any of the following::

- Report you to one or more credit-reporting agencies if your payment is just 60 days past due
- Obtain a judgment placing a lien against your assets
- Assign your defaulted loans to the Department of Justice for collection
- Offset any IRS tax refund you might receive
- Publish your name, address, and amount of loans in default in the Federal Register (which invariably makes it to your hometown newspaper)
- Release information about your default to "other interested organizations," including professional and specialty organizations, hospitals, and state licensing boards
- Exclude you from Medicare and Medicaid reimbursement

Clearly, you don't want to default on any educational loan. There are simply too many ugly things that happen if you do. There are also a number of loan-forgiveness programs and other options that make repayment easier if you've hit a snag.

## Loan-Repayment Forgiveness Programs

There are several loan programs under which you promise to work in exchange for reduced levels of debt. While they require a time commitment, they can reduce the size of your educational debt tremendously.

### *National Health Service Corps Loan Repayment*

Program physicians may receive repayment of health-professions loans—$50,000 for two years of service—in exchange for serving full-time at a designated NHSC site. Participants are also reimbursed for increased federal, state, and local income taxes resulting from the loan repayment. Service commitments range from two to four years; priority for selection is given to doctors who have completed their residencies in fields of need at the time of application.

### Indian Health Service Loan Repayment Program

Participants are paid up to $20,000 per year toward loan repayment for each year of full-time clinical practice at a designated IHS location. Priority is given to physicians in specialties of need as determined by the IHS.

### Military Loan Repayment Programs

Various branches of the armed forces—active, reserve and guard—offer loan repayment programs in exchange for a fixed term of service. Visit each service's healthcare recruiting website in order to learn more.

### State Loan-Repayment Programs

Many states have initiated programs of loan repayment for doctors who agree to practice in high-need areas. These programs are often modeled on the National Health Service Corps Loan Repayment Program; however, service is based in the state in which funds are received. Some states get matching grants from the government to assist physicians in public clinics or private, nonprofit practices. Unfortunately, no federal money is available to assist those doctors going into private practice, although some states may use their own money to do this. Check with the financial aid office for details.

## PRIVATE LOAN PROGRAMS

Many medical students find that a combination of scholarship funds and federal loan programs is not adequate to meet expenses. Over the last few years, several private loan programs have emerged to fill the gap. Contact your financial aid officer for information on private loan programs such as MedCap, Access, MedFunds, TERI, Grad EXCEL, and T.H.E.

# DEBT MANAGEMENT

You've read the material on financial aid and loans. You've done the worksheets about paying for your medical degree. How much did you calculate you'd need to borrow? This is the time to figure out if you'll actually be able to manage your projected debt. If your projected indebtedness seems unmanageable, now is the time to try to figure out ways to reduce your borrowing.

## Step 1: Calculate Your Monthly Payments

Use the worksheet at the end of this chapter to calculate your monthly repayments after graduating. In estimating your indebtedness, remember that you're likely to need similar funding for all four years you're in med school. Multiply all the loan amounts in your financial aid award letter by four to arrive at the total amount.

| Monthly Loan Payments* | | | | | |
|---|---|---|---|---|---|
| For a $1,000 Loan | | | | | |
| Rate | 60 Months | 120 Months | 180 Months | 240 Months | 300 Months |
| 5% | $18.87 | $10.61 | $7.91 | $6.60 | $5.85 |
| 6% | 19.33 | 11.10 | 8.44 | 7.16 | 6.44 |
| 7% | 19.80 | 11.61 | 8.99 | 7.75 | 7.07 |
| 8% | 20.28 | 12.13 | 9.56 | 8.36 | 7.72 |
| 9% | 20.76 | 12.67 | 10.14 | 9.00 | 8.39 |
| 10% | 21.25 | 13.22 | 10.75 | 9.65 | 9.09 |

\* Minimum monthly payment may apply regardless of the loan amount.

Use the table above to help you calculate most monthly payments on a level-payment plan over 5 to 30 years. For example, suppose you had a $5,000 loan at 8 percent interest and a 10-year payment term. As the table shows, the monthly payment for a $1,000 loan would be $12.13. Multiply this by 5 to get $60.65.

Bear in mind, however, that you may need to calculate several payments. You should calculate the payments to each lender, under each loan program, separately. For example, if you have several Federal Stafford Student Loans issued by a single lender, add them up to arrive at a single balance. But, if you have two additional loans issued under a private supplemental loan program, consider them separately. Calculate the separate payments, then add them together to determine your total payment responsibility.

### Step 2: Estimate Your Starting Salary

The average resident starting stipends are around $50,000 and increase by a few thousand dollars annually during your graduate medical education. Once you begin practicing, it's very likely that your salary will increase. Try to get more specific information from your school's financial aid office or Student Affairs Office, or from physician salary surveys available on the Internet, about salaries for particular specialties and types of practices you're considering.

### Step 3: Fill Out the "Will My Paycheck Cover My Expenses?" Worksheet

The worksheet at the end of this chapter is very important. It'll help you find out whether your projected postschool paycheck will cover all your expenses. Many of the expenses in this chart are flexible. It'll be up to you to stretch your salary to meet your projected expenses.

---

**Just the Facts**

The *AAMC Data Book* is a good place to begin considering your projected earnings vs. your projected debt. Published annually, the book contains a variety of statistical information, including the following:

- Mean tuition and fees for first-year med school
- Career choices and specialty plans of graduating med students
- Median net income of physicians before taxes and after expenses

To order, contact:

AAMC
Publications Department
Phone: (202) 828-0416
Website: www.aamc.org/data/databook

---

### Step 4: Consider Your Financial Options

After doing the "Will My Paycheck Cover My Expenses?" worksheet, you'll have a better idea of your post-med-school financial picture. If things look tight, you could plan to reduce items in the "Discretionary Expenses" category. Another option is to lower your monthly loan payments. This may be accomplished at the time of repayment through loan consolidation.

## Creative Payment and Repayment

As medical school debt climbs, some private practices and hospitals are using bonuses to attract educationally indentured young MDs.

### The "Northern Exposure" Plan

Some medical students are making arrangements with hometown hospitals to pay their medical school tuition. This comes with an agreement that the doctor return there to practice for a specified period of time. Agreements are signed converting tuition payment to a loan if the doctor fails to fulfill the obligation.

### Group Practices

Medical groups are also getting wise to the loan-repayment woes of new physicians. It is not uncommon now for a large group to offer loan-repayment options to lure new doctors who have amassed a large debt. Practicing physicians (who are good risks to lenders) can do this by securing a low-interest private loan at, or just above, the prime rate. They use the loan to pay off the higher-interest loan and let the new doctor pay off the lower-interest loan. The beauty of this arrangement is that the loan secured by the practice is a business loan and, therefore, tax deductible by the practice.

### Headhunters

Search firms that place doctors in hard-to-fill practices are also finding ways to use loan repayment as a carrot, encouraging independent practices to tailor debt-assistance bonuses to be competitive with HMOs and hospitals that are buying up family practitioners. Some offer a lump-sum payout of as much as $100,000. Others provide "earn-out agreements" that spread the practice-paid loan repayment over an agreed-upon time., while still others offer a combination of an up-front bonus and an earn-out agreement.

When you're projecting your loan repayments, you need to remember that, while the payments will stay relatively stable, your salary will (presumably) increase over the repayment term of the loan. The loan payments will be less onerous as your salary goes up. On the other hand, the longer you are out of school, the more major expenses you're likely to have: a house, a car, children, and so on.

## Will My Paycheck Cover My Expenses?

**Income**

1. My annual salary/wages   $_____
2. My spouse/partner's salary/wages   _____
3. Other income (source/amount) (e.g., interest, self-employment, etc.; don't include gifts that may not be available each year)
4. Total annual income (sum of lines 1–3)   _____
5. Monthly income (line 4 divided by 12)   _____

**Mandatory Expenses**

6. Taxes   _____
7. Monthly mandatory deductions from salary (e.g., health insurance, required pension contribution)   _____
8. My monthly student loan payment (assume $125 per $10,000 of student loans)   _____
9. My spouse/partner's monthly student loan payment   _____
10. My total monthly personal debt payments (credit card and other personal debts; assume minimum payment of 3 percent of total credit card balance)   _____
11. My spouse/partner's total monthly personal debt payments   _____
12. Total of what I have to pay each month (sum of lines 6–11)   _____

**Discretionary Monthly Income**

13. Total monthly income (line 5)   _____
14. Total monthly mandatory expenses (line 12)   _____
15. Monthly total available for living expenses (line 14 minus line 13)   _____

**Living Expenses/Discretionary Expenses**

16. Rent/mortgage and maintenance fees   _____
17. Utilities and phone (local and long-distance)   _____
18. Groceries and meals away from home (including lunches at work)   _____
19. Clothing, laundry, dry cleaning   _____
20. Medical and dental care, prescriptions   _____
21. Recreation, entertainment (also include newspapers, magazines, TV/cable)   _____
22. Car (payments, parking, gas, insurance, repairs) or mass-transit expenses   _____
23. Vacation/travel   _____
24. Dependent care or childcare   _____
25. Insurance (home, life, medical, dental, renter's)   _____
26. Personal care   _____
27. Gifts, miscellaneous   _____
28. Savings, emergency fund, retirement (emergency fund should equal 3–6 mo. salary; recommended level of savings/retirement investment = 10% of gross monthly income)   _____
29. Total monthly living and discretionary expenses (sum of lines 16–28)   _____
30. Total monthly amount of money remaining and available for savings, investment, improved lifestyle (line 15 minus line 29)   _____
31. Annual amount of money remaining (line 30 times 12)   _____